MADE IN CANADA:

A BUSINESSMAN'S ADVENTURES

IN POLITICS

MADE
IN CANADA

A Businessman's Adventures in Politics

Alastair W. Gillespie

with Irene Sage, PH.D.

Foreword by John English

ROBIN BRASS STUDIO

Published 2009 by Robin Brass Studio Inc.
www.rbstudiobooks.com

ISBN-13: 978-1-896941-59-2
ISBN-10: 1-896941-59-1

Printed and bound in Canada by Friesens, Altona, Manitoba

Reasonable efforts have been made to trace the source of material quoted or shown for the purpose of giving credit. Information enabling us to rectify errors or omissions will be gratefully received.

Library and Archives Canada Cataloguing in Publication

Gillespie, Alastair, 1922–
Made in Canada : a businessman's adventures in politics / Alastair W. Gillespie with Irene Sage.

Includes index.
ISBN 978-1-896941-59-2

1. Gillespie, Alastair, 1922–. 2. Cabinet ministers – Canada – Biography. 3. Canada. Parliament. House of Commons – Biography. 4. Politicians – Canada – Biography. 5. Businessmen – Canada – Biography. 6. Canada – Politics and government – 1968-1979. I. Title.

FC626.G45A3 2009   971.064'4092   C2009-905111-7

This book is dedicated to Diana,
who shared so many of the "ups and downs."

CONTENTS

FOREWORD

Nortel, once the gem of Canadian scientific research, is sold off piecemeal to foreign bidders; and energy shocks disrupt political and economic planning at regular intervals; and Canadians fret about the inability of their businesses to compete on the world stage. Rare is the political biography that bears important messages for our times, but *Made in Canada,* with its fascinating stories and analysis of how Alastair Gillespie confronted energy crises, takeovers of Canadian industries and economic volatility in the seventies is one such book. Gillespie served successively as Canada's science, industry and energy minister during that difficult decade when it seemed capitalism no longer worked and Canada faced challenges unimaginable only a few years before.

Alastair Gillespie is an extraordinary blend of a first-rate mind, a successful businessman, a senior federal cabinet minister and a western Canadian who is a Canadian nationalist. He is, frankly, unique, and we shall not see his like again because the experiences that shaped him are part of Canada's past. Yet his perceptions of what those influences mean speak clearly, if poignantly, to the problems Canada confronts today. As science minister, for example, he probed why Canadian research so seldom brings commercialization and gained insights of value to policy-makers today. As industry minister, he drew up guidelines for foreign takeovers which would assure that foreign companies buying Canadian companies would bring benefits to Canada. As energy minister, he wrestled with reconciling the demands of Alberta and the need of all Canadians to have a secure supply of energy and an equitable distribution of economic windfalls. His book brings lessons for today's politicians as they confront similar dilemmas. Gillespie's biography rhymes with our own times.

Yet Gillespie's biography is a life story that stands on its own as a tale of a young British Canadian who grew up on Vancouver Island, the descendant of some of the major names in Victorian Britain and its empire. British to the core but Canadian in his heart, Gillespie valiantly fought in the Second World War and lost a beloved brother in the battle. A Rhodes scholar, Gillespie became part of Canada's good generation, which fashioned a prosperous and vital Canada in the postwar years. Although his formative years in business occurred when vast flows of foreign investment poured into Canada and created much Canadian wealth, Gillespie shared Walter Gordon's concern about what foreign ownership meant for Canadian entrepreneurship and research capacity. His interests blended with his family's commitment to public service and led directly to politics during the heady days of Trudeaumania in 1968.

By that time, there were few successful businessmen in Canadian politics. Most preferred the security and copious benefits of the boardroom, but Gillespie and his family were willing to face the often bitter winds of political life. A millionaire when he entered politics in 1968, he had lost half his fortune by the time he left public office in spring 1979. But he has no regrets, nor should he. This biography convincingly demonstrates that politicians can make a difference and shape a country's direction. Gillespie was, by far, the most significant businessman in Trudeau's cabinet, and he often challenged his colleagues who questioned the motives of the business community. Although he shared some of Trudeau's own criticisms of Canadian business, he was a devoted supporter of the free market and an admirer of the entrepreneurial spirit, which he embodies so completely himself.

Alastair Gillespie has written one of the finest autobiographies of a Canadian businessman. But *Made in Canada* gives its readers much more: the remarkable life of a western Canadian, who has reflected and shaped the major events of Canadian history during the last eighty years. *Made in Canada* is thoroughly a Canadian product – just like its author.

JOHN ENGLISH

ACKNOWLEDGMENTS

I should like to acknowledge, recognize and thank the main political staff assistants that helped me, first as a member and second as a minister. At the outset, Ruth Cruden took over the constituency office – responsibilities which lasted nearly eight years. She was followed by another people-oriented person, Bea Yakimoff, who saw me through the remaining years.

Jeannine Enright handled my Ottawa office. She was universally respected, a wonderful link within the system. Jeannine also acted as a marriage broker when it came to my special assistant Ian Webb and my daughter Cynthia.

During my years as a cabinet minister, I recruited a number of first-rate helpers. Some handled Toronto area responsibilities. I think of George Dupuis, Derek Brown, Ian Webb, Peter Maguire and Betsy Stikeman. Peter was pinched by the Prime Minister's Office (PMO). He was not the only one. What do you say when the PM calls and asks you to accept his wish to hire one of your most productive staff? Paul Manning was too, as was a loyal and very hand-working assistant, Mike Gillian, the husband of Joyce Fairbairn, who was legislative assistant to the PM. Alan Lutfy (now Chief Justice of the Federal Court) made his mark when he handled FIRA matters. He was "stolen" by the PM's office too. On my appointment as energy minister, I was fortunate to recruit a very knowledgeable, energetic, somewhat combative, politically astute executive assistant, Jamie Deacey. He is still enlivening the Ottawa scene as a consultant since my departure.

This book would not have been possible without the assistance of many players. It started out with the encouragement and support of Professor John English, Pierre Trudeau's official biographer.

I want to thank my collaborator and dear friend Irene Sage for guiding me through the many twists and turns of writing this memoir. Her sensitivity and nuanced understanding of the political economy of my time in office was invaluable.

Irene and I have been the recipients of much good advice and secretarial assistance. Susan Kerr, who started with parts of the early manuscript, never lived, I'm very sorry to say, to see the finished product. Josephte Belcourt has been a tireless source of energy, researching expertise and product development. It is she who has worked over the manuscript.

Lastly, my publisher, Robin Brass, has brought determination, guidance and encouragement to this memoir.

I am profoundly grateful to them all for the finished result and for the memories.

If there are errors, they are mine. The memoir looks back over an impressive number of years.

ALASTAIR W. GILLESPIE
Toronto, September 15, 2009

MADE IN CANADA:

A BUSINESSMAN'S ADVENTURES

IN POLITICS

INTRODUCTION

Today's news is full of echoes from my past: financial shocks, oil spikes, startling rises and falls in the price of food, and politicians struggling to tame the wild bear of a collapsing stock market. Is the current disorder a depression or a recession? I grew up in the Great Depression and felt its profound impact upon my family and my country. In the 1970s when the Bretton Woods system collapsed, I was a Canadian politician faced with the challenge of dealing with simultaneous energy and food crises as well as rampant inflation. Looking back, I believe there are lessons we learned as we struggled with new unknowns. Today's financial collapse is unprecedented since the Great Depression, and it seems to me the product of an irresponsible American administration and a bloated financial sector that became consumed with greed and an inflated sense of power. As we fight these battles once more, I offer these memories of earlier struggles. We won them but not without costs. Perhaps these reflections will contain some glimmers of hope that will lighten our current discontents.

I was born in Victoria, British Columbia, not long after the First World War when many of its sons gave their lives fighting for the British Empire and for Canada. We were part of that great Empire, but we were Canadians too, proud of what we had accomplished since Confederation and already resentful of the British colonial mentality. Since my kindergarten days, I have reacted against the bully. As I matured I learned that the world was full of bullies, sometimes warlords or dictators like Hitler and Mussolini. As a young Canadian, I fought against them in the Second World War. Hitler and Mussolini fell, and later so did Stalin, but the democracies who triumphed in the forties faced challenges themselves as special interests, demagogues and bullies tried to gain power. I learned that countervailing forces are fundamental to the success of democracies, and that under-

1

standing guided my public life when I first began to be active in politics. Influenced by the outward looking vision of Lester Pearson in the sixties I entered politics in 1968 during the heady times of Pierre Elliott Trudeau and Trudeaumania.

In my youth, the British Empire still was dominant in much of the world and my family believed in it. But like most imperial powers, it held its power by bullying others. London saw itself as the world's centre of power, and the trade policies it pursued were all about the benefits to be derived by importing and upgrading foreign commodities and then exporting the manufactured products back to those who had supplied the raw materials. Those who imported Canadian raw materials thus created and captured the value added, and British entrepreneurs, my ancestors among them, created the great wealth the country enjoyed in the nineteenth and early twentieth century. Today, the British Empire is a distant memory, but the United States has become the predominant international force through its efficient and far-seeing multinational companies. However, as I write these words, the American empire is tottering as its careless invasion of Iraq and its irresponsible domestic economic policies threaten the economic future not only of Americans but of Canadians and billions of others throughout the world.

I came to believe in the essential need for countervailing forces between government and business, within governments, and among countries. Although I grew up steeped in British values, I was distrustful of British imperialism, particularly the bullying parts of it. Those who criticized the British in those days were denounced as anti-British. Similarly, today criticism of the United States, our neighbour and largest trading partner, is labelled as anti-American and not as pro-Canadian. This attitude is a trap. When the United States fails to honour international agreements, should we stay silent? When the great military power of the United States is directed towards narrow American interests, should we wince and turn the other way? When the doctrine of pre-emption becomes the new Manifest Destiny, should we not object as our Canadian ancestors did over a century ago? When unilateralism becomes the guiding light and the sanctity of international treaties is regularly abused, should Canadians remain silent? I think not, but in recent times "Nervous Nellies" urged Canadians to avoid challenging such behaviour when George W. Bush bullied us and others. If we raised our voices, they claimed, we would be "anti-American" and harmful to our national interests. Yet Bush's audacious successor, Barack Obama, did not say silent, and the American people stood up. In my mind, our habit of kowtowing is often humiliating.

My attitudes were formed in my adolescence in British Columbia, hardened in the wartime battle, and reshaped as Canada became closely integrated in the American economic giant that emerged in the postwar period. I came to regard Canada's government as a necessary countervail to the powerful forces of the American empire. During the 1960s I believed that Lester Pearson was creating a base for a new vision of Canada, with a distinctive Canadian flag and a vigorous Canadian identity, an alternative to the American way of life. In this sense, Expo 67 was more than a celebration of Canada's 100th birthday. It represented a coming of age, a generator of confidence, and the reflection of a new Canadian "can do" spirit," one that the sudden emergence of Pierre Trudeau captured in his remarkable march to the prime minister's office in 1968.

My business career in the 1960s brought me into contact with Walter Gordon, a minister in Lester Pearson's government and a mentor to some of the brightest young Liberals of the time. Although an accountant and a very successful businessman, Walter was an economic nationalist, wary of the growing influence of American interests in Canadian economic and political life. In the fifties he headed an important Royal Commission on Canada's economic future, which called for government support for Canadian companies that could compete internationally. In the sixties as Canada's finance minister, he promoted nationalist policies that prevented powerful American banks from overwhelming our smaller financial institutions. Thank God he did or we would today face the fate of the Wall Street giants that have collapsed completely. He also encouraged Canadians to halt shipping our raw materials abroad for processing and instead to process those materials in Canada, thus building strong Canadian companies able to compete on the international stage. As I write today, with Nortel bankrupt, Inco and Falconbridge gone, and our American branch plant auto companies threatened as their American head offices pull back their foreign earnings to their home land, how I wish he and the governments I served had succeeded better. Why did our businesses fail so often to meet the challenges? When did they succeed? There are no simple formulas, but I offer some thoughts in the following pages about what we did right and where we went wrong.

I was swept into political office by the incredible wave of Trudeaumania that erupted in the spring of 1968. I was elected as the member of Parliament for Etobicoke, then a young western suburb of Toronto, and Trudeau almost immediately gave me serious responsibilities, which became greater over the following decade. The Trudeau government had many brilliant politicians – intellectuals, lawyers and others – but few businessmen. For me that was sometimes an advantage, at other times a disadvantage. Although my business career in Toronto had brought me much satisfaction and the material goods to support my family, I relished the rare opportunity my election gave me to put my beliefs about Canada into practice. Trudeau first asked me to head a new Ministry of State for Science and Technology, where I learned the limits and the opportunities for Canadian science and technological development. Then, Trudeau asked me to head the new Department of Industry, Trade and Commerce, where I had the responsibility to develop the controversial Foreign Investment Review Agency (FIRA) and to promote Canadian business interests internationally as major crises of the seventies erupted in the western world. FIRA became the butt of much unfair criticism from Canadian business interests and journalists, egged on by Americans and others who resented any requirements that would assure that Canadian raw materials were not simply shipped out of the country for processing. Many business leaders and business journalists did not share the Trudeau government's view that corporate takeovers of Canadian businesses by foreign interests should bring some clear benefits to Canada.

The seventies were a time of economic tumult, particularly in the energy sector. In 1975 I moved from Industry, Trade and Commerce to the Department of Energy, Mines and Resources. Out of the frying pan, into the fire. These were crisis years as the federal government tried to balance the interests of the producers, who were concentrated in Alberta, with those of consumers, who mostly lived in central Canada, at a time when industrial workers faced increasing challenges from lower tariffs and swelling unemployment. In my ministerial responsibilities, I tried to recognize the importance of countervailing powers – government against the power of multinationals and central Canadian provinces against the energy dominance of Alberta. FIRA, for example, was an institution of countervail, maximizing Canadian advantages against the power of American corporations and the huge, daunting economy that spawned them. I was never anti-American and I criticized those who overstepped fair criticism to denounce American institutions and even American themselves. I thought the *Toronto Star* sometimes went over the line, and so did my mentor Walter Gordon, who occasionally could not resist poking the American eagle in the eye. And yet, Walter and I shared a deep sense that Canadian interests needed the protective arm of the Canadian state, which alone could provide a countervailing force against the tremendous energy of American private interests and public authority.

After I left politics, Canada drifted far away from such beliefs. The Mulroney government made FIRA totally ineffective and famously declared that Canada would be open to business, no questions asked. Later Liberal and Conservative governments alike embraced "globalization" and its promise of lasting economic growth and prosperity. Governments became hesitant to perform their countervailing role and to intervene in the workings of the free market. Most business people cheered these changes. Although I returned to business after my political career ended in summer 1979, I refused to join in the cheering. Make no mistake: I share profound reservations about the often-clumsy interventions of governments in the economy. I learned those lessons at great personal cost when I tried to establish a major economic development project in Cape Breton to develop synfuels. Before I entered politics and in my post-political career, I saw that governments can behave irresponsibly and even fraudulently. I watched in horror as our major development project to establish a marine oil terminal at Point Tupper suddenly lost its support, even as the notorious Karlheinz Schreiber sucked away government incentive funds to support his Bear

Head Industries, whose purpose was to produce armed personnel carriers for Saudi Arabia, production that never occurred – fortunately.

At my core, I am a businessman first. I have served on and even chaired major corporate boards. I invested in the famous Creemore Breweries and have participated in some of the major private sector decisions in the final years of the twentieth century. The business world is the one I know best, but today it seems badly out of shape. The Canadian economy, despite solid fundamentals, is staggering as the result of the greed of modern-day bullies on Wall Street, who faced no countervailing forces from Washington or elsewhere. And what about Canada's future? We negotiated a free trade agreement with the United States in 1988, yet our goods are often blocked at the border and the American Congress blithely ignores our legitimate complaints. Our natural resources flow even more freely over the border in huge quantities nearly all without Canadian processing, while our manufacturers and farmers often face great difficulties in securing American markets. Of course some companies have benefited. One of the highly publicized benefits to Canada of free trade was, supposedly, the free entry of refined petroleum products to the American East Coast, one of the largest import markets in the world. The Canadian independent Irving Oil Company took advantage of this opportunity. However, the American-controlled refineries and the province of Nova Scotia did not. Indeed, the opposite occurred. The multinationals spent their energies on *reducing* the supply capability of the existing Canadian refineries. In fact, they even broke up the Ultramar refinery in Halifax and shipped off the remnants to the Middle East. There are too many tales like this sad one and too few good ones like Irving's.

When I was Minister of Industry, Trade and Commerce, my role was to protect and advance Canadian companies and Canadian influence. Canadian-controlled multinational corporations were, in effect, our commercial ambassadors, and I worked closely with these representatives of Canada. I recall well the great companies with whom I interacted: Alcan, Inco, Falconbridge, Stelco, Dofasco and Algoma Steel. My ancestors of the North West Company had competed with the great Hudson's Bay Company, others had bought their goods from Eaton's catalogue and, until

Creemore, I drank Molson's beer. Today, these companies are gone; they no longer bear the Canadian flag. This outcome seemed unthinkable in the seventies. Frankly, I find it incredible today.

In that turbulent decade we struggled with the strong international forces that came to be called globalization. We heard the calls from Milton Friedman, Ronald Reagan and others to end regulation and open borders. We were wary. We resisted and established Petro-Canada as a national oil company, and when the American multinational Atlantic Richfield withdrew from the development of the oil sands, we made a direct investment to assure that their early promise was realized. Had government not intervened, the oil sands would not be satisfying America's energy thirst today. As Minister of Industry, Trade, and Commerce, I developed the "Gillespie Guidelines," which offered foreigners clear directions on how their Canadian investments should be made for the benefit not only of their shareholders but of Canadians generally.

For a while, the apostles of deregulation, the opponents of government intervention, and the prophets of globalization overwhelmed the centre stage of public debate. Rare was the Canadian businessperson who raised his or her voice against these views. Now, as Wall Street giants like Lehman Brothers and Merrill Lynch crumble, we are slowly realizing that governments do have a role, that business needs rules and that Canada has distinct national interests. Today is the time to relearn the clear lessons of the past that, at great cost, we had forgotten.

CHAPTER ONE

COLONIAL INFLUENCES

I was born in beautiful Victoria, British Columbia, on May Day 1922 to a family of Scottish extraction that had moved across the continent as Canada expanded westward. Victoria was founded by the Hudson's Bay Company in 1843 as a fur trade fort. The total population was 400 for 15 years until the gold rush on the Fraser River. In 1868, Victoria became the capital of the Crown Colony of British Columbia. Named for the greatest symbol of the British Empire but, far away from Buckingham Palace and across an ocean and a continent, Victoria remained true to her name and British faith as the 1920s began. The memory of the First World War, in which so many had fought, was deeply etched in the hearts and minds of Victorians, especially in my own family, whose men had served overseas and whose women had rallied to the cause in a variety of roles, including medical corps and volunteer services.

Our family was proudly part of the British Empire, comfortable in our identity in a corner of the empire where boys played cricket and rugby and where almost one-third of the city's 38,000 residents were Anglican and many were recent immigrants still with British accents. My father, Erroll Gillespie, was a civil servant, a somewhat reluctant one I believe. Unlike others in the family, he had survived the war without wounds, although I later believed that his silences masked deeper wounds that never vanished. Like other veterans, he returned to a province where jobs were few and the civil service offered security to a newly-married young man. Physically hardy, my father was a careful man who, in the fashion of the early civil service, would never say what his politics were. Even to his wife and his children, he was close-mouthed about who the good and bad guys were. He did, however, spend hours with his kids, studying a huge map of the world and quietly explaining what seemed like an endless array of relationships among nations. When the subject was sports, he always had strong opinions that he sometimes demonstrated by wrestling his three contesting sons to the ground simultaneously. He challenged us in all sorts of ways, probably because he grew up in a family of seven athletic brothers – like the time he did a straight-arm circle on the bar he had mounted between two oak trees in the back yard. He swung around the bar with a straight arm without losing his balance and his life. He could have worked for Cirque du Soleil today.

My mother, Catherine Oliver, was an activist who readily argued with anyone, even my father's boss. She was a passionate Canadian nationalist, albeit with a strong Western flavour. She was never embarrassed about speaking her mind, especially when she believed that politicians were sacrificing long-term objectives in favour of short-term gain. On drives into the country, she would erupt into consternation about some dreadful wrong, but my father attempted to keep the dinner table clean of politics, a subject not palatable to him as a civil servant. She was, in many respects, like many "respectable" young women of the day, largely self-educated. She never went to school and was raised by a governess. Yet she was outspoken in defence of women's rights and displayed a quiet admiration for Carrie Nation and positive enthusiasm for Canada's first female MP, Agnes McPhail.

As my father's wrestling efforts indicate, we were brought up to revere strength in all its forms. Strength of character in particular. My mother, a very compassionate person, had no time for those that did not measure up to her standards. That is not to say that she ignored or avoided the less fortunate. Anything but. She believed in helping those who could not help themselves. She volunteered in hospitals and, during the war, she ran a drop-in centre for servicemen. But she also had a creative side.

My mother liked art and artists and he had been a student of Emily Carr, British Columbia's greatest painter and a bit of an eccentric. I remember her interest in Fenwick Lansdowne, a paraplegic born in Hong Kong who became one of Canada's most famous wildlife artists. In the early days of the Second World War, his mother got them out of the war zone in Asia. Fenwick was a budding artist short of money. How to finance his training? He had already shown great promise, particularly in his paint-

My father, Erroll Gillespie, just before his marriage.

My mother, Catherine Oliver, in the early 1920s.

ings of birds in their natural habitat. A well educated woman herself, Mrs. Lansdowne dug in and found work cutting lawns. My mother liked that kind of self-reliance and saw it in Fenwick's work. She was one of his very early customers.

My father adored his wife and always deferred to her judgement on matters that he considered intellectual, such as politics, the church, history and current affairs. I was blessed by parents who took an enormous interest in their children's accomplishments, challenges and disappointments – always providing encouragement when needed. My mother and father were very much outdoor people, which is not surprising since they were descended from early pioneer families in B.C. We used to spend many a weekend at a beautiful and secluded lake not far from Victoria learning all sorts of skills with an axe, a gun and a fishing rod. My father had inherited Matheson Lake from his father. In his declining years, he transferred the ownership of the nearly 1,000 acres to the provincial government in order that it be established as a public park. He wanted to preserve that magnificent first-growth timber for the enjoyment of future generations. Although it was an inheritance lost, my brother, sister and I never regretted his generous gift to the province we love.

ENTREPRENEURS AND PIONEERS

My Canadian Gillespie ancestors came to Canada in the late 1700s as fur traders. George, my great-great-grandfather, and his brother, John, were partners of that most famous explorer, Alexander Mackenzie – the first European to reach the Pacific Coast of North America over land. Alexander Mackenzie and Company morphed into the famous North West Company. Some of George's other brothers who stayed in Scotland opened up a supply business to the fur trade – based in London – to provide food, drink, trade goods and other essentials, including financing. They also acted as marketers in Europe of the fur sent from Montreal. They were pioneers and entrepreneurs in every sense of the words, at home in the North American wilderness.

Much of the fur trade was operated from Mackinac Island in what is today part of Michigan. There, George got to know John Jacob Astor's

American Fur Company. A competitor, Astor had a large vision and appetite. He was urged by Washington, still fired by the spirit of the American Revolution, to take a group to the Pacific Coast. He established a presence by building Fort Astor at the mouth of the Columbia River – all part of a move to establish American sovereignty at the turn of the nineteenth century over the Pacific Coast region. But the initiative was blunted somewhat by the fact that Alexander Mackenzie had got there first. Astor was late. Subsequently, during the War of 1812-14, Fort Astor was captured, with the assistance of the North West Company, by British forces. Today, the town of Astoria stands as a monument to these contests.

When George returned from the fur trade country at the Head of the Lakes to Montreal, he enjoyed the long bibulous nights as a member of the famous Beaver Club. He became a member in 1794. Although his entry in the *Dictionary of Canadian Biography* claims he joined the club in 1799, his Beaver Club medal, which remains in the family today, reads, "George Gillespie, Fortitude in Distress 1794." Engraved just above these words are a fast-moving canoe of voyageurs and the "bourgeois" (boss) approaching a veritable waterfall. On the medal's reverse side is a beaver working on a maple tree with the words below, "Industry and Perseverance." These values were ones which we learned to respect. They were touchstones to live by which guided our family through many perilous moments.

The Beaver Club had been founded in 1785. It was the exclusive social club of the fur trading community when in Montreal. You had to have spent at least one winter in the Pays d'en Haut and receive the unanimous vote of the other members to be admitted. There were only forty ordinary members by invitation and eight honorary members. The rules of the club indicated that there would be five toasts drunk after dinner, including one to "voyageurs, wives and children," after which each member could "drink as he pleases and retire at his pleasure." One can imagine how many would be "retired" after such copious food and drink. They were mostly Scots who enjoyed their drink, hard work and lively company.

No doubt inspired by memories of good times in Montreal, George Gillespie, together with three of his brothers and a number of other entrepreneurs such as Sir Alexander Mackenzie and Simon McGillivray, found-

Great-great-grandfather George Gillespie's Beaver Club medal.

A replica North West Company freight canoe sets out to run the Ottawa River from Ottawa to Lachine in 1973. A group of historians re-enacted the passage. I'm in the middle with the Tam O'shanter hat.

ed the Canada Club in London to promote trade between Canada and the United Kingdom in 1810. Today, it meets at the legendary Savoy Hotel and years later, as a descendant of co-founders, I was proud to be a speaker to this club so rich in tradition. It continues as one of the oldest dining clubs in London, with the very same focus it had two centuries ago.

After creating the firm of Gillespie, Moffatt and Company in Montreal, George returned to Scotland, where he purchased the estate of Biggar Park. But Canada remained in his heart. His son Alexander returned to Canada with the daughter of one of Wellington's generals as his wife and joined

Gillespie, Moffatt and Company in Quebec City, then very much a British city with a strong French presence. They named their son (my grandfather) George. George Jr. was born in Quebec City in 1849 and became a banker in Victoria with the original Bank of British Columbia, which was chartered in London and included in its ranks the future Canadian Prime Minister, Sir Charles Tupper. When the bank was sold in 1901 to the Canadian Bank of Commerce, he became its first manager. Despite the good distance between Victoria and our Scottish homeland, Scottish roots were constantly cultivated. The completion of the Canadian Pacific Railway in 1885 helped enormously in allowing the now-western Gillespie family to travel across Canada and back to Scotland. Grandfather Gillespie, who wore a moustache and had strong convictions, sent my father and his six brothers to Loretto, the leading private school in Scotland. Cousins in Scotland took the boys in for the holidays. Each would stay four years before his return to Victoria, which meant there was a Gillespie at Loretto for twenty years. They must have been hardy young men, because they became sought-after members of various school teams. And of course they started the day with a cold bath, a part of the get-up-and-go mentality of the boarding school. The values emphasized were duty, loyalty and perseverance. The British Empire was the product of that ethos, and the Empire was not English. By the dawn of the twentieth century, it was thoroughly Scottish, and Scottish soldiers with their kilts and bagpipes carried the Empire's banners in battles throughout the world. It was also Canadian. When war broke out in August 1914, my father and three of his brothers responded eagerly to the call to arms. Our participation derived directly from our heritage.

My father was, therefore, very much a product of this trans-Atlantic upbringing. His was a family of entrepreneurs, powerful athletes with a strong sense of public duty. In the fashion of the times, Grandfather George Gillespie had eight children (seven boys and a girl). They were a lively lot, especially Sholto, who became my godfather. He was a tall, immensely powerful and good-looking man – a charmer whom I adored. He served in the army during the First World War and was wounded in Greece. After the war, he left Victoria for China, where he joined his older brother Ronald, who had established himself as a senior manager with Imperial Chemical Industries Limited (ICI). Ronald, a tall, aristocratic-look-ing man, had served in France and was taken prisoner by the Germans. In an adventurous attempt to escape from the prison, his fellow escapee broke his leg and Ronald stayed with him and was retaken prisoner. The German commandant was so impressed with the help he gave his injured compatriot that he gave Ronald a copy of the *Complete Works of Shake-speare* to keep him occupied. Ronald was later repatriated to France on a prisoner exchange. After the First World War, ever the adventurer, Ronald chose China for his future career, but alas, when the Japanese captured Hong Kong in the Second World War, he was taken prisoner once again.

Another brother, Dugald, became the president of the Distillers Com-pany of Canada, the leading importer of Scotch whisky and other major brands, such as Hennessy cognac, to Canada. More interestingly, he mar-ried four times and my father was the best man at every wedding. At the last one he told him, "Dugald, I have stood up for you four times. This is the last time I'm going to do it." Dugald managed to remain a Presbyterian in good standing because two wives died and one marriage was annulled, after only a week. Apparently the marriage was not consummated and he realized it was a mistake. Not long after, he found a very charming, young-er, good-looking woman as his final partner. Despite or perhaps because of his marital record, he was a popular man.

Despite the distance and differences, we were a close family. We cher-ished letters from China, and the other brothers respected my father, obvi-ously a more reserved person, for looking after their parents. It was in all likelihood because of this care that he inherited the wonderful property at Matheson Lake that he passed on to the province.

My mother's family was, if anything, more flamboyant. Her great-great-grandfather was Duncan McLaren, the Lord Provost of Edinburgh, who left home at the age of twelve in 1812 to work as a draper's assistant and became a draper himself in 1851. He became the Liberal MP for Edinburgh for sixteen years and was so closely identified with Scottish interests that his Westminster colleagues called him "the Member for Scotland." The flavour of the family is captured by the description of Duncan's beliefs in the *Dictionary of National Biography*: "anti-drink, anti-establishment, anti-trade unions and anti-home rule." He had, it was said, a "prodigiously long upper lip and the firm chin of a calculating Scot." My mother inherited the firm chin. At the age of forty-eight, he married the famous Liberal John Bright's sister, Priscilla, with whom he had, at an advanced age, three children. The dictionary in its biography of Priscilla, a "campaigner for women's rights," says that Duncan and Priscilla were "alike in party politics and single-issue agitation; Priscilla McLaren and her husband were equal partners, though they disagreed from time to time on matters of tactics and policy."

My mother's grandfather, William Curtis Ward, an Englishman, came to Victoria with his sixteen-year-old bride several years before Canadian Confederation. As was the custom, they sailed from Portsmouth round the Horn. When the seas were raging, she was strapped to the mast but somehow she endured the voyage, which lasted nearly four months. William started as a clerk with the Bank of British Columbia, rising to the position of manager, which, upon his retirement, he turned over to my Gillespie grandfather, George. William Curtis Ward was also the founder/owner of the famous Douglas Lake Cattle Ranch in B.C.

My mother's Liberalism was, therefore, bred in her bones, but, as we have seen with Priscilla and Duncan, it was not a Liberalism that was conventional, not least because of my great uncle and other godfather, Frederick Scott Oliver, brother of her father, William Edgar Oliver. F.S., as he was called, was highly successful in business (an owner of Debenhams, one of the most successful department stores in the United Kingdom) and a respected author. I used to visit his grand estate in Scotland and shoot grouse and pheasants in the presence of the obliging game warden, but his real love was political controversy. My mother kept in close touch with him as he became one of the leading political polemicists in Britain. *The Times* of London described his book *Ordeal by Battle*, published in 1915, as one of the most important written during the First World War. He published a number of books and supported imperial unity, a sentiment that found many followers in Victoria, the most British of Canadian cities. He was, of course, the pacifist John Bright's nephew and had been forbidden to play with toy soldiers as a child. Perhaps because of that denial, the contrarian

F.S. became one of the champions of compulsory military service early in the twentieth century. He broke with British Liberals on conscription during the First World War and on other issues but remained a Reformer to the end. On his death the great Liberal historian G.M. Trevelyan, in *The Times*, described him "as one whose intellectual power was tempered with a quaint, sweet humour, testifying to the breadth and kindliness that underlay his revolt against sentiment." The *Dictionary of National Biography* adds: "He also had a roving eye for pretty women." My mother was silent about that intriguing trait.

My maternal grandfather, F.S.'s brother, William Edgar Oliver, was an expatriate Scot, a Victoria lawyer and an active developer of the city. He was the partner of Supreme Court Justice Lyman Duff, but he rejected politics as a most dubious profession. Nevertheless, he did become the first reeve of Oak Bay and developed that jewel which now is part of the City of Victoria. His style could be unusual and even eccentric. When he suffered a badly sprained ankle, he had his Chinese gardener, Ah Foo Yong, wheel him daily to the streetcar in a wheelbarrow. At the end of the day at a designated time, Ah Foo Yong would meet him with the wheelbarrow and take him home.

There were many questions about how the injury was sustained. My grandfather grew weary of repeating the circumstances and wrote a letter

Grandfather William Oliver on his way to the office. Illustrated by Susan Dunlop from the 100th Anniversary Commemoration Book of the Victoria Golf Club. Established in 1883, it is the oldest golf club in Canada still on its original site.

outlining what had happened, which he carried with him and handed to people when they enquired. He wrote it out to explain precisely what had occurred, the cause and the incrimination of a negligent Green Committee at the Victoria Golf Club, the nature of his injury and the progress, his thanks to those enquiring and a request for no further discussion of the matter. According to the club, this incident contributed to a lively, if not contentious, period of the its history.

His wife, Nelly Ward, was the daughter of William Curtis Ward, the principal owner of the Douglas Lake Cattle Company. Many letters from F.S. to my grandfather and a few of his to F.S. written during the war years were published as *The Anvil of War* in 1936. The editor, Stephen Gwyn, says that his letters show my maternal grandfather to be "a Scot rampant." Like his brother, he was "a very disputatious man" who argued ferociously with his brother while sharing a common pride in their Scottish origins and, in Gwyn's words, "a desire to undertake public duty ... accompanied by a rage against public duties ill done." With a sense of duty deeply felt, my grandfather tried to sign up for the war but, at the age of forty-nine, his body was not up to it. He was a man of strong opinions, and one he held was that my mother would learn more through travel and a governess than at school. He was close to her and took her on trips to Europe for her education. My mother was devoted to him.

GROWING UP

My father's emphasis on the importance of physical strength and training derived from his own war experience and his father's beliefs. Although we lived in the city, we thrived in the country, especially at Matheson Lake, which we visited almost every weekend. We had to walk almost a mile along the railway line (now part of the Trans Canada Trail) to reach it. There was a small boathouse on the lake and a big raft where my brothers and my sister and I learned to swim. In that magnificent setting surrounded by giant Douglas firs and Western cedars, we learned the lessons of the outdoors. My father, not a rich man, eventually donated much of the land to the Regional Municipality of Sooke, with the knowledge and cooperation of the provincial government, because he could not bear the thought of those trees falling to the loggers' axes. He taught us the arts and craft of the forest and shrewdly knew that handling axes for three young boys was a useful way to use up energies often applied to fighting. My sister, Catriona, was nine years younger than me. Even though I was scarcely around as she grew up, we were close. We adored each other. She lived and died by the family motto: fortitude in distress.

I had two brothers, Ian and Andrew, and we were a spirited lot. My father attempted to apply some discipline to our rough-house ways by teaching us boxing. It didn't always work. I remember one occasion when Ian and I had a tremendous fight that ended with the shattering of my mother's cherished antique chair. Like today's hockey referees, my mother could do nothing to end the mayhem and simply announced, "Let them have it out". We did, but then my father came home and we got a caning. Sometimes he even used a riding crop. He would tell us that he had been caned at boarding school and it was always for a good reason. We never resented it because we also knew we had earned the punishment. It became a badge of honour and we never confessed that it hurt.

The manly arts, as they were then called, served us well when Ian and I went off to boarding school at Brentwood College, at the south end of the Saanich Peninsula, near Butchart Gardens, where hazing was an unfortunate tradition. One of the seniors told us we were the next set of new boys to be hazed. We had a couple of robust friends, and the bunch of us told the seniors that "if you try it with us, we'll knock the shit out of you." One tried, and we did. The result of the first victory of freshmen over seniors was the end of hazing at Brentwood College.

The weekends in the country were idyllic parts of our youth. Unlike many, if not most, of our contemporaries, we did not spend much time in church. My mother's family had been Presbyterian and my father's Anglican, and I was baptized as an Anglican. However, religion mattered little to us, apart from the traditional Christian ceremonies of Easter and Christmas. Even in the case of the former, I remember my father would head to Matheson Lake on Easter Sunday bearing a bit of guilt, which my mother and siblings dismissed with such comments as, "Well, Dad, when you're in the country you're nearer to God than when you're in church." Perhaps it was the war, or maybe my mother's radical and questioning spirit, or perhaps it was simply the good life that came in the twenties, but whatever the reason churchgoing was not a part of my early life except for formalities at school.

The post-Great War depression lifted just after my birth, May Day, 1922. The 1920s were good to British Columbia, Vancouver Island and Victoria, but although our family was very much a part of the Island establishment of those days, we never became wealthy. We were fortunate, however, in our good health. Like kids of the time, I had mumps, which was a worry for me as my teen friends claimed it would affect my virility. I did some stupid things and paid the price: I had some friends who lived beside Dunsmuir's Craigdarroch Castle, on a steep hill which turned onto Fort Street, one of Victoria's main streets. Once, when there were some unusually cold days, we took buckets of water, threw them down the sidewalk and created a splendid ice slide. I jumped on the sleigh, gained speed rapidly, could not keep control on the corner and smashed right into a telephone pole at the very moment my father stepped off the tram. He towed me home, somewhat the worse for wear, with a fractured arm.

My parents, with fairly limited means, believed in the discipline provided by private schools, although thankfully I escaped the cold baths of my father's school at Brentwood. I am sure we got some help from my grandmother for our education but we got pocket money only when we did chores such as splitting wood for the stove or shovelling coal at night, a common ritual in those days before oil or gas became the source of home heating. Fortunately, winters were mild in Victoria. I remember at Hallowe'en how we chased around Victoria after booty, with the prize being the dollar bill given out by a wealthy American who lived in our area. Compared to so many others, we lived well. We were even fortunate enough to belong to a fine golf club. My mother golfed superbly, to my father's undoubted envy, at the Victoria Golf Club at Oak Bay. Her father was a founder and champion, and the first captain of the club, the oldest golf club in Canada still on its original site. Our grandmother gave us junior memberships, which then cost $10 per year. We bought our own clubs. Perhaps my entrepreneurial spirit derives from an enterprise to make money from rich Seattle businessmen. They were invariably challenged by the fifth hole, which required a drive over a saltwater bay. We would make a little raft of logs and float out into the bay holding a prong on a stick. Plop, the ball landed in the water.

"Boy, get my ball," the businessman demanded.

"Sir," we would reply, "there is a lot of seaweed and the balls are hard to find."

"I'll give you twenty-five cents," we then heard.

"But it's so hard to find," we replied.

Suddenly, at "fifty cents," miraculously the ball would appear. Perhaps my lack of awe of American business acumen dates from this early experience.

Golf was one of the sports that occupied some of the spare time of my holidays. My mother, incidentally, allowed us to buy only a number five iron or mashie to begin with and would not allow us to buy another club until we showed that we could make it work. Unfortunately, my collection of clubs came slowly. My game improved to the point of being runner up to Billy McColl for the Victoria Junior Championships and a handicap of 6. I wish I could do it today.

Golf, of course, was a Scottish sport and within the British tradition, but it is a mark of the place and the times that in the twenties and thirties in Victoria the sports I principally played were team sports – cricket and rugby, not baseball or hockey. My first school was St. Michael's, where sport was central to building the young boy. I attended it from September 1931 to June 1937 and have very fond memories of Kyrle Symons, the headmaster, who could not abide laziness and insisted on cleanliness. The latter was difficult when, after a hot game of rugby, we'd come back to take a shower and, thanks to the headmaster's well-known parsimony, there was no hot water. A strict disciplinarian with an unerring aim, he would fling used pieces of chalk to gain a student's attention. There were some difficult times. Much later only the best memories endured when Kyrle Symons supported my nomination for a Rhodes scholarship. He wrote a letter of recommendation in which he commended my marks but characteristically emphasized that I was the "Captain of Games" and extolled my skills at rugby, where I had captained the team. It struck exactly the right note for the Rhodes committee, which valued "manly" ways.

There were many fond memories, but looking back on those times recently, I reflected on how much the Great Depression, which began in 1929, affected us and our friends. Certainly the good times of the twenties came abruptly to an end when Black Monday began to spread its ill effects throughout North America. I saw the evidence in the struggles some friends had, kids who withdrew from boarding school because they could not pay the fees and men wandering the roads out of work. Still, as a teenager, I was not much aware of the outside world that was falling apart in the thirties, particularly in Europe. We had our own world at boarding school, one that Benny Goodman and the big bands animated. Our world was largely sheltered by the rules and security of a boarding school culture. Through athletics we learned something about competition, achievement and the character of others. Little did I know in the mid-thirties those lessons would mean so much to me in the next decade. At school, we were strangely distant from the Depression, aware of a little but not a lot. Even in the thirties, I remember the summer holidays as being golf in the morning and tennis in the afternoon. There were trips down the coast, even to Northern California.

The Douglas Lake Cattle Ranch founded by my great-grandfather was a frequent summer retreat. Uncle Frank Ward ran the largest ranch in North America in his own way with the help of the local aboriginal population. In the afternoons he rode the range on an English saddle. In the evenings, he insisted on dinner in black tie. I became an apprentice cowboy and quite expert with a lasso. I once challenged Jack Horner, the MP from Crowfoot riding, to a lassoing contest; Horner, who prided himself on being a rancher, refused to accept the challenge.

I don't think we understood the broken dreams of our parents' generation, especially as they began to realize that the war to end all wars was yet another broken dream.

Even though I was a teenager in the Depression, I think my generation actually inherited the hopes of the early 1920s, the dream of a prosperous, modern society where a League of Nations would preserve the peace and where the marvellous inventions – the car, the radio and the movies – were making life so much more exciting. When I left St. Michael's in 1937, war clouds were gathering in Europe but they were only thin mists in Victoria when I entered Brentwood College that fall. My brother Ian and I went to Brentwood together, even though Ian was over a year younger than I. My parents, it seems, thought the two of us were so close that we should not be separated. So off we went to school in the new uniforms, confronting the seniors before they hazed us and preparing to fight other battles on the playing field. Athletics played a formative role in our school life and in our overall development.

Ian and I had a healthy rivalry, but that did not mean that the Gillespie brothers did not come together to fight battles together. He was my closest friend and physically we were equals. We did our homework together and, in doubles competition, he was my constant partner. I have a copy of the Brentwood College Magazine for 1941, our last year together there. The cadet corps had been organized, but the games of peacetime were still played. I note, with enormous curiosity and puzzlement, that I "was invited to read the lessons at Evensong in Christ Church Cathedral following a Youth Rally Service in May 1941." In the School Roster, I was pretentiously titled "Head of School." Ian and I were both prefects, and I am listed as captain of football and cricket while he was captain of badminton and squash and the editor of the school magazine.

In a decisive 61-0 rugby triumph over Shawnigan Lake School, Ian, "brilliant fullback of the team," converted eight tries for sixteen points. Although I was the team captain, the comments were more about my leadership and determination ("good and determined tackler") while those about Ian were more exuberant: "It is not too much to say that the whole side had absolute confidence in him as their last line of defence." In cricket, I reportedly captained well but, it must be admitted, the analyst said I had "bowled consistently well though, at times with but little luck." More troubling perhaps was the comment that my batting was "still variable, being too inclined to have a 'bang' before he has got set, with the result, he has got himself out far more quickly than he should have done." Ian was damned with stronger praise by this rather caustic critic.

A winning cricket team. The Brentwood College and St. George's School first elevens in June 1941. I am third from left in the front row. My brother Ian is front row left and my brother Andrew is top row, second from right.

The best high school rugby team in British Columbia. From left to right, front seated row: My brother Andrew, John Schinbein, Alan Brown, Jack Shields, my brother Ian. Middle row: Pip Holmes, Dick Whittall, AWG with rugby ball, A. Underbakke, cousin John Gillespie. Top row: Norman Worsley, Moe MacKasill, Tonkin Clark, Coach "Tiny" Levine, John Berry, Sasha Angus.

Trophies won by the Gillespie brothers, Ian (left), Andrew (centre) and me at St. Michael's and Brentwood College.

My brother and I loved to compete. Sport was at the heart of the life of the Gillespie boys. In the senior track sports, I won the 880 yards and Ian came third, but in the high and long jumps, Ian came first and I took second and third respectively. My younger brother Andrew was perhaps the best of the bunch, taking firsts in the high and long jump and the 440-yard race and later becoming Canadian half-mile champion. Andrew did well at all sports, but Ian and I were seniors together. When we did not compete, we played together, winning the senior doubles in badminton, after which Ian beat me for the singles title. We won the doubles in tennis too when Andrew won the juniors. Sports in school united us. It developed character and a healthy competitive spirit. It prepared us for what we soon would face.

The school magazine from which I quote was published in August 1941, six months before Pearl Harbor. We knew by then that this world as we knew it was coming to an end. And it did, all too soon.

CHAPTER TWO

THE SHADOWS OF WAR

When war broke out in September 1939, our family was on vacation at Radium Hot Springs on the Alberta/B.C. border. We had driven to Banff very much aware of the talk of war. My father became very anxious as we were heading home, but being young and thinking we were immortal, my brothers and I did not share his sense of foreboding. My father's anxiety undoubtedly arose from his own memories of the First World War. He was also well aware that his sons had been raised with an ethos of military service. He himself had survived as a machine gunner in France and six of his eight family members had served overseas. Two of my father's Gillespie cousins died in the trenches of France. My father felt the uneasiness that remains with survivors and yet he and my uncle Ronald enlisted once again in the Second World War, my father as a reserve officer and Ronald in Hong Kong, where once again he was captured by the enemy, as he had been in the First World War in France.

Still, things seemed to proceed normally in the early months of war. Brentwood College, like other schools, did form a cadet corps, of which Ian and I became a part. We started to learn some of the rudiments of military training. Ian like many of us wasn't much interested in parade ground stuff. His sights and thoughts were in the skies. On his eighteenth birthday, in September 1941, he and an old friend and classmate, Derek Todd, signed up for the Royal Canadian Air Force. The RCAF won its wings in that war as it gained freedom from the British Royal Air Force. It became recognized as a premier fighting force with some of the most daring pilots who fought the war.

While Ian chose the air, I chose the sea but no call up came for me. On graduation from Brentwood College in June 1941, I enrolled in the Applied Science Faculty at the University of British Columbia. I wanted to be an engineer – a chemical engineer. It was becoming clear to me that plastics

My father, Erroll, a lieutenant in the First World War, re-enlists at age forty-seven as a buck private.

were going to play an enormously important part in world commerce, and I wanted to be part of that growth opportunity. During my one and only term at UBC I played rugby for the Thunderbirds and was finally called up just as the autumn term in 1941 was finishing. It was just after Pearl Harbor. I wrote to my parents on that fateful Sunday night of December 7, 1941, "What a terrible day this has been. I guess really it is one of the most momentous the Pacific coast has ever had. The news this morning floored me and it still seems a bad dream. What does Dad have to do? Wonder if it will hurry up my call to the navy?"

Pearl Harbor had changed everything and my call for the navy came at Christmas 1941 and I was ready. I told my parents that I "did not feel like studying any more. After all my work, I felt like chucking it. I just didn't feel I could stay down." My parents said little about my decision. They did not need to say anything because they expressed without words – and I understood how they felt – that our family had a deep sense of service. The decision to join, we all acknowledged, expressed our family's sense of duty and our traditions. They were as proud as they were terrified.

The Royal Canadian Navy began the war unprepared and weak with only 3,500 permanent and part-time sailors. It ended the war with over 100,000 men and women and 365 ships. Because of its initial weakness, the British wanted to have the RCN become a part of the Royal Navy, but Mackenzie King refused. Nevertheless, the RCN had to prove itself not only to the British but also to the Americans as the defence of North America had become crucial. Sometimes the British officers with whom we trained and worked treated us as bothersome colonials, but by the end of the war, the British and Americans recognized that the Canadian navy was one of the most important in the world, the third largest, and that its service in winning the Battle of the Atlantic had been decisive. I was privileged to be a part of that grand Canadian experience.

ROYAL ROADS

I started my naval career with four months training as a probationary temporary acting sub-lieutenant at HMCS Royal Roads. The government had purchased the magnificent estate Hatley Park, created by a local entrepreneur, Robert Dunsmuir – at one time reputed to be the wealthiest man in Canada. Dunsmuir had made his fortune from coal mining and railways and was an important ally of Sir John A. Macdonald. The Royal Roads experience bonded together the trainees, and it was here that I met my oldest and still my closest friend, Bill Wilder. Bill and I have enjoyed a lifetime of friendship and several business partnerships. I graduated at the top of the class, a distinction which I suspect had as much to with my skills on the rugby field as my academic achievements.

My first posting was to a Bangor minesweeper, HMCS *Canso*, on anti-submarine duty up the west coast of Vancouver Island and further north. The Japanese, always called the "Japs" then, had moved up from Pearl Harbor and torpedoed a merchantman off this coast and fired on a lighthouse. I wasn't long at sea because other plans, which I of course knew nothing about, were hatching. After three months, I qualified as an officer with a Watch Keeping (WK) Certificate. The government had decided to convert Royal Roads into a permanent naval college for the training of 16-, 17- and 18-year-olds as potential future permanent officers. It was a two-year course. My job was to take charge of the junior term, some fifty students from all over Canada, and to coach and captain the rugby team. I was the sports officer as well. Our team, fortunately, won every senior rugby competition in the province that year, much to the delight of the command-

The young sub-lieutenant naval officer in 1942 at Royal Roads.

Accompanying the Governor General, the Earl of Athlone, as he inspects the graduating class of sub-lieutenants at Royal Roads in the spring of 1942.

ing officer, Captain John Grant. I think the accomplishment advanced my promotion to lieutenant somewhat earlier than normal. Royal Roads was close to the established naval base at Esquimalt. The conversion of the Dunsmuir property to accommodate about 250 young males was not without its surprises. After all, the property had been used by family and friends as a residence and place for entertaining such VIPs as the Prince of Wales. It wasn't long before there were problems with the plumbing. The septic tanks proved inadequate for the new naval establishment. They had become clogged by an enormous accumulation of condoms.

This was a time too when the Allies were worried about the threat of fifth columns such as Hitler had used effectively. In British Columbia this led to a belief that Japanese-Canadians were unreliable for the same reason. There were a great number of Japanese fishing boats at the start. As a person who was on guard against Japanese submarines, I feared the same thing.

In the summer of 1943, I was posted to HMCS *Saskatchewan*, a destroyer on the East Coast, and the senior ship of the C-3 escort group. This was a trans-Atlantic anti-submarine and convoy protection assignment. Our two bases were the magnificent harbour of St. John's, Newfoundland, "Newfie John" as we fondly called it, and Londonderry in Ulster, Ireland. Our job, along with a number of other destroyers and corvettes, was to escort merchant convoys over and back. We had to keep the supply routes open at all costs. If Hitler was able to cut off the supply of fuel, oil and other materials of war to Britain, all would be lost.

The sophistication and number of German submarines gave the enemy the capacity to deprive the Allied war machine of its essentials. And Hitler's Admiral Doenitz knew it. In many ways he was a superb architect, who knew what was needed and how to do it. All he needed was the support of his boss to deliver the necessary number of U-boats. Up until April 1943 Doenitz was succeeding as his submarines were decimating Allied merchant shipping. He was within an ace of winning the critical Battle of the Atlantic.

Then the fortunes of war turned and shipping losses were greatly reduced. An unexpected ally presented itself in the form of great Atlantic storms in which U-boats could not operate effectively. The advent of long-range, land-based aircraft was also crucial to our success in winning the

Battle of the Atlantic. The situation improved but for sailors life was not pleasant as the storms buffeted us as well as the Germans. I described one rough crossing to my parents:

"I came for my breakfast with some of the other officers and as it was particularly rough we were using the cafeteria serve-yourself method. I grabbed myself some cornflakes and a spoon and sat down on a leather settee. I was managing to find my mouth without blackening both eyes when, all of a sudden, a ruddy great big one hit us. I tried to dig my toes in, like Mousey the wild-eyed horse, but failed miserably and consequently started across the wardroom – plate in hand – doing a juggling act till I was travelling really quite rapidly and as a result, banged my shins a hell of a whack. To alleviate the pain and with the aid of the ship, I must have jumped upwards. This proved my undoing for, with my forward momentum, nothing could stop me. I plunged the full length of the table, still balancing the Kellogg's product in what my fellow officers described as the most perfect swallow dive they've ever seen. Somewhere along the line, my head knocked the chandelier completely out of commission so that it was hanging by one thread. My feet in the meantime, with heavy issue boots, dragged right through the fiddles, smashing each one as it came and sweeping the silver ahead. I landed with a colossal thud against the electric heater and bulkhead with a bit of broken plate in one hand, cornflakes stuck to the bulkhead which must have resembled dirty stucco, a broken wrist strap, all the silverware and broken woodwork, and the end chair in an inverted position above me."

The whole disaster took less than three seconds. It was small wonder that for me service in the air was becoming more tempting than service on the water.

Although initially lukewarm to the British naval policy of escorted convoys (learned from the experience in the last world war) the Americans eventually came around but only after disastrous losses of unescorted merchant ships off their shores in 1942. They had been asleep in the Pacific too as Pearl Harbor revealed, but they still thought they knew best how to deal with the dangers of the Atlantic; they would learn how wrong they were the hard way.

The success of the escorted convoy system depended on a well-informed and disciplined group of merchantmen accepting a certain set of rules for their protection by naval escorts. After Doenitz's huge successes in 1942 and 1943 the balance swung in our favour when air cover was obtained from land bases such as Iceland. At the same time the convoys began to be supported by a few Swordfish aircraft flown off converted grain ships (the Mac carriers).

Air cover was the greatest factor. Indeed, the record speaks for itself: more submarines were sunk or disabled from the air than by surface ships by the end of the war. Admiral Doenitz developed the "Wolf Pack" tactic – wolf packs were groups of U-boats acting together rather than being deployed singly along the well-known ocean routes. These wolf packs along with new technology, including the snorkel and acoustical homing torpedoes, proved to be a major threat. The Allies countered with their own innovations, such as forward-firing depth charges and better radar. New mid-ocean attack groups were also formed, which operated independently from convoys.

But I digress. I served as a watch-keeping officer on the destroyer HMCS *Saskatchewan*, the senior ship in a group known as C-3. We were captained by an experienced British commander, R.C. Medley, a very competent but at times emotional skipper. He was known as JC, a nickname, short for Jesus Christ. It would be his responsibility to plan and manage his group in the event of a U-boat attack.

I remember on one middle watch (midnight to 4 a.m.) listening to Captain Walker, RN, deploy his mid-ocean group against marauding wolf packs. He was a superb tactician, an innovator like no other and relentless, surely the greatest U-boat destroyer of the war. Walker conducted his attacks all in plain language, no code, on the RT (radiotelephone). On one occasion as officer of the watch I listened in fascination as he directed his Bird Class sloops in a co-ordinated attack on submarines. It was 3 in the morning when the fight occurred, not far from our ship.

Our group, C-3, was fortunate. We never lost a ship. Large storms often interceded to protect us against awaiting wolf packs. Our destination was always Londonderry up Northern Ireland's River Foyle. We would detach our convoy and hand it over to British escorts to take it to its final destination, often Liverpool. In Londonderry we had ten days or thereabouts, for refits, repairs, courses and a little time off as well. It was on one of those occasions that I was able to meet with my brother Ian in Edinburgh. On another occasion I had tried to see him at his air station in the north of Scotland at Wick but without success.

Our group's normal practice was to leave the sanctuary of "Newfie John" and to escort a fast convoy (they were organized as fast or slow convoys) across the Atlantic. (Slow convoys would take ten or twelve days or more.) After the layover in Londonderry we would pick up another convoy of mostly empty ships and head back to Newfie John, whose welcome was always warm to the feisty boys returning home. The layover in St. John's was a short one and usually fun. I remember, however, one ugly incident. We had encountered a bad storm with freezing rain which had built up as ice over some of our sensitive equipment. We were put into dry dock in Newfie for repair, but without any heat. A destroyer is a thin-skinned vessel with no insulation. The ship's company refused to do the work – technically a meeting, I think, it was an outright challenge to the officer in charge. Somehow an escalation of disobedience was avoided. I think peace was bought with several extra shots of rum ration. Sometimes the turn-around at St. John's coincided with Captain D's Saturday cocktail party, an opportunity to fraternize with officers from other ships and of course with Wrens from the base and local girls. And who can forget the Crows Nest, an officers' club up two long sets of stairs in an abandoned warehouse where we would head for bacon and eggs and a glass of rum. The Crows Nest still operates and contains a treasure of naval memories.

At Newfie John our layovers were brief, sometimes no more than two days, but at "Derry" they could reach ten days. During one of our layovers we learned of a special gift, a piano for the wardroom. But how to get it down the small watertight hatch? Rules forbade any tinkering with such watertight openings. But matelots are invariably imaginative. First, wait for the captain to go on course. Second, put down a good coat of paint to cover the re-welded surroundings of the subject hatch. It worked perfectly and we had our piano.

John Nichol of Vancouver, later a senator and president of the Liberal Party, was a brother officer and a good piano player. He got us started on "Paper Doll," a favourite that we all could sing. Then, two days later the executive officer of the U.S. destroyer escort (D.E.) alongside us came over for drinks. We had dined in his wardroom a little earlier, but there was no booze on the D.E. The Canadians had the booze, but the Americans brought Eddy Duchin, probably the most famous piano-playing orchestra leader in the U.S. at that time. And the great Duchin christened the piano. It was a "helluva party" enlivened no end by some lively Wrens who danced the night away.

Letters to my parents were a relief for me, and in reading them now I'm surprised how open I was to them, especially about my dates, my marks and my stupidity. Like my chums, I waited eagerly for the mail sacks to arrive, and my own letters are full of bitter complaints about the post. Letters from home were treasures, not just because they had news of the family but also of my friends and my country. In 1944 and 1945, many letters contained news of missing friends but they also brought continuing excitement as the Allied forces triumphed. I was angry with the Canadian government for its hesitations and mismanagement, but I am surprised about how seldom I spoke about political events in my letters home. I regularly sought news of Andrew's successes as he became a young medical student at McGill University and thanked my sister, Catriona, for the socks, hats and sundry other gifts she and my grandmother knitted and sent to me. My family was with me at every step of the way.

Like so many young officers, I wanted to obtain my wings but the Canadian naval air service did not become organized until later. In the meantime, Ian had become a flying officer. His enthusiasm for flying was infectious and I had caught the infection.

Ian was flying with 404 Squadron, which in 1943 was stationed at Wick at the top of Scotland. His mission was to target German shipping and escort vessels, especially off the coast of Norway. His motto was "ready to fight" and the 404 "Buffalo" Squadron with its powerful Beaufighters was in the air constantly throughout the summer and fall that year when the war's tide finally turned. It was exciting but dangerous work. Although the powerful German war machine had been stopped in its tracks in the Soviet Union, its forces on the Western Front remained formidable, well-trained and determined. We could not relax, and Ian never did.

On December 22, 1943, Ian went out on a patrol in a Beaufighter looking for German U-boats and destroyers. About mid-morning, off the Norwegian coast, his patrol spotted a destroyer and a surfaced submarine. Ian, who had great confidence in his two-engine Beaufighter, attacked with the same determination that had made him one of the finest rugby fullbacks on the West Coast. On January 5, 1944, my father received a letter:

> You will have received official notification from the Air Ministry that your son, Flying Officer Ian Gillespie, has been reported missing as a result of air operations against enemy shipping off the Norwegian coast December 22nd.
>
> Ian's aircraft, in company with seven others, took off about mid-day to attack shipping reported early that morning on the southern part of the Norwegian Coast. They sighted a target just as they reached the coast and the formation turned to attack. Ian's attack was seen to be pressing home with such great determination that one of his comrades said the anti-aircraft fire from the target vessel was silenced. Ian's aircraft must have been hit on the attack run as it was seen to partially recover from the attack and then observed to hit the sea about one mile from shore.

The letter's author was Wing Commander Chuck Willis, the commanding officer of 404 Squadron (and whose brother had been with me at Esquimalt). He said that because of their mutual sporting interests, he knew Ian "much better than any of my pilots." They had played tennis two or three times a week and usually shared dinner on Sunday "at the home of a lady who originally came from Chilliwack." Ian had been the sports officer for the unit and, in Willis's words, "never failed to inspire enthusiasm among his fellows where his responsibilities were concerned, and that persistent sparkle in his eye was always the certain indication that your son took great pride in his fitness for duty and always set the pace." The sparkle endures for me; and it haunts me. Let me reflect on what we lost.

Ian was a very "cool cat." Fiercely independent – the second son of three boys and one daughter, he surveyed the field, then stalked his prey. He moved quietly, purposefully, then quickly, powerfully. When he pounced there was no escape. His friends called him Pussy. So too, out of respect, did his teachers, the school masters at St. Michael's and Brentwood College.

There were fields and rock walls and trees and an old stone castle in the Rockland Avenue district where he grew up. This open environment provided all sorts of challenges – Everests to be conquered. He loved to climb. The metal drainpipes at the old Dunsmuir Castle on Craigdarroch posed a special challenge – as did avoiding the watchful caretakers. Trees were for building tree forts. If he fell, and occasionally he did, he always seemed to land on his feet, just as his pet cinnamon cat did too. At gym class, at the age of ten, it was just the same. Flying upside down on a trapeze he kicked off and always landed neatly right side up. His life as he lived it over the next eight school years went from strength to strength. He loved physical competition. If there was risk so much the better. He knew no fear. Boxing, wrestling, gymnastics, soccer, rugby, cricket, racquet sports (tennis, squash, badminton), sailing, track and field – in these he excelled.

He didn't like bullies. More than one bully learned the hard way and paid a nasty price with a broken nose. He also had a temper which sometimes got the better of him. Such as the time he was applying a neck lock on a particularly obnoxious bully. Only the intervention of Pussy's friends saved the blue-faced bully from premature death.

Ian was a superb athlete. He possessed what today would be described as phenomenal hand-eye coordination. He wasn't tall – rather short in fact, but immensely strong. He admired sportsmanship in others. He despised the pretentious and fakes – except he liked the deceptions of magic. Drennan Hincks, the maths and sciences teacher at Brentwood, was his hero. In his early teens Ian became very interested in chemistry. With the permission, if not the full encouragement of his parents, he set up a lab in the basement. Extraordinary smells and not a few explosions followed. He was intellectually curious and liked to experiment. His lab came ahead of girls and parties. He didn't show much interest in the opposite sex – at least not until he left Brentwood – but there were Canadian girls he liked a lot, and at least one English girl in London.

Ian Gillespie, photographed in Victoria after receiving his RCAF wings.

His letters to me in 1941 and 1942 tell mostly of the boredom of barrack life; the inefficiency, as he saw it, of his training program, the incompetence of his superiors, the frustrations generated by a system still in slow motion. But he maintained a saving sense of humour. And more than that, he was thinking about and planning for his future after the war.

His energy, strength of character and determination manifested itself in many ways. He was accepted as a leader, a protector by younger boys and as a reliable ally on any team sport. Indeed a Brentwood College classmate, Colin Graham, immortalized him in a poem, *1943*, that he published fifty years later to remember Ian's life and death.

In the changing room
after the Navy game
he said, "Indian,
I've joined the Air Force."

Through the steam from the showers
he was already a ghost.

"Live forever, Pussycat," I said.
"I promised you, you'll live forever."
We're all immortal
    when we go to war.

You were posted missing in action,
the next I knew. Your Beaufighter
went down on bomber escort
over the Channel.
At Runnymede, I saw your name
twenty years later. It seemed
a terrible waste
of the best fullback
the world had ever seen.

The citation said
you'd died drawing enemy fire.
What else?
You'd call for the mark
solid as houses. You tackled
like a rattle-snake.
You didn't leave the kitchen
when the fire got hot.

I promised you you'd live forever.
Well, almost. While I live,
    so do you.

Neither Graham nor Brentwood nor I ever forgot.

In May 2004, we dedicated Brentwood's Gillespie Field, where there is now a plaque that commemorates the rugby team of 1940-41 as one of the school's "great sides." It points out that in that year there were four Gillespies at Brentwood, myself, Ian, my brother Andrew and my cousin John. John, like Ian, was killed in action. Ian, the plaque states, "is remembered by all who knew him as an extraordinary athlete and a fearless war hero."

At the time, Ian's death only reinforced a sense of duty and my own

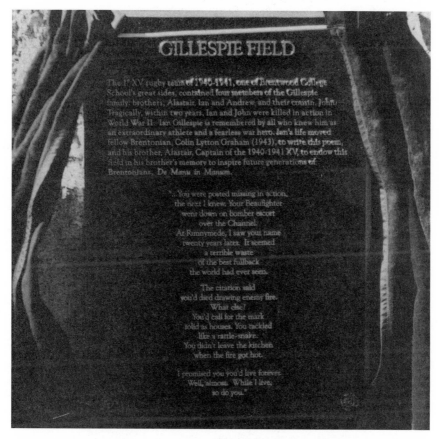

GILLESPIE FIELD

The 1st XV rugby team of 1940-1941, one of Brentwood College School's great sides, contained four members of the Gillespie family: brothers, Alastair, Ian and Andrew, and their cousin, John. Tragically, within two years, Ian and John were killed in action in World War II. Ian Gillespie is remembered by all who knew him as an extraordinary athlete and a fearless war hero. Ian's life moved fellow Brentonian, Colin Lytton Graham (1943), to write this poem, and his brother, Alastair, Captain of the 1940-1941 XV, to endow this field in his brother's memory to inspire future generations of Brentonians, De Manu in Manum.

"... You were posted missing in action,
the next I knew. Your Beaufighter
went down on bomber escort
over the Channel.
At Runnymede, I saw your name
twenty years later. It seemed
a terrible waste
of the best fullback
the world had ever seen.

The citation said
you'd died drawing enemy fire.
What else?
You'd call for the mark
solid as houses. You tackled
like a rattle-snake.
You didn't leave the kitchen
when the fire got hot.

I promised you you'd live forever.
Well, almost. While I live,
so do you."

The plaque at Gillespie Field honouring my brother Ian.

determination to get my wings. I was in the mid-Atlantic on board a destroyer escorting a slow-moving convoy when I received the news of Ian's death at the precious age of twenty. The signal message I received said that he was "missing in action," but I, like my family, knew he was dead. I cried like a baby – as I never have since – for we had been so very close. Off watch, I cried for several nights in the privacy of my own cabin. My ship, the *Saskatchewan*, became a sanctuary as I mourned a brother, a model and a friend. I had tried to see Ian in London just before he was killed but, as I wrote to my parents on November 23, 1943, I had very bad luck as far as spending any time with him the last trip over. He was doing a special course and I absolutely could not get any leave. "The sore point is that he is now enjoying two weeks' leave in London and I'm just about as far away as

I could be on this run." I deeply regret missing him in November and again in early December when we failed to connect once more. On this occasion, I had travelled in the most miserable twenty-four-hour train ride from the bottom of England to the top of Scotland. I had filled my typewriter case with oranges, which I had bought in the Azores, where our destroyer had had to refuel on the way back to Londonderry from Newfie John. There were no oranges in Great Britain's shops. It was a very cold, bleak journey when I finally arrived at his air station. I was informed he was out "on operations." There was little I could do. I had to get back to my ship and that meant the train, which was due to leave in an hour. In my letter to my parents I said I had never felt as depressed as when that train pulled away. I left the oranges but never did hear whether he ever got them.

Although my family was irregular in the observation of its faith, every night during my boyhood years I would pray to a God I thought benign and a source of strength. My prayers would at times be directed to some sort of future goal. More often, they were to some immediate priority and always for the protection of close family members. The prevailing culture of my childhood seemed to believe that "God is an interventionist – just pray and ask your friends to pray. If you pray hard enough, your prayers will be heard." It was a question of faith. At that time, death was not often an issue of immediate concern. We were young and fatalistic, and I had not yet heard a bishop's declaration that God was not an interventionist. Ian's death became for me a betrayal of my trust. How could God have let this so talented and alive brother die so young? I have never again felt the same way about faith in God or the power of prayer.

THE FLEET AIR ARM

When we docked in St. John's, Newfoundland, just after Ian died, there was a signal from Naval Headquarters asking for volunteers to train as pilots for a Canadian Fleet Air Arm. Canada did not have one at that time. There were Canadian aviators flying with the British Fleet Air Arm but there was no Canadian aircraft carrier. The government had decided (perhaps with the Pacific theatre of war in mind) that there should be a Canadian Naval Air Arm. Stu Keate, a distinguished Vancouver journalist, collared me for an interview. He said that he believed that Ian's death had created in me an "avenging force." Perhaps it had.

I put my name in, was accepted and given a short home leave. To get to Victoria from Newfie John, I flew off with Trans Canada Air Lines. TCA was flying Hudsons in those days, a relatively small and, as I recall, unpressurized aircraft. We had to put on oxygen masks when crossing the Rockies, whose splendour I glimpsed for the first time from the air. The Hudson had limited range, which meant that after an overnight flight we landed in Winnipeg. The captain said, "We can't proceed to Victoria (he may have said Vancouver) – bad weather. You will have to wait for clearance – perhaps eight hours – until things clear up."

As we were getting off the plane a distinguished older man asked me what my destination was. I told him and he said, "Come and clean up at my place and have some breakfast; you can stay until your flight is called." These sorts of acts occurred in wartime as a uniform opened doors and prompted generosity unknown in peacetime. On the way in from the airport he volunteered, "We have a famous Victorian here, Bruce Hutchison." I still didn't know who my host was. We arrived at a substantial house on a big lot, in a very upscale neighbourhood, Wellington Crescent. He showed me my room and said, "You can stay until you are called by TCA." When I got downstairs for breakfast I saw an envelope addressed to a Colonel Victor Sifton. A few more inquiries established that he was on loan – a dollar-a-year man – to the Canadian government as well as being the publisher of the Winnipeg *Free Press*.

After breakfast he said, "It may be a long wait. Would you like to have lunch with Bruce Hutchison at the Press?" And so it was. In those days Bruce Hutchison was perhaps the most effective author/historian in explaining Canada to Canadians. I had been impressed by his book *The Unknown Country*. In that book he had a fascinating chapter, "Men in Sheepskin Coats," in which he described how Victor Sifton's father, Sir Clifford Sifton, a member of Laurier's cabinet, had helped to populate the West with Ukrainian immigrants. I think meeting Hutchison, who loved British Columbia and the Island as much as I, made a profound impact on me.

My week-long leave in Victoria was restful but I was anxious to get on with my training. I was first stationed in Belleville, Ontario, where I received my initial training. The Initial Training School occupied the building that had previous taught the deaf and the blind, hardly the qualifications for pilots. The course lasted about six weeks and although the training was quite intensive, there was at least a little time for fraternising with some of the local girls. This ground training was followed by a stint at St. Eugene near the Ontario/Quebec border, where we received our first practical training at the Elementary Flying School. We trained on Cornells and strove for the day to fly solo. Although it was in many ways an exciting time, somewhere deep inside me the sadness of Ian's death lingered. But, typical of those days, his death did not create a fear of flying in me. I remained committed to fight the war against Hitler.

One day, at St. Eugene, I was called to the phone: "A lady wants to speak to you." Who could this be? No recent dates alas. Probably a wrong number. But it wasn't. Colonel Sifton had tracked me down. It was his wife asking me for the weekend to their family summer headquarters, Assiniboine Lodge near Brockville, Ontario. They couldn't have been kinder. I had formed a very high opinion of Victor Sifton – he was my first contact with a government leader and, looking back, he had a profound impact on my interest in public service. He was a very focused man who exuded confidence. He knew where the reins of power were held. Assiniboine Lodge was a gorgeous summer place, right on the crystal-clear St. Lawrence River. One of my pleasant duties was to teach Caroline, their teenage daughter, how to sail. She was a fast learner. I was fortunate to enjoy their hospitality on a number of weekends.

The next stage of my training took place at Kingston, where our planes were exchanged for the more powerful and versatile Harvards. Manoeuvres were much more complete and included night flying, instrument flying, acrobatics and close formation exercises. At the end of the two-month training period, I received the coveted prize – my wings.

I went overseas again at the end of 1944, this time as a fighter pilot. Given the attrition rate and the demand for pilots for the newly-constructed aircraft carriers, Canada had to send reinforcements. Victory now seemed assured but both the European and Japanese wars were still raging. Ex-

Getting ready to fly the powerful Corsair in early 1945.

ploding V-2 rockets in Britain were a reminder that the Germans retained much punch, and the initial successes after the landings on the Normandy beaches in June 1944 were followed by fierce German counterattacks. Like others, I was ready to fight but impatiently yearned for the war's end. On February 5, I wrote my parents: "The Russians certainly are going forward in great style – if only they can reach Berlin." I wrote to my family on April 15, 1945: "Apart from the exceedingly encouraging and momentous war news that day by day ever grows better, I cannot help but feel that the death of Roosevelt is one of the greatest blows that has befallen the Allied nations and free peoples of the world since the beginning of this hateful conflict. I honestly consider his passing on as a personal loss. Most of the people over here feel about the same way." He was, I wrote, the leader who came forward in "humanity's hour of peril."

Much peril remained, and I had some close calls in the last months when I trained on the Corsair, a very powerful machine designed espe-cially as a long-range fighter strike aircraft for fleet operations. At that time it had the most powerful engine of any single-engine aircraft, and this power made it a brute to land. There was very limited visibility when coming in to land with a huge gas tank and radial engine looming between the pilot and the propeller. Unless a landing was perfectly executed, the plane would bounce. More than one pilot was killed on landing when he tried to get airborne again to try another landing. The trouble was that the torque from the huge propeller could, under full power, turn the aircraft on its back. But it was another Corsair trait, which nearly did me in: I miraculously survived an upside-down landing.

My training concentrated on how to land a plane on a carrier, which was always tricky. We did our training at a RAF station where the runway was marked out to the same dimensions as an aircraft carrier deck. The landings were called ADDLS ("Assimilated Dummy Deck Landing"). Our approach was governed by an officer who guided us into landing, waving something like an illuminated ping-pong bat to direct the incoming pilot. If we got a "wave around" from the BATS officer, who would stand slightly to the left at the rear of the runway, we were instructed to break to the right and go round again at the RAF station. We then proceeded to try our skills on carriers. After three successful landings, my fourth attempt at a carrier landing generated a "wave around" by the BATS officer. I broke right as I had been trained to do. I had full flap, hook down, wheels down and, as in all carrier landings, had brought the plane virtually to a stall. Suddenly, the bridge, masts and funnel of the carrier showed up. I did a steep turn to the left in front of the bridge. I remember seeing the captain diving for the deck with his gold-braided cap rolling off his head into the scuppers. My hook nearly took him by the neck. It was a miracle that the plane did not stall and crash.

I then completed another circuit. When I landed, the public address system announced loudly, "Would the pilot that just landed report to the bridge immediately." I clambered up the various ladders to the captain's bridge with a big smile on my face. After all, I had survived. The captain was not at all amused. "Wipe that smile off your face, you f*&$*ing idiot, you bloody colonial. You nearly decommissioned this ship." He wasn't interested in my comment that the training procedure needed to be synchronized with the RAF's or that I had survived. He brusquely sent me away to do more ADDLS. After several weeks of penance, I was assigned to another carrier. I did eight or ten more landings but never again did I break to right on a "wave around."

(Above) My unconventional
Corsair landing.

Not much of an
escape hatch.

At the Fleet Air Arm station St. Merryn in Cornwall, I had another training incident. On this, it was air gunnery practice. When I started to taxi for
take-off, I realized there was something wrong with the brakes of my Corsair. I returned the plane and asked the mechanics to fix them. About an
hour and a half later, they assured me the brakes were now fine. I took off
and did my gunnery practice but as I landed, the brakes suddenly seized.
The nose of the airplane went down, the tail came up. We moved forward
in pogo stick style, and then the plane flipped over on its back. I was inside, unconscious, hanging by my straps, upside down. It would have been
hilarious but the fuel pump was still operating. Gasoline was everywhere
and could easily explode. Any spark would ignite it. Despite the very real
danger, Clifford "Clunk" Watson persuaded a few brave souls to try to get
me out. They arrived with a crowbar and axe and cut the fuselage open.
They left me unconscious in the harness. They knew if they released me
from the harness, the fall would break my neck. It had happened to others
in similar situations. Somehow, they got me out. Clunk (the brother of the

Clunk Watson reported on the landing and the rescue.

CBC's Patrick Watson) had saved my life and, wonderful artist that he was, captured the humour of the moment in a marvellous cartoon.

Soon after the war, Clunk, who had survived a crash on land and many carrier operations in the Mediterranean, was killed at the CNE Air Show at Toronto. An error by a flying shipmate doing close formation acrobatics caused a midair crash. What a sad ending to a very brave, talented and stimulating shipmate and friend.

Obviously, training for the naval air service was demanding and dangerous, and I constantly tried to reassure my worried parents. In a letter of June 20, 1944, I told them that my station was "extremely safety conscious and has one of the best records in the Eastern command." The carriers were much shorter than current ones, and they were not really designed for the kind of aircraft that we flew. When you came towards the carrier from the air, it looked like a postage stamp sitting on a vast ocean. You had to come in right on the stall so that when you cut the power, the plane would drop. You hoped desperately that the hook would catch one of the five or six arrester wires.

Four of my close friends, Mike Little, Frank McGarry, John Feeney and Jack Grogan, were killed in the U.K. during training exercises after VE Day when they were preparing for service in the Pacific. Ironically, on stationery dated May 15, 1945, my horrified parents received a letter that read, "Dear Mr. and Mrs. Gillespie, I regret to inform you that your son Alastair has been hospitalized overseas suffering from bruises, abrasion and shock due to a non-operational aircraft accident in the United Kingdom." It was cruel and I was livid, especially since the injury was mild and I had said nothing to them. It was an all too typical screw-up. In fact, I had survived the war.

The European war, of course, had ended on May 8, 1945. I wrote at the time and still believe today that we in the West had been granted our deliverance – "our deliverance from all the evils of the German system and the vindication of the democratic way of life." The night of May 7, I got together at a pub with a bunch of my Canadian friends to sing our favourite songs long into the night. The only ones I recall through the haze of drink and time are "Paper Doll," "I'll Be Seeing You" and various obscene ditties. The next day, there was a formal ceremony at 11 and then we partied again long into the night. We ended up closing the WREN officers' mess early in the morning. The war against Japan continued, and I was awaiting a posting there, which I had requested. Pacific service was voluntary, but I still wanted to serve. But VJ Day came first. On that unforgettable day, I was staying with friends in Cornwall on leave. We got into a tiny little convertible, roared through the countryside and did not leave a pub unvisited as the calm British countryside experienced, not for the first or last time, rambunctious Canadians at play.

In truth, I had not wanted to go to the Pacific. I was ready to return to Canada for the best of personal reasons: I had fallen in love. To speed my return I went up to Scotland, where I was posted to a destroyer that was run by one of my old friends, Geoff Davidson, from the escort and Royal Roads days. I was put to work as a watch-keeping officer once again and helped to bring the ship back to Halifax, this time without worrying about U-boats.

CHAPTER THREE

NEW DIRECTIONS

When the war ended, we did not talk about a war to end all wars as my father and uncles had done. For most of us, Europe had been Canada's major focus, but not on the West Coast, where the Pacific War brought the direct threat. The atomic bombs that exploded over two Japanese cities in mid-summer 1945 brought the Pacific War to an end and changed the world forever as we became citizens of a nuclear world. Little did I know years later, as Minister of Energy, that I would be dealing directly with the issue of nuclear proliferation. When the war ended, I was simply a lucky soldier going home. Canada emerged from the war far stronger economically and politically. We came home ready to take on the world, and we did. I'm not sure we were the "best generation" as the American broadcaster Tom Brokaw claims, but we were damn good and damn determined.

For all the perils and pain that the war years had delivered, there had also been a few exquisite moments. In the autumn of 1944, when I had just received my wings at Kingston, there was a long weekend coming up. My much-married Uncle Dugald asked me to stay in Toronto with him and Madge, the first of his four wives. Aunt Madge called her friend, Madge Hogarth, and asked her if her daughter Margaret was free that Saturday night. Alas, she had a date but she said she would ask her best friend if she might like a date with a young soldier. The friend, Diana Christie Clark, set out tough conditions for the blind date. If, on initial encounter, I seemed a hopeless nerd or a real pill, Margaret must agree to take her home.

Diana's father looked me over. His eldest son, Gavin, had trained at Royal Roads in the same class I had. I think that may have impressed him. In any event, I believed I had made a good impression on him when we had a drink together. Then, Diana came in. I thought, "My god, this must be the maid." But it was Diana, my stunning blind date. The world melted

An early date with my future wife, Diana, undistracted by the couple behind.

from sunshine when she smiled. Two weeks later, I wrote to my parents about my second encounter with "that beautiful girl." I had taken her to dinner and a show and she had told me that she wanted to become "active" with the RCAMC and would be going to Camp Borden. I lamented that that was "miles from here" and that I would not be seeing her soon. Nevertheless, the enchantment remained.

As a student at a boy's boarding school from 1936 to 1941, my contact with women had been much less frequent than students enjoy today. We did have one school dance per year at Brentwood College, and girls came from as far away as Vancouver. Family occasions dominated my social life outside school, but I do recall escaping once when I was fifteen or sixteen to meet a girl. Movie theatres were the centre of social life in the thirties and early forties and who can forget "Gone with the Wind" or "Casablanca." After the movies, we would go to the White Spot, where they would put a tray that extended from the car window on the right to the car window on the left to serve hamburgers or sandwiches. It acted a little like a "bundling board" and forced you to keep your distance. It was just as well because I was hesitant with women, no doubt the result of my male boarding school education. I finally broke out of my shyness at Royal Roads in 1942 when I began dating and enjoying the delights of female company.

But this little bit of experience with women had not prepared me for Diana that Saturday night in her father's library. We were smitten with each other at once. Nevertheless, I was soon to be shipping out for Europe and given the uncertainty, neither of us forswore other dates.

In the bloody autumn of 1944, Canadians were dying at sea, in the air and in the fields of France and Italy. There was still a war to be won but I knew that the Axis was crumbling and that I had to consider what I would do when peace finally came. My original intention was to become an engineer but now I was restless about my future plans. I recall a conversation with a brother officer one night on watch as we provided anti-U-boat protection for a slow-moving Atlantic convoy. He told me to focus on policy and politics: "Those are the things which create wars and can prevent them." It wasn't long before I came to the conclusion that there would be a lot of engineers after the war and that the world would not miss one. I decided to take a commerce degree with an economics accent. Through that work, I hoped I would make enough money to consider a political career. Public service and public life had come to matter to me, but I knew that failure could leave deep wounds on the ones you loved as well as election debts.

A year later, the guns silent, my future seemed very uncertain. Bickering among the victors quickly quelled my celebration of the war's end. I wrote to my parents on May 20, 1945, "Even now, with all the bickering and negotiating, I cannot help but feel somewhat depressed, but then at the moment, I am in a horrible mental depression." My dear friend Jack Grogan, one of Victoria's great rugby players, had been killed at my air field in a training crash, just as the war ended. He had been a close friend. I had to sort through his belongings to be sent home. I wrote to his father, "He was loved by all – always full of life and so gay – worshipped by his subordinates" and treated with "admiration and respect by his senior officers" – such memories of war would endure.

Staying on in Britain with the European war over was boring. I complained to my parents in a letter about going to a steamy, smoky gymnasium to watch an Errol Flynn film where the chair was too hard for my buttocks and the air too fetid for my eyes. Then, just as the climax of the film came, the projector broke. Typical, I complained, of the times and the service. The movies were part of an aimless life in those days. I liked Bob Hope. "See Bob Hope's 'Princess and the Pirate,'" I told my parents, "I'm sure Dad and Blos'm (nick name for my brother Andrew) would like Lauren Bacall in 'To Have and Have Not'. OWOO!" And I complained about Canadian politics: "I was very glad to see that Mac. King lost his seat through the overseas vote. It should give him much food for thought and help to jolt away a little smugness." And I must admit that I cheered the Conservative gain and hoped it would be greater, but I did express regrets that the Liberal lost in my home riding of Victoria. In hindsight, my political leanings had not yet fully formed.

Fortunately, the Canadian government and universities treated the war veterans better than they had after the First World War. We were an unusual bunch when we came home from the war, earnest but also a little nervous. A letter dated September 24, 1945, from Andrew's rooms at McGill captures this uncertainty:

> I find it quite unbelievable and at the same time just a bit disquieting. For now the impact of postwar readjustment is being heavily felt. Not only the different way of life that must be mine soon but also the thought of embarking on a civilian career that is likely to become a life's work … tends to give me certain misgivings. This new task ahead appears to me to be quite as severe as any I have ever had to face and always there is the uncertainty of security after university training. I am not worrying so much about my future as perhaps it seems but I do have a very unsettled and anxious mind.

I'm sure my brother's death remained an ever-present preoccupation. It was also unsettling to say goodbye to old friends in Halifax, but more troubling was the strong pitch made by the military to have me stay on. I easily resisted the temptation but had to find an alternative. I thought of law school in Toronto or returning to the University of British Columbia, but I remained uncertain.

When I got back to Victoria after the long train trip across Canada from Halifax, I made the decision to go to McGill University rather than return to UBC. Montreal was close to Diana but not too close to affect my concentration (or so I thought). McGill had an outstanding reputation for commerce and economics. As I mentioned earlier, the Gillespies had deep Montreal roots in the fur trade, the merchant supply business and the Beaver Club, important parts of Montreal's history. However, first among the advantages of McGill was the presence of my brother Andrew, who was studying medicine. He was a great comfort, and I joined him in his residence at Douglas Hall.

McGill, like English Montreal itself, was an enclave, a place apart from the French-speaking population of Quebec. To my enormous regret, I never found the opportunity to improve my somewhat tenuous British Columbia French. It was, by B.C. standards, not bad but by Montreal standards, not good. The uneasy relationship between the French and English communities was reflected in many complex and difficult ways. There was, however, a very amusing example which involved Montreal's Mayor Camillien Houde. He had been interned during the war for his anti-war attitudes. Houde, who won the mayoralty after his internment had ended, was really quite a character. Anxious about its place in the mayor's office, McGill asked Houde to perform the ceremonial kick-off at a football game in Molson Stadium. Perhaps to the surprise of McGill he accepted. The line of dignitaries formed, the football was placed and Houde grabbed the microphone: "C'est un grand plaisir pour moi to kick hoff the football. I 'ope you will hask me back so I can kick hoff all your balls."

Whatever its deficiencies in the eyes of Mayor Houde, McGill was an exciting and excellent university in the postwar years as veterans crammed the classrooms and professors from throughout the world taught with an enthusiasm that was probably later lost. My major professor was Kenneth Boulding, the remarkable Englishman who became one of the pre-eminent American economists of the day. He was only in his thirties but already possessed an international reputation for a two-volume study, *Economic*

Analysis, published when he was thirty-one, and an important article on "A Liquidity Preference Theory of Market Prices," published at thirty-four. My other teachers were excellent in courses in money and banking, commercial law, accountancy and calculus.

I was not long at McGill before I was nominated for the B.C. Rhodes scholarship. My name went forward in 1946. Although I was not able to travel to British Columbia for the interview, my various schools on the West Coast – St. Michaels, Brentwood College, UBC and Royal Roads – rallied to my cause. The decision came on December 12, 1946. I was told that I had been chosen and should get in touch with the Warden, Rhodes House, Oxford. In those days, people sent telegrams immediately and phoned briefly and rarely. My parents used the economical language of the telegram but their emotions overflowed: "Joyfully overwhelmed by wonderful news you awarded Rhodes scholarship. It's the talk of the town our chests bursting with pride. Stand by for long distance call nine o' clock your time tonight. Love & heartiest congratulations for all." Few words have ever mattered so much to me.

The memorable congratulatory letter came from an old Royal Roads friend, Gerald Graham, one of my referees for the Rhodes. He later enjoyed a very distinguished career as an author and historian at the University of London. He wrote:

Obviously an awful mistake has been made, and in the interests of the Empire I shall do my best to repair the damage. I am writing immediately to the Rhodes Trust to say that when I remarked that were Cecil Rhodes alive today he would have chosen Gillespie as a Canadian representative: it was intended only in good fun – a joke, ha ha – like nominating Bob Hope for the Presidency; who would have thought they would take it seriously. The other humorous element, of course, is the fact that an old crock like me trimmed the pants off you in a pentathlon at Royal Roads, and you were reduced to artifice and guile in the shotput to bring your pants up to a reasonable level.

He then gave good advice.

You should undoubtedly get your Blue in rugby, but don't let it swallow your life. I hope you will work like the devil and soak up learning. Everything is in favour; architecture, tradition and some famous men; drink it up – for it can mean wisdom – which this world could do with in quantity.

However, Diana's comment was the best. We had already decided to marry. In reaction to the Rhodes, she simply said: "I'm marrying him. It's the best recommendation anyone could make." And it was for me.

In the postwar years, the requirement that Rhodes scholars be bachelors was eased for veterans. By the time of my nomination, Diana had charmed my family – even my brother Andrew, a most demanding critic, who gave my parents "an independent opinion and eulogy on Diana." That was in the spring of 1946. But it wasn't plain sailing in planning our lives together. McGill contributed to our troubles by scheduling classes on Monday and Friday, thus limiting my trips to Toronto. We met infrequently, and I kept my parents informed of the developing relationship. Reflecting those conservative times, I wrote about one visit. "Then on the Friday morning we went away for a glorious weekend." I added: "Don't be alarmed ... Eleven of us went up to Diana's parents' summer place ... her brother Gavin was along and seems to be greatly improved and really very likeable. I get on with him quite well now. A young married couple went along as chaperones and proved themselves most popular and capable."

Distance created barriers but it certainly did not dim our ardour. I told my parents that they would really like her, "She is quite one in a million." In the summer of 1946, they came east for the Canadian track and field finals at which Andrew became the Canadian half-mile champion. They finally met Diana and together we told them we had decided to marry. They welcomed Diana immediately and warmly into the family. Their reaction meant a lot to me, and I reflected my thanks in a letter to them that asked: "How could I be prouder of my parents for all that they have done for me"? I so often wondered how I could express my real gratitude adequately. I never really could put my emotions about their love for me during these times into adequate words, but that inability reflected the depth of my feelings.

I returned to McGill in the fall and took every occasion to see Diana. I continued to enjoy inter-collegiate sports such as squash and rugby, of which I was coach and captain of the McGill team, while scampering off to Toronto to plan the wedding. I made the error of inviting Diana to a rugby game between Toronto and McGill in November 1946. It shocked her. She wrote my mother that English rugby was "so much rougher, so very much worse than ours ... After watching someone fly head long into a stone wall and Alastair underneath the whole of the two teams, I decided it was a very barbarian game. Alastair doesn't agree of course and thinks that I will probably learn to appreciate it in time!" I'm not sure she ever did. And she did have a point about the rough ways of English rugby. Once again that fall I ended up in hospital with my shoulder dislocated.

When Diana's mother heard about the Rhodes, she actually became a bit worried that I would take her precious daughter, who had not yet learned to cook, off to Britain with its cold rooms and postwar rationing. Nevertheless, she kept her concerns to herself, and on June 17, 1947, Diana Christie Clark became my wife. The Clarks gave us a magnificent society wedding – tailcoats, even spats and top hats, and long dresses – all the trimmings.

Although her family was of both Irish and Scottish extraction, Diana had more of the feisty character of the former and less of the dour style of the latter. Her grandfather had been the founder of Christies of biscuit fame. On her mother's side, her family came from the Goderich area, where her grandfather had been the mayor and a doctor. In fact, several of her relatives were doctors. Her father, Christie Clark, was a very successful businessman and one of the senior officers and shareholders of Rolph, Clark, Stone, which was the leading lithography company in Canada. Christie Clark was great company and left an indelible mark on Toronto. He served as president of the Toronto Club, was active as a racquets player and golfer, and served on boards of directors and took an active part in civic affairs. He and his wife built a wonderful summer home on Lake Simcoe, where we golfed and fished together. One of Diana's brothers is Ian

The beautiful bride. We were married at Grace Church-on-the-Hill, Toronto,
on June 17, 1947.

Christie Clark, who has been a major figure in Canadian diplomacy and
cultural politics and served as Canada's ambassador to UNESCO in Paris.
Gavin and Sheila were the other children and splendid in-laws throughout
my life, despite the initial wariness between Gavin and me.

AND THEN TO OXFORD

We went off to Oxford the next fall, excited and fearful of what awaited us. I knew England well, but as a Scot, of course, I had some doubts. We were met at Liverpool by an old Brentwood College friend, Harry Rogers, who had served overseas and married a beautiful English girl, Helen Fitz George Parker. They took us on a "familiarization" tour before we ended up at Oxford. It was a wonderful introduction to our new life together and to the English practice of the pub crawl. In future years we shared many with the Rogers.

Our two years at Oxford were full of unforgettable and happy experiences. We were blessed with new friends, foreign travel, new places and ideas and regular "Care" packages from home. Unlike Canada, post-war England was still relying on the rationing system to distribute food. However, Diana, despite her mother's fears, learned to cook extremely well although postwar rationing did limit her choice – a few ounces of beef every three weeks for example. On some occasions we had rolled oats for all three meals in a single day. It did take imagination to make a memorable meal, but we managed well, as did the English people around us.

What can I say about Oxford after the war? It was all that I had expected and more. In many respects, it was a two-year honeymoon away from many cares of the real world. It was also the perfect way to salve much of the pain of the war years behind me.

Our first apartment was a small one on Heddington Hill – a bed-sitting room, with a small fireplace as the sole source of heat. Like a lot of other things in postwar English life, the fireplace was hopeless. All we had was green wood. Furthermore, we had to share a kitchen where the flat's owner always seemed ready to make raisin scones whenever Diana wanted to make an evening meal. Too often cold and hungry, we decided to move and at the end of 1947 we found a better place at 5 Norham Gardens overlooking the University Parks. It was also close to Rhodes House. The landlady, a very imperial Mrs. De Vere Hunt, told us we were living on Oxford's Park Avenue – and charged us accordingly. We adopted an even more frugal lifestyle in response. As part of the rehabilitation of former servicemen, the Department of Veterans Affairs paid married students attending university $90 a month. That together with the Rhodes scholarship stipend and some of my savings was all we had to finance our Oxford enterprise. At least we were warmer in the new flat and finally had an oven of our own.

At Oxford, I chose to read Philosophy, Politics and Economics (PPE). Why did I choose PPE? And why did I choose Queen's College? PPE was the logical extension of the work I had started in the commerce faculty at McGill. My interests had increasingly been focused on a business career and on public policy issues. On my return from the war I think I realized that if at some point I were to seek elected political office I should be financially independent. The pay of a politician was meagre in those days, and I wanted my new wife and my future family to enjoy a comfortable standard of living. A successful business career could underwrite my dream of a comfortable political career. And I chose the historical Queen's College on the advice of my McGill economics professors, Burton Kierstead, John Rollit and Kenneth Boulding.

They had told me of a rising economic star at Queen's, Charles Hitch, an American Rhodes scholar. He was one of the first American Rhodes scholars to become an Oxford don when he became a Fellow of Queen's. Our first meeting was memorable. "Why have you come to Oxford?" I said I was interested in economics as a preparation for a career in business. He looked at me, stony-faced: "That's the first mistake you've made! Nothing in economics courses you read here will be of the slightest use to you in business."

I liked his iconoclastic outlook on life – but wondered.

When Robert McNamara became Secretary of Defence for President Kennedy in 1960, he recruited Charles Hitch, who had moved back to the U.S. to work at the Rand Corporation on defence budgeting. Hitch became the Assistant Secretary of Defence in charge of the business side of the department, at that time probably the biggest business in the world. It was too good an opportunity to miss: I wrote Hitch a note congratulating him on his appointment, recalled our first interview and wondered whether he still considered an Oxford economics degree to be of so little value. He wrote back, "Come on down to Washington and we'll talk about it." Our lives, alas, became too busy. When we finally did meet in the mid-seventies, I was Canada's energy minister and was taking part in a lively debate about conservation and energy. The Club of Rome's famous *The Limits to Growth* had become a focal point of debate. Active groups opposed to nuclear energy sprang up and new hopes were wrapped up in conservation and renewable energy. Hitch, who served as the president of the great Berkeley campus of the University of California between 1967 and 1975, had also been the president of an important consortium, Resources for the Future, which pondered the types of questions I had to ask as a minister. We had a good lunch helped along by a little wine as we discussed whether our values ever really change.

Post-war Oxford made a number of changes to accommodate the influx of veterans. The one-on-one tutorial system was often modified by doubling up. I shared my tutorial with Hitch with a Nova Scotia socialist, Alan Blakeney, a fellow Rhodes scholar, who at the time of my 1977 lunch with Hitch was a rising political force in Canada. As Premier of Saskatchewan he was nationalizing potash mines. As Minister of Energy I was trying to get the private sector involved. Nothing in our value systems seemed to have changed. He remained on the left and believed (at least then) in nationalizing natural resources while I believed in the greater effectiveness of market forces and the private sector. Hitch and I laughed at the way our arguments in tutorials thirty years earlier were now mirrored in Canadian political life. We both agreed, however, that those tutorials on economics had never prepared us for the energy crisis we faced in the seventies and the economic troubles it caused.

Perhaps the biggest surprise of PPE was the impact of philosophy upon me. I had never had any courses in philosophy and didn't know what to expect. "There is no preparation for it, Alastair, we will just do it," so said Tony Woozley, my pipe-smoking philosophy tutor. As I think back I believe I benefited more from the course on moral and political philosophy than I did from any economics courses. What was the main benefit? It taught me very simply how to think.

As I was pondering the joys of philosophy, Diana was learning the idiosyncrasies of English life. Just after our arrival, we were travelling with the Rogers and stopped to visit some friends of theirs in the gorgeous Lake District. I reported the experience in a letter home:

"We had already started on our drinks when there seemed to be kind of fuss going on outside. The host, Roderick, and a friend of his, Malcolm, complete with monocle, were somewhat mystified…. the ladies reported that Diana had got herself locked in an upstairs lavatory! A ladder was procured. Diana helped me in through the minute opening but it was no use – the door would not open. She had ripped her panties. Malcolm kept muttering to himself, in a rather slow drawl, as he was shooed away from under the ladder, 'But I say, dash it all old man, Canadians don't call them lavatories, they call them bathrooms.' Suddenly Malcolm's monocle seemed to pop off as Diana descended and, to the delight of all present, her panties were in full view.

By Christmas 1947 we had learned to grin and bear the peculiarities of postwar English life. We had, in truth, begun to adore Oxford. Our Christmas letter home that year declared Oxford "a fascinating place." I told my parents about our attendance at a ceremony where American General George Marshall, now the Secretary of State, was granted an honorary degree. Prime Minister Clement Attlee and Anthony Eden were in attendance along with many other notables of British public life. Attlee, I wrote, "is a very ordinary looking man-a complete nonentity at first sight. He looked most tired & haggard – little wonder at the present time."

Having family friends in England made things much easier for us in those first months, but very soon Diana's charm overcame British reserve and new friendships flowed from each encounter. I recall one night with Lionel Curtis, a famous writer and great Imperialist. He invited twelve of us to his rooms at All Souls, the intellectual heart of Oxford. The influence of Great Uncle Fred S. Oliver, a former associate of Curtis, prompted the invitation. One of the guests I recall was "an enormous Fiji Islander," who entranced Diana, the only woman present. She had "the time of her life" among the motley colonials gathered around Curtis. On another occasion, Sir Oliver Franks, the retiring provost of the Queen's College (he was appointed British ambassador to Washington) invited us to a reception. He was so taken with Diana that word quickly spread that we had made a mark. My (Canadian) view expressed to my parents was that, in contrast to Diana, "Oxford women are notoriously dowdy and plain. In many cases they are probably too preoccupied with Plato or Aristotle to give their appearance a second thought." Mind you, the black gowns they wore to class didn't help, but the truth was Diana brought North American glamour to bland times in Britain.

My interest in British politics was growing. Although I was not personally impressed by Prime Minister Attlee, whom Churchill unfairly mocked as a modest man who had much to be modest about, I liked some of his initiatives. My first experience with medicare "left a very favourable impression," I reported to my parents I spent a week in hospital in 1948, recovering from surgery designed to restore my rugby-shattered shoulder, which kept coming out at inconvenient times. I told my parents that I was impressed "not the least of all because I could see what a difference it made to my dozen or so ward mates psychologically. They did not have the spectre of unpaid doctors' bills hanging over them. Their personal dignity was not impaired & they enjoyed the service not as charity but as of right." I was not a socialist, but I firmly believed the state should take responsibility for the welfare of its citizens.

Oxford was a much different educational experience from UBC and McGill. The lectures were few and not compulsory; the required tutorials were the core of the education. I was constantly writing essays and reporting on what I had read to my tutors. Even on vacation I was given large reading lists. The academic and social life was carefully structured, and I came to believe that "tea" was a wonderful institution where one could meet wonderful English eccentrics, wise scholars and fellow students. We regularly received invitations to nearby country homes, including that of Lady Tweedsmuir, whose husband John Buchan (a friend of my great Uncle Oliver) had been Canada's Governor General and a great author. Mrs. Allen, wife of the warden, helped new brides to adjust to the English culture of the Rhodes trust.

Like most Canadians, Diana and I were irritated by how Canada rarely appeared in the British press, particularly our sports. Even Barbara Ann Scott's figure skating triumph in the 1948 Winter Olympics almost entirely escaped press attention. *The Times* declared after she won that "Barbara Ann Scott skated slowly." It was almost the only comment and it infuriated us.

On the spring break (Hilary term) we went to France and celebrated our birthdays (May 1 for me and May 4 for Diana). After a rough train ride, we reached the Riviera and stayed on that fabled coast for $3 per night including *petit déjeuner*. We dined at the Monte Carlo casino and, in postwar austerity where dollars ruled, lived far beyond our means. In the summer, we wandered again and saw Europe's charms and enjoyed the hospitality of Lady Francis Ryder's home visits for overseas Commonwealth students in Ireland and the Midlands. At the Christmas break, it was once again France and skiing in Switzerland. Somehow, we lived high on the cheap.

The fall of 1948 was a profoundly troubling time for Europe as the wartime alliance completely disintegrated and the Cold War began. I wrote home about the international situation and the tensions between East and West Germany. Italy seemed on the verge of collapse. "Things haven't looked as black for a long time – what possible hope is there for an eventual reconciliation of two views which are so utterly conflicting and divergent?" There would be none for two generations.

Europe and Oxford left enduring memories, but I was ready to return home. It seemed that past quarrels of the continent had not ended and Canada seemed ever more the land of the future. I told my parents in September 1948 that "for my part I am anxious to return to Canada and start earning an honest dollar. Besides there is the very great desire to get settled down with a secure job and start to raise a family. We're both very anxious to make you grandparents twice over." I told them that, unlike many other Canadians at Oxford, I had no interest in the Department of External Affairs, which offered a tedious life in the early years and, too often, political interference. My aim was to enter business with the hope that I might later have a chance to make Canada "play a more & more significant role" in the world. In the spring of 1949 I sent out letters inquiring about positions. Fortunately McGill gave me credit for some of my Oxford courses with the result that I left Oxford with a McGill B. Comm. and an Oxford M.A.

As we prepared to leave England, I expressed my appreciation of Oxford in a letter to my parents: "The prospect of leaving Oxford is a sad one indeed – we've both been so very happy here. Everyone has been extremely kind – we've met many interesting people and made some wonderful friends – I can't imagine any educational institution that could duplicate the manifold possibilities offered by Oxford." I still can't.

With Basil Robinson, Oxford blue, in the fathers/sons match with son Ian's Upper Canada College cricket team, May 1971. We won. We won. Basil was another Canadian Rhodes scholar whom I'd known since before the war. He was my captain in the Canadian Interprovincial Junior Cricket Tournament which British Columbia won in 1939. He served as the under-secretary of state for external affairs and earlier was Prime Minister Diefenbaker's foreign policy adviser.

CHAPTER FOUR

GETTING STARTED

Diana and I returned to Canada in the summer of 1949. She was pregnant with our first child, Cynthia, who was born in February 1950. Obviously, I truly needed a job. Fortunately, the times were right for a young war veteran returning home. After an initial hesitation at the war's end, the Canadian economy began an unprecedented period of economic prosperity that lasted for almost two decades. Unemployment hovered about 3 per cent, inflation was low, investment was strong and economic growth was continuous. I came home brimming with entre-preneurial spirit, determined to make my mark in a business world that offered rich opportunity.

My friends, and especially my father-in-law, Christie Clark, were very helpful in making the connections that are often critical to business suc-cess. I spent some time looking for the right job in the right place. I went to Montreal, Ottawa and Vancouver, where I had studied and had friends. In British Columbia, I had the chance to spend some wonderful times with my family, who were overjoyed to see me. I contacted no less than thirty-five companies and I had two tempting offers. One was in the investment department of the internationally known Sun Life in Montreal; the other was from W.J. Gage & Co., a Toronto publishing firm. I took the latter partly because I thought I would be a minor cog in a huge operation at Sun Life whereas at Gage, the largest educational book publisher in Canada, I would have more chance to influence operations – making a difference. Moreover, postwar Toronto attracted us.

For Diana, Toronto was home. For me, her family played a major part in making Toronto my home. Her father was a prominent businessman, who knew his way around the business circles in a city that was becoming a major international business centre. His own business, lithography, had some relationship to Gage, which was involved in the manufacture of sta-

The family, in the garden in Victoria in the early 1950s. Back row: My brother Andrew, my father, AWG. Middle row: Andrew's wife Betty, my mother with my son Ian, my grandmother Ward (Gaggie) with Andrew's daughter Gail, my sister Catriona, Diana. Front row: Two of Andrew and Betty's children, Dawn and Ian, my daughter Cynthia.

tionery as well as in publishing. Toronto was not yet Canada's largest city, but the foundations of its economic dominance were firmly established by a number of factors: its expanding stock exchange, the building of the St. Lawrence Seaway in the 1950s, the growth of its financial sector and the rapid expansion of the automobile industry that was centred in southern Ontario. The Golden Horseshoe that swept around the west end of Lake Ontario was acquiring its glitter.

We purchased a small house at 154 Lascelles Boulevard, which marked the beginning of our new life in Canada. On February 7, 1950, Diana gave birth to our beautiful Cynthia. In those days fathers were not allowed to participate in a child's birth as they are today. I tried to be patient, but when I approached Diana's room a very stern nurse told me to go away. She said I had done enough damage already. Of course our lives were changed for-

At home in the mid-1950s. Our daughter, Cynthia, looks over her younger brother, Ian.

ever with the birth of our daughter. A household that had been relatively quiet and tidy became a flurry of activity. Like so many couples in that optimistic postwar period, we embraced the idea of expanding our family.

Two years later, on March 27, 1952, we were overjoyed with the arrival of my beloved son Ian (officially Alastair Ian Gillespie). If life changed significantly with one child, it changed exponentially with the second. Our children joined the ranks of what came to be known as the "baby-boom" generation.

Gage was the corporate descendant of a Montreal publisher, Robert and Adam Miller, which had been established in 1844. William Gage, later Sir William, bought out the Millers' Toronto business in 1880. It was located originally on Wellington Street and then, after the Great Fire of 1904, moved to a solid old wood and brick building at 82 Spadina Avenue in downtown Toronto.

I was first assigned to the book warehouse on the fourth floor, there to learn the stock. Despite my degrees, I had to start at the bottom and did so without complaint because I knew that the best business leaders knew what went on at the bottom. On my second day, I arrived with fifty feet of thick rope. This created quite a bit of interest. What on earth was this new boy doing? A group quickly assembled. "Well," I explained, "none of us would ever get out of here alive if there were a fire. So, let's put some knots in it, tie one end to the radiator there in front of the window and neatly coil it up." This initiative was accepted quietly but probably convinced the supervisor that this eccentric newcomer was not likely to last very long. But I did, for thirteen fruitful and happy years.

When I joined Gage, the general manager (and soon to be president) was another navy war vet, Gage Love. He had ambitious plans for the future. A new warehouse was erected in 1950 on O'Connor Drive, and more would soon follow. In 1958, a large (5 acres under one roof) modern manufacturing plant was built on Birchmount Road in Scarborough, a new suburb where most employees then lived. In May 1953, the *Globe and Mail* printed a photograph of a serious young man along with the announcement that I had become an assistant general manager. A slightly less serious photograph of me appeared on April 5, 1958, announcing that I had become Vice-President, Operations. I remained at Gage as an employee until 1963 and as a director after I entered public life in 1968.

While Gage and the family were major preoccupations, I decided soon after my return that I would attend school on a part-time basis, this time at the University of Toronto, which was establishing a new business school, the Institute of Business Administration. My first work at Gage was as a market research analyst, a field for which my Oxford education, however valuable, did not prepare me fully. My salary was $200 per month, uncomfortably modest for someone who had bought a new house, started a family and was financing the purchase of a new car. It was a powerful incentive to move ahead. I planned to take a master's degree in commerce, and my first course was in advertising and market research. I wrote to a friend from Oxford: "How strange that must sound to Oxford ears. How vulgarly practical." But practical I needed to be. Not only did I attend the school but they soon had me teaching part-time, which provided welcome financial assistance. The students were interesting, Peter Newman, the future famous Canadian author, being one that I remember well. Although Canada was booming, the cost of living was rising and expectations were high. It was a time when a young businessman knew he could and should take chances, and I was no exception.

I was always on the lookout for new opportunities. In 1952 I went on a business trip to Western Canada and met an old school friend, Sasha Angus, who was working in Alberta. He had just acquired an automatic vending machine franchise for Kwik Kafé and invited me to taste the coffee. It was my first experience with coffee from an automatic dispenser – and it was surprisingly good, not least because the coffee was kept as a liquid concentrate under refrigeration and served with 18 per cent fresh cream. Even more impressive were the business numbers: the coffee sold at 10 cents a cup. The cost, including the cream, sugar and paper cup was only 3.5 cents. That left a big margin, the key to business success. Sasha suggested that I try to get the Ontario franchise and I decided to do so.

Upon my return, I contacted some Harvard Business School graduate friends, my old companions Bill Wilder, Doug Matthews and McGill friend Ed Ballon – all of whom had full-time jobs. We obtained the franchise for the Rudd-Melikian equipment and formed a company called Coffee-Mat Services Limited, of which I was the president. We were given exclusive rights for York County and first consideration for the rest of the province. In the end only Ottawa and adjacent counties escaped our grasp. Our first problem occurred with the need to adapt first to 25-cycle and then to convert our vending machines to 60-cycle power in Ontario. Within a year we had begun to expand. Sales for the first full fiscal year were $41,649. In the mid-1950s we added other products as automatic machines gained greater acceptance in Canada. By the end of the decade, we had vending machines throughout Ontario, many at large businesses, for example, twenty-five at Canada Life alone. Our annual product sales were well over $600,000 and, taking into account machine sales, close to $1,000,000. We moved three times to larger premises and had twenty trucks on the road. By this time, Coffee-Mat had grown too large to remain as a "sideline" enterprise, and we all had other jobs. We looked for a buyer. After some difficult negotiations, we sold the business to Canadian Food Products.

Being an entrepreneur always thrilled me but it did not invariably reward me. Sometimes I failed to recognize potential profit, notably in the case of a major innovation of those times: push-button telephones. I had raised the possibility of push-button phones with a former science teacher, Drennan Hincks, in 1951. Drennan thought the best approach was to incorporate the method used on juke boxes for the selection of records. I was convinced that people would rather push buttons than turn a rotary dial. However, I was too busy with my job, my home and selling coffee vending machines to take the idea forward. I wrote to Drennan on March 4, 1953, "If you can make some money on it, so much the better." Although he did not take it up, somebody else did and certainly made lots of money.

I lost a bit of money and time on a scheme called Areon, the brainchild of a naval engineer named Adrian Philips. Philips had the idea that the hovercraft principle could be used to build a flying saucer. In the fifties, flying saucers were the rage with reports of appearances everywhere. Philips had the idea of building a hovercraft in an airfoil shape (much the same as the wing of an airplane). It would gain speed over the water in normal fashion for take-off speed and then the jets would be made to tilt the craft upwards for the take-off. He created a prototype and managed to get a reckless navy flier to volunteer to be the test pilot. Since we believed secrecy was paramount for this grand idea, we went out to Oakville for a 5:00 a.m. test on Lake Ontario. Of course, it never took off and neither did my $1000 investment. I have kept the share certificate as a souvenir.

GETTING OUT OF THE CITY

My money was much more productively spent on a property that I bought in 1958 at Claremont, which is near Pickering, northeast of Toronto. By the late fifties, I was financially secure although not wealthy. Diana and I recognized that hard work can be only part of life, and we began to develop other interests which were typical of Toronto business people of those times. On one splendid October day, I came upon this land with no road but with a forest of hardwoods ablaze in fall colours. As I walked up an old

Fishing with Diana in the early 1950s. The West Coast salmon are big like the trees.

maple syrup trail, I came upon a wonderful view of Lake Ontario glistening in the distance. There was water enough to create a pond. Recalling what our Victoria retreat with its lake had meant to our family, I said to myself that this was a place for Diana, the children and me. I discovered that the owner of the land was a Toronto advertising man. He was also an unsuccessful hobby farmer who had lost money on sheep and then pigs. He accepted my offer and we began to dream of building our own log house.

My friend and partner Bill Wilder had bought a nearby property, a farm with a stone house and the original settler's cabin beside it. The cabin was in bad shape and well over a century old. Bill said, "It's a hell of a mess and it's too close to the house anyway." Two days later I got a call. "Take it down and take it away – it will cost you nothing. The same applies to the old barn on my property. If you want any of the lumber in it you can have it, but you have to take it down." I numbered the logs, hired some workers and a horse and wagon. There was no road. Many of the old pine logs were two and a half feet wide. It took two years to convince the local authorities that I should have a building permit. Together with the family we built the house, and Ian learned how to use an axe and hammer. It started as all original log houses with no water, no electricity. We added to this house and eventually put in a tennis court, and in time the whole family became extremely proficient at tennis. Some went on to compete and Cynthia's daughter Katie put herself through university by teaching tennis.

Cynthia's eldest daughter Vanessa learned to play tennis so well that she became an internationally ranked star and a member of Canada's Olympic doubles team in 2000 at the Sydney Olympics. When she was at Duke University, she was the first foreigner, as the *New York Times* reported, to win the U.S. Inter-college (NCAA) Women's Tennis singles. Claremont, or Highwood as we call it, after the family's house at Gillespie Place in Victoria, became a central part of our family life.

In 1963, we added to our family fun by spending weekends skiing in the Collingwood area. We had a cabin/chalet there and were members of Osler Bluff, the popular ski club of those days. Increasingly, I was active in Toronto clubs that were important to business life.

Another important association was that of the Canadian Institute on Public Affairs, organizers and sponsors of the annual Couchiching Conference. I served as a director from 1954 to 1967 and was chairman of the executive committee for several years. The Couchiching Conferences were conceived and developed in the early 1930s as a venue to debate measures to deal with the Great Depression. All manner of political issues, social concerns and, of course, Canada's economic prospects were the standard fare. Speaker-participants came from all over Canada, the U.S. and Europe. The conferences were held on the lovely shores of Lake Couchiching near Orillia, Ontario. They expressed the excitement Canadians of the time felt about the country's future and the challenges we faced.

The CBC was a partner in the planning and presentation of these conferences. Bernard Trotter, Art Stinson, Frank Peers, Reeves Haggan, to name just a few from the Public Affairs department, were very important to its success. The CBC, then a proud promoter of Canadian content and public debate, devoted at least two hours each night for the week, broadcasting the proceedings, the speeches, the debates and most importantly the questions from the audience on the floor. Canadian political leaders, senior mandarins, academics, foreign leaders, journalists, in fact almost any Canadian who was a somebody would come to enjoy, to debate, to proselytize, to put the record straight, to network. Like a Middle Eastern bazaar, it attracted an enormous variety of colourful people sizing up the offerings of others. There were pastors, professors, socialists, business people and the so-called "ordinary" citizens, all eager to share their thoughts and eat.

POLITICAL BEGINNINGS

Diana became active in the arts community, especially in the area of ceramics, a subject she knew well. After the birth of Ian in 1952, we moved to a new home at 27 Wilburton Road. We led a busy social life, often at an athletic club. One reason the clubs thrived in the forties and the fifties was the absence of good restaurants in Toronto. Another was the tight restrictions on liquor and hours of opening that melted away in the 1950s as immigrants and new ideas replaced the puritanical ways of Toronto's past, where there had been no sports or fun on Sundays or after 11 in public places on other nights.

Gage Love encouraged me, as a young business person, to take part in community activities and the broader public debate, as the Gage family itself had done. They probably were not so happy when I did so quickly in an angry letter to the *Globe and Mail* on August 7, 1951, I went after the mayor and city council for the rise in property taxes. I argued that the mayor had been badly advised when he claimed that taxes had increased in response to the rise in the cost of living. The increase in taxes was far greater than the rate of inflation. I concluded emphatically: "The Taxpayers are entitled to know that the Mayor and City Council are aware of this fact. They certainly won't stand for misrepresentation or ignorance." It was my first letter to the editor, and my first public contribution to Toronto political debate.

My political concerns went beyond municipal politics. Despite my doubts about Mackenzie King, I remained a good Liberal; Diana was a vociferous one and loved political arguments with our many Tory friends, for Toronto was then a Tory city. Liberals tended to be Italians and Catholics, and we were among the fairly rare Protestant Liberals. I had followed politics in Britain when I was there. I went to the House of Commons and saw Anthony Eden lead one of my heroes, the great Winston Churchill, out of the chamber for a vote on divisions. Another occasion stands out in my memory. It was at the University College on the occasion of a commemoration ball. Prime Minister Clement Attlee was wandering about the College and, astonishingly as it seems today, no one was paying any attention to him. Along with a friend, Erskine Carter, we invited him to join our party in a room full of Canadians. He accepted without hesitation. He said to us: "I understand you have an election in Canada." It was 1949. "How do you think it will go? Do you think the CCF has a chance?" I told him," No." My opinion reflected my sentiments, but, of course, not Attlee's.

On another occasion at a swish event for Rhodes scholars hosted by the chairman of the Hudson's Bay Company, Sir Patrick Ashley Cooper, at Ontario House in London, the Agent General, James Armstrong – a Tory appointment – told me over lunch that I should join the Conservative Party. It would help me get a job. I still recall his reaction, his look of shock, when I bluntly replied, "I'll never join the Conservative Party."

But I wasn't a truly partisan Liberal then. I just didn't like Armstrong's attitude. In those adventurous postwar days when the Liberals seemed the inevitable government, I was concerned about many directions in public policy. While I understood and welcomed American leadership of the democratic world, especially since I remembered the isolationism before Pearl Harbor, I was troubled by some aspects of that leadership. In 1950, in the first stages of the Korean War, I wrote to a British friend that it seemed there was "much unfounded hysteria and confused thinking about current international events. I wish I didn't feel that much of this confusion was caused by the political leaders of the United States. As a Canadian, I cannot say that I am any too happy in the knowledge that our country, economically and, broadly speaking, politically on the international level, is largely dominated by American thinking and leadership. But if, for no other reason, than their willingness to accept the task ahead of them, indelicate though some of their methods may be, I still have to admire them – but it's a qualified admiration." The comments summarized well my mood then, and, frankly, unlike that of some of my business and political colleagues, it hasn't changed much over the years.

I recognized the tremendous role American investment had made in the economic boom of the 1950s, but I was concerned that in our critical resource sector raw materials were exported and the value added in their processing was realized in the United States, not in Canada. The resource industries did not seem to be particularly interested in getting into the manufacturing or further processing of their raw materials. They had their markets, and some of those markets were covered by intra-dependency in which our in situ companies were subsidiaries and the manufacturing capability lay elsewhere. There was little vertical integration. Moreover, the financial institutions, which had earlier been the backers of Canadian business, were making vast amounts of money not by backing Canadian firms but by being agents who helped to sell Canadian companies to American interests. The appointment of Walter Gordon's Royal Commission on Canada's Economic Prospects in 1955 brought this issue to the forefront with its warnings about too much dependency. I did not know at the time that Gordon himself was to play a significant role in my future life.

At W. J. Gage, the ambiguous positive and negative impact of living next door to the vast U.S. market became very clear in the later 1950s. During that decade, the Gage textbook division provided most of the profits for the business. That division benefited enormously from being the Canadian agents for American textbook publishers who had undertaken much of the research on subject matter – but it was research related to American cultural values. I wrote to the president of Gage in 1966 (after leaving but still a director) that we had "overlooked the unpalatable economic facts of life implicit in such a course," i.e., reliance on a U.S. editorial point of view. The company was now bearing the costs of assuming in the past that "we were doing the right thing. We were doing it well. And besides, look at the figures – we knew what we were talking about."

But we didn't. The company was facing a crisis. The major American publisher Scott Foresman was demanding full control of the marketing of the financially lucrative Dick & Jane readers in Canada, of which Gage had the exclusive right to market Canadianized versions. Gage Love was advocating selling the textbook division. I told him that our reliance on others' editorial competence had made us vulnerable. Surely we needed to do more than simply "Canadianize" American texts. While economists produced lofty theories praising, correctly, the benefits of foreign investment, those of us who put together the nuts and bolts realized that there were real costs that were not captured in their stark and lifeless equations.

During the sixties, I developed a deep concern about, and interest in, Canadian politics and public life. When television arrived, I wondered whether politics would ever be the same. It wouldn't. More than the style, it was the substance that fascinated me. As I gained financial security, I had more time and probably more confidence, and both allowed me to take a greater part in public affairs. Some of my energies were devoted to business groups, where I advocated a more international approach to Canadian business. Within Gage, I pushed us to look at new markets such as Jamaica, where I made a real effort to have Canada lead in producing educational materials. A less successful attempt to expand markets occurred when I tried to expand into the Nigerian market. I had determined that Nigeria was importing virtually all of its scribblers and exercise books. I felt a subsidiary manufacturing company with key properly-trained Nigerians would have the contacts to exploit the vast Nigerian market. Alas, it did not work out but my resolve remained: I thought and still think that our business leaders should look to Europe and elsewhere and not concentrate so much on the United States. Unfortunately, such views were not widely held in the late 1950s, and in Canada political tides were changing.

The Liberal Party met defeat in 1957 and then disaster in 1958 as John Diefenbaker's Conservative Party took office in Ottawa. As Mike Pearson tried to rebuild the party, he agreed to hold a Study Conference on National Problems at Queen's University in Kingston from September 6-10, 1960. Although it soon became clear that the main purpose of the conference was to get the Liberals re-elected, the debate about Canada's future direction was lively and full of meaning. Of lasting influence was the debate about social programs, where a shrewd British journalist, Tom Kent, who had recently arrived from the *Economist* to edit the *Winnipeg Free Press,* and Quebec economist and future politician Maurice Lamontagne played a large part. There was already a developing rift between the conference chair, Mitchell Sharp, who had been C.D. Howe's deputy minister and who was more inclined to welcome American investment, and Walter Gordon, whose royal commission had identified his deep concern about the scale and influence of that investment. The major point about the conference was that policy discussion mattered in the Liberal Party once again, as it did not when they were in government in the fifties and as it does not seem to matter now.

DUKE OF EDINBURGH'S COMMONWEALTH STUDY CONFERENCE

A Canadian cannot understand country-wide public issues solely by participating in a political party. Another exposure to public policy issues was my participation in the Duke of Edinburgh's Commonwealth Study Conference in 1962, "The Human Consequences of Industrialization." A Commonwealth study conference for business and labour in 1956 at Oxford in the U.K. started the ball rolling. Its success led to a call for a second conference to be held in Canada, and Canadian labour and business offered financial support. The emphasis was very much on business and labour participation from all over the Commonwealth. Gage Love encouraged me to join the ninety-member council, which, under the leadership of former Governor-General Vincent Massey, planned the event, to which participants would come not as delegates representing a particular interest but as individuals. According to the May 12, 1962, *Financial Post,* participants were picked because we were "on the way up." The conference began on May 16, 1962, in Montreal and study tours went off from there to various parts of our country. I was one of fifteen group chairs; specifically, I chaired Group W, which visited a number of Newfoundland and Labrador communities. We travelled to Bell Island for discussions with representatives of the town of Wabana about the death of a one-industry town. Its played-out iron-ore mine stretched miles under the sea. Another Newfoundland community was Gander, a growth community, the air transport hub for flights from North American to Europe. Happy Valley in Labrador was the community adjacent to the great military base, Goose Bay. Its citizens relied exclusively on the needs of the base. There was a strong Inuit population in Labrador; at Northwest River in Labrador, we visited the first Indian band that wintered under canvas, across the river from the Grenville Mission.

The tour showed how each of these communities had developed as an isolated and remote entity and had responded to the pressures of development. The study group saw how each community had accommodated change to the many external forces beyond its borders and beyond its control. An unforgettable memory came in Happy Valley, where we met an Inuit woman who had two prosthetic legs. Her father was a hunter trapper who had set out in winter leaving a pregnant wife behind. Survival for both depended on such a lifestyle. He did not manage to return before their baby daughter was born. When he returned later than planned, the mother had frozen to death, the baby was blue and gangrene had already set in in the baby's legs. He grabbed her by the hair, cut off her legs with an axe below the knee and then dunked her in a barrel of flour to staunch the bleeding. She was an active woman when we met her – a person of courage who reflected the great endurance and resilience of our native people. These were truly Canadian experiences, the kind Canadians need to know and ones that intrigued the foreign participants in the conference.

The central focus of the conference was the question: Where do we find leadership? Be it Happy Valley, Labrador, in Ottawa, in our corporate or union offices or in the world. In proposing the conferences, Prince Philip had said that the armed forces train their officers for their most senior positions, but the private sector trains them only "for their next job up." He wanted to encourage young people to have vision. Among my group were three Canadians, two Britons, two Australians and individuals from Uganda, India, Trinidad, Malta, the West Indies and Nigeria. Bob Hawke, one of the Australians, became that country's prime minister. He was not a favourite – uncooperative and very self-serving. I believe the Nigerian, J.O. Enigbokan, was murdered in one of the tragic periods of unrest in that county.

We then travelled westwards through Toronto and Ontario into the far west on the transcontinental train. It was a wonderful experience that brought labour and managers together and introduced me to a diverse group of Canadians, many of whom I would never have otherwise encountered. As a great bonus, we met wonderful people from all parts of the Commonwealth. Those were troubled times for the Commonwealth as it dealt with apartheid in South Africa. There were also moments of great hope as the former British Empire disappeared and decolonization created many new states. Those states, unfortunately, have had many troubles, but most have remained in the Commonwealth. I like to think that the conference relationships assisted in the process of the new states finding their way forward, however difficult that path might have been.

Perhaps it was my appearance at the Liberals' 1960 Kingston Conference that brought me to the attention of Walter Gordon, although I had known Walter and his brother Duncan earlier in their role as senior partners in the accounting firm Clarkson Gordon and the management consultant firm Woods Gordon. Walter had become much more serious about politics after his Royal Commission involvement and had organized Mike Pearson's campaign for the Liberal leadership. He funded Pearson and recruited a bunch of young people to work for him, including the shrewd political strategist Keith Davey and others. Walter himself was elected to the House of Commons in 1962 and was certain to be a minister if Pearson came to power, which he did in April 1963. He had created a very successful firm called Canadian Corporate Management (CanCorp) which acquired Canadian companies whose owners were looking for responsible buyers. CanCorp's mission was to add value after the acquisition. Knowing that he was leaving, Walter asked me to join the firm in 1963. It was a great opportunity to work for a firm that reflected my own beliefs about the importance of Canadian innovation, processing and business leadership. I left Gage and embarked on a new venture, one that seemed to fit well with both my experience and my beliefs.

CHAPTER FIVE

BECOMING A PLAYER IN THE PARTY

Becoming linked to Walter Gordon meant that I would be close to the political action, and I had long cherished the excitement. Just after the war, I was already interested and bold enough to tell the Rhodes scholarship selection committee that politics were my future ambition. At Oxford, moreover, I had taken the classic training for future politicians, "PPE" (philosophy, politics and economics). Politics and public service had played an important part in the careers of some ancestors, mostly on my maternal side. They included the nineteenth-century Liberal Duncan MacLaren, member of the British House of Commons, and later Lord Provost of Edinburgh. There were also the twentieth-century writer/politician Frederick Scott Oliver, my godfather, and his brother, my grandfather, W.E. Oliver. I made no secret of my ambitions because – undoubtedly prompted by my mother – I believed politics was a responsible calling, one that demanded commitment, responsibility, energy and, preferably, a sound financial base. What intrigued me about politics was what you could do. More than any other career, you could hope to influence the future course of your country.

Although my family, my job and other interests took most of my time and attention in the 1950s, public service and political work occupied increasing hours as the decade progressed. When John Diefenbaker trounced the Liberals in 1958, the Liberal Party's collapse paradoxically offered great opportunity. The broken pieces of the once-great political machine were there for the quickest and brightest to pick up. At the Kingston Conference in 1960, I noticed the tension between the "old guard" like Paul Martin and Jack Pickersgill, who appeared leery of "amateurs" talking about "policy." Policy was for leaders, not for a bunch of people who had never held elective office. But the conference brought together people like Tom Kent, Mitchell Sharp (who chaired it), Walter Gordon, Maurice Lamontagne, Montreal business leader Bud Drury, and many others who were to be the dynamic force that rebuilt Canadian Liberalism in the 1960s. They set much of the agenda that governed and changed Canada dramatically when the Liberal Party finally regained power.

Martin and Pickersgill did have a point, the same one that Tip O'Neill famously made: "All politics is local." You had to have roots, friends and financial supporters. Living in Toronto, playing squash and tennis at various clubs, raising a family and participating in public events creates a network, one where you can send out messages about what you believe and what you can do. The remaking of the Liberal Party in the 1960s began at the grassroots, and riding associations were never as lively as they were in those days when we believed we were not simply winning a riding but changing Canada. I joined the St. Paul's Riding Association of the Liberal Party in 1960, the same year that I attended the Kingston Conference. Ian Wahn, a fellow Rhodes scholar, had secured the Liberal nomination for St. Paul's. I organized and chaired "citizen forums" for him where voters in St. Paul's could give their views on the issues of the day. We would get one or two speakers, debate the issues and then get to know each other in a school auditorium. It was a beginning adopted by other ridings. In 1962 Wahn defeated another Rhodes scholar, the formidable Roland Michener, the Speaker of the House and an Oxford classmate and doubles partner of Liberal Leader Mike Pearson. His own leader, Prime Minister John Diefenbaker, distrusted Michener, whom he regarded as suspiciously close to Pearson, and his suspicions gained, for him, substantiation when Pearson appointed Michener Governor-General of Canada. Later, when I was sworn in as a cabinet minister, and over a glass of ceremonial champagne, I told Governor-General Michener that I had helped to make him available for his high office as a member of Ian Wahn's victorious team. Michener gave a wry smile; Prime Minister Trudeau stared into the bottom of his glass. I did not like the oath of office swearing allegiance to the Queen; I thought it should be an oath swearing allegiance to Canada.

When I first became involved in politics, Toronto was not traditional Liberal territory and the Liberal defeat in the general election of '57 and again in '58 was a bad beginning for the leadership of Mike Pearson as the Tories swept Toronto, the town of his birth. Despite the tremendous postwar boom under the Liberals, the business community was inclined towards the Tories, although Diefenbaker's western radicalism began to trouble them in the early 1960s. The Tories, however, had many Toronto business-men who gave them credibility in the 1950s and 1960s: the Bay Street law-yer Michener; Donald Fleming, the powerful Minister of Finance; dashing George Hees, the popular veteran and Minister of Trade and Commerce; and Wallace McCutcheon, a giant on Bay Street. But a new and younger generation was beginning to smell victory, and it was willing to work hard. Ian Wahn, for example, canvassed almost daily in the evening. The St. Paul's riding was multicultural with a large Chinese-Canadian community, and the new arrivals were not so attracted to Tory ideas and ways.

One of Wahn's not-so-secret weapons was Doc Yip, of Chinese extrac-tion. He appealed to large communities of Chinese-Canadians on behalf of Wahn, a name he pronounced as if it were spelled Wong. Doc was an agile fellow; he became Treasurer of the party and he almost always got a seat up front at Liberal meetings. He would always have a camera around his neck. He aimed it frequently but I sometimes wondered if it ever had any film because I never saw the photos. Nevertheless, it got him a good seat and lots of attention as he passed the hat.

I had one unforgettable encounter. It occurred at an apartment building at about 8 o'clock in the evening. I knocked on the door and announced myself as a Liberal working for the Liberal candidate. I waited ... and then the door opened. She had just stepped out of the shower and the only thing she was wearing was a smile. "I'm Liberal," she said, "come on in." The Liberal Party is full of wonderful surprises.

That election of '62 was the beginning of the end for the Diefenbaker government. The Tories fell from over 200 seats to only 116. Whereas the West remained fairly loyal to "The Chief," Quebec abandoned him, as did Ontario. His total in Ontario fell from 67 to 35 while ours rose from only 14 to 43. We made deep inroads in Toronto, and Wahn, Paul Hellyer, Don Macdonald, Mitchell Sharp and Walter Gordon formed a solid Liberal phalanx to advance on Ottawa. Walter was now the organizational leader, and he recruited Keith Davey and Richard (Dick) O'Hagan from the *To-*

ronto Star to provide the kind of media skills that were essential in modern politics. Walter had considerable influence with the *Toronto Star*, which never failed to put his comments on any matter on the front page. He was, for the *Star*'s publisher, Beland Honderich, the voice of common sense, political wisdom and, above all, Canadian nationalism. I'll never forget the headline in the *Toronto Star* when Walter's second budget was presented, "Walter Does It Again."

At the national Liberal rally in Ottawa in 1961, nationalism was very much in the air, as was the need to respond to the strong winds blowing from the election of the Jean Lesage Liberal government in Quebec in 1960. The so-called Quiet Revolution set off a storm in Canadian politics, the gusts of which still blow through Ottawa. In English Canada, many were sharing my concerns that our prosperity in the 1950s had been too dependent on American direct investment and that we had become an inward-looking nation. Gage was a good example, as I mentioned in chapter 4. Its experience mirrored the influence of American direct investment in the fifties. I had worried about our unwillingness to spend money on editorial staff that became essential when the nature of the textbook market changed in the sixties, partly in response to Canadian nationalism. Just before I left Gage for Canadian Corporate Management (CanCorp) in 1963, I wrote a memorandum urging stronger attention to Canadian programs and lamenting that we had not paid enough attention to Quebec.

CanCorp was an exciting and, for me, a highly profitable experience from 1963 to 1968. I suppose that Walter Gordon developed the idea for the company through his work at Woods Gordon, where his firm covered the waterfront, including the leading Canadian chartered accounting firm, management consultants and bankruptcy specialists. He would have learned how many solid Canadian companies were poorly managed and unable – through lack of capital or succession problems – to take advantage of opportunities. CanCorp was a company which purchased controlling interests, most often full ownership, of Canadian firms that the owners were looking to sell – often to American investors. When Walter entered politics, his brother Duncan became the "designated hitter" for the family, which maintained a controlling interest. I suspect Walter knew what we were doing, but I was never aware of any action by him during his political life that directly affected the value of CanCorp. In my company work, I had little contact with the Gordons after Walter first met me in a restaurant in the old *Toronto Star* building and asked me to join the firm. I became the vice-president and Larry Bonnycastle, another Rhodes scholar, was president. He dealt with the Gordons, who kept a discreet distance, especially after Walter entered politics.

CanCorp in itself was, deliberately, a partial demonstration of Walter's nationalist theories, which he had reflected in the Royal Commission he had headed. It was partly the inspiration for a much debated, public-private Canada Development Corporation which Walter announced in the 1964 budget and which was one of my cabinet responsibilities in the seventies. The premise was that Canadians did not own enough of their own industries and that Canadians should invest more in equities. The Canada Development Corporation would give them a nationalist vehicle. In the case of CanCorp, we took full advantage of the boom of the 1960s. It wasn't always easy if even possible to find Canadian purchasers Our board was distinguished, and I worked with some of the outstanding business people of North America, including Hartland Molson of breweries fame, Grant Glassco, the president of Brazilian Light and Power, R.A. Laidlaw from Canada and Godfrey Rockefeller, Douglas Stuart and Winfield Ellis from the United States. We bought firms, turned them around and then sometimes sold them – for a very nice profit.

Although I never spoke with Walter about the matter, it struck me as very odd, given his Canadian nationalist views, that his brother Duncan (who held a controlling interest) sometimes would sell a company to American buyers. In his study of the career of Walter Gordon, Stephen Azzi quotes me as saying that it is "one of the ironies of Walter's life that he made a substantial amount of money by selling Canadian enterprises to Americans." He adds that I speculated that this inconsistency was known to his critics and may have accounted for much of the anger generated towards Gordon when he tried to limit American ownership in Canada.[1]

1. See Stephen Azzi, *Walter Gordon and the Rise of Canadian Nationalism* (Montreal and Kingston, 1999), 68.

I collected a bunch of directorships that reflected the kind of companies that we ran. I got to know the inside of many manufacturing, wholesale and retail businesses, including powdered metal technology, forging, steel casting and the metal valve businesses, railway supply businesses, printing plants, electric baseboard heating, cash and carry lumber for the do-it-yourself market, and the paper converting businesses. It was invaluable experience for public life, one that was probably rare for politicians. It gave me a sense of the strengths and weaknesses of our manufacturing sectors, including the advantages and disadvantages of foreign-based manufacturing licences. By 1968 when I finally entered politics, I was the president of Welmet Industries and Canadian Chromalox and the senior director of Richardson Bond and Wright, International Equipment Co. Ltd., Larkin Lumber, Mechanics for Electronics in Cambridge, Massachusetts, and, of course, the non-CanCorp company W.J. Gage. CanCorp boomed during the 1960s, and I acquired the financial independence that greatly facilitated my public life.

WALTER GORDON: ANOTHER BUSINESSMAN IN POLITICS

In April 1963, Mike Pearson won a minority government. The minority made life difficult, but his government in retrospect was one of enormous accomplishment. I believed in his activist liberalism and worked my butt off for the Liberals as a poll captain. A few years later in 1966, I attended the National Liberal Federation Policy Rally in Ottawa, where Gordon and Sharp fought a pitched battle on the subject of Canadian nationalism. By that time, Walter had left the cabinet. He had been singled out for Pearson's failure to win a majority. It had been his recommendation that Pearson call the 1965 election and the result was another minority. Walter became bitter towards Pearson. This bitterness started to develop soon after the troubles with his first budget as finance minister in 1963. In that budget, Walter had retained some outsiders in the preparation of his budget (David Stanley, Geoff Conway and Martin O'Connell, a most conscientious and very bright Torontonian; he was later elected in 1968, appointed to Cabinet and then defeated in 1972; he briefly became principal secretary to the Prime Minister after the election). The finance department much resented Gordon's lack of confidence in them and its bureaucrats did not approve of the substance of his budget. The distrust undermined the ability of Gordon as minister and the department to work together to advance public policy. The use of outside consultants was portrayed as a very serious lapse in the secrecy of the budget's preparation. It became increasingly an issue of confidence and Walter offered his resignation as the Pearson government stumbled forward.

Of course, I sympathized with Walter. Yet the budget did trouble me. There was a punitive aspect to it, especially in its treatment of American investors. In fact, there was a punitive aspect more generally in his approach to government. I've often speculated why he took such an approach and thought that it might be the product of his education at Royal Military College, but who knows? In general, he had tended to emphasize sticks rather than carrots, and that may have caused some of his problems in government. However, Walter was very kind to me and I believe that he deserves much credit for awakening the country to its over-dependence on American markets, and the negative consequences of too much foreign control of Canadian businesses. One of the most important contributions was his readiness as one of Canada's most significant businessmen to devote most of his energies to public life. He would say: "Look at the country. Parliament needs businessmen as well as lawyers." Not enough businessmen heard his arguments, but I certainly did.

The Pearson government could count on some outstanding businessmen, and they were liberal in spirit and Liberal in their commitments. Some of these businessmen promoted wide-ranging and enduring social legislation including the Canada Pension Plan, Medicare, Canada Student Loans and the national flag. His government also negotiated the very successful Auto Pact and managed to balance the budget every year. In Pearson's cabinet, besides Walter, were leading businessmen such as Mitchell Sharp, Walter's brother-in-law Bud Drury, Albertan Harry Hays, contractor Paul Hellyer, Arthur Laing, who had worked for a leading agricultural firm, and Bob Winters who was head of the Canadian international firm Brascan. No one could say that the Liberal Party was hostile to business or that the voice of business experience was lacking. I was impressed with what the government was achieving despite all the scandals and controversies of minority government and began to wonder whether there was room for one more businessman in Ottawa.

It was a lively time, an awakening. I participated in a fascinating conference on Canada's economic future in 1964 on Georgian Bay, where we considered the question of what happens when "Canada faces the World." Marshall Crowe, then with the Canadian Imperial Bank of Commerce, which sponsored the meeting, warned us that we should more aggressively advance Canada's trade and economic interests. He believed as I did that we exported too many raw materials and partly-manufactured industrial materials. Mitchell Sharp, who was then the Minister of Trade and Commerce, also attended this small workshop and said we had to get better access to other markets outside the United States. It was a theme that Diefenbaker liked too. Sharp later developed the "Third Option" when he assumed the External Affairs portfolio under Pierre Trudeau. Mitchell had been deputy minister to yet another famous Liberal businessman, C.D. Howe.

I attended other meetings like the one in Georgian Bay where we discussed ideas, but elections are not won by ideas alone. I quickly got an education in the hard realities of politics when I became the treasurer of the Liberal Union (an Ontario initiative) and its co-chair in 1967-8. I think I was chosen for my organizational abilities and my business background. I divided the province into about twelve to fifteen regions, each with a designated chairman, and established quotas for each. These were based on marketing statistics. Essentially, the job of the regional chairman was to enlist donor/members at an annual fee of $100, very much like the Laurier Club today. It was well organized and proved very productive. Party fundraising in those days was much different. There was no tax deduction for contributions, much less the generous tax credits that exist for donors today. The records of who gave were closely held among a small group of people. I would gather together a bunch of people, divide up the list matching those who knew or were owed a favour by someone. The experience convinced me that there was a better way, and I began to argue before I was a Parliamentarian that, at the very least, political donations should be tax deductible as church, school and other donations were. Eventually, changes were made. The fundraiser today has had to adjust to a different set of challenges.

CHANGING PARTY LEADERS

In 1966, there were already rumblings about leadership. Pearson was turning seventy; several ministers were elbowing each other to stand first in line. Because of my activism in Toronto, I had become better known among Liberals. I was not only a party fundraiser but an active participant in the constituencies and district meetings. By this time I lived in the Forest Hill area of Toronto at 376 Russell Hill Road, but I remained a member of St. Paul's. In poring over my papers, I note with interest that I was elected a delegate for Marvin Gelber's riding of Forest Hill in November 1966 along with Michael Ignatieff, then a student at the University of Toronto. I had always thought Ignatieff had joined the Liberal Party in support of Trudeau, but apparently his Liberal affiliation preceded Trudeau. It is curious that he chose a riding far away from the University of Toronto, where he was then a student. He was typical of the many bright young people, energetic business people and others who were becoming involved.

When Pearson announced his decision to step down in December 1967, one quickly had to decide whom to support. After casting about, I decided that I would support John Turner, a younger member and a Montreal lawyer. I had not then met Pierre Trudeau. I did not know John very well, but I admired his credentials. We had had several contacts over time. He was, like me, a British Columbia Rhodes scholar but unlike me, an Olympic standard athlete. He had sometimes called on me when he visited a canoeing pal, our next door neighbour Don Wright. When he asked me, I agreed to be his Ontario fundraiser. He was young, vigorous, articulate and bilingual. The others at the starting gate were either old warhorses like Paul Martin or unilingual English Canadians like Allan MacEachen, Joe Greene, Paul Hellyer, Bob Winters, Mitchell Sharp and Eric Kierans. The day of unilingualism had ended. Turner seemed by far the best choice. Then came Trudeaumania.

Strikingly handsome and extremely articulate, John Turner was a newly

John Turner speaks to a group of young people. I welcomed John's support in the 1968 election campaign.

minted minister in the Pearson cabinet. He had a Kennedy-esque physical appearance, great energy, a quick wit and a modern contemporary view of Liberal policies. Many an attractive girl melted before his piercing blue eyes, as romantically compelling as those of Frank Sinatra – or Pierre Trudeau. For John, Trudeau's entry presented a real problem.

Political leadership conventions are like nothing else. Music, hoopla, staged demonstrations, a sea of gyrating partisans' signs and not a few gyrating dancing girls. For all the appearance of a totally out of control, uncoordinated, even chaotic scene, there is still a pervading discipline among the separate delegates. A great deal of expense is lavished on establishing goodwill with potential supporters among and within the separate delegations.

Much has already been written about that convention and I need not add much. Pierre Trudeau had an exceptionally well organized and well orchestrated set of supporters. As an experienced businessman and devotee of modern management practices I was impressed. John Turner's campaign chief, Senator Daniel Lang (of the famous Lang Michener law firm), tried to offset this Trudeau tidal wave of energy with arguments that attacked PET as a "philosopher king." The inference was that Pierre Trudeau lacked leadership experience, was prone to the theoretical or academic, and not a person who would perform in a practical way. Besides he had never been in a military uniform. I never really bought into the argument but I was still a partisan like everybody else and mouthed the Turner arguments.

The convention, as I look back on it, was a turning point in my life. I made many friends amongst the various delegates. I had had the opportunity to size up the various contenders at close range, all of whom became senior members of Pierre Trudeau's first cabinet with one exception. The exception was Bob Winters, who had finished second and might have been the leader had not Sharp opted for Trudeau before the convention and Turner decided to stay in for the last ballot. A discouraged Winters returned to the private sector. His decision to abandon politics had an unexpected effect. It opened a Toronto riding, and I became his successor.

I had supported Turner because I believed him the right choice, and Trudeau had not impressed me. My first impression of Trudeau was unfavourable: he really didn't participate in small talk and, to my surprise, had a weak handshake. Yet as events unfolded he rushed into the lead. When Mitchell Sharp endorsed him, he began to gain support but I was not convinced that support was enough. I was working hard for Turner, especially in the fundraising area, where I encouraged him to call for transparent campaign contributions. I thought it would bring him much editorial support and capture the media attention that was so critical to success. I continued to think he would win until the last moment. Such is the enthusiasm of the true believer.

Gradually it became clear John would not win. I made some notes on what happened during the convention on April 4-6, 1968. In them, I concluded that we were victims of our own propaganda. When we did not do well on the first ballot, we suddenly became demoralized. I believed that Turner was right to stay in on the final ballot when Trudeau battled with

Robert Winters for the prize even though Turner was strongly criticized for that decision. After the convention I remained a Turner supporter, one of the 195 who stuck with him. He made a good show, one that placed him in the forefront of the government that Trudeau formed. In my reflections written immediately after the ballot, I summed up the candidates:

> Trudeau: After Mitchell Sharp's endorsement first rate-and on an
>   upbeat
> Winters: Skilful and good humoured
> Hellyer: Efficient like a greyhound but for all that rather pedestrian.
>   The package is more imaginative than the product
> Joe Greene: A steadfast reliance on the rural metaphor and in the faith
>   that if you can wound the real enemy your friends will discover
>   your greatness.
> MacEachen: A steadfast faith. Period.
> Martin: Faith, hope and charity.

Despite my support of Turner, the convention and Trudeau's victory left me more enthusiastic than ever about the possibilities of a political career. Following the convention I returned to my job as vice-president of CanCorp. Today CanCorp would be described as a small conglomerate. Its shares traded on the "over the counter market" and they stood at a level which provided me the financial independence which I had promised myself before seeking a political career.

Walter Gordon had long known of my political interest. I had told Walter when he interviewed me that I would like the job at CanCorp but that I, like him, might, at the right time, seek a career as a member of Parliament. He noted the comment, hired me but said nothing, although Walter, the master political recruiter, filed the information in his capacious political memory. That was in 1963. A few weeks after Pierre Trudeau's victory as the new leader in 1968, I was in San Francisco with our company lawyer, Edward Saunders – later a much-respected Justice of the Ontario Superior Court. I was trying to complete the acquisition of a major U.S.-owned fabricated steel valve manufacturer. It would complement our other valve businesses in cast steel and stainless steel.

We were staying at the Mark Hopkins Hotel with its legendary Top of the Mark bar: "A long distance call from Portugal for you Mr. Gillespie."

"Alastair, this is Walter Gordon. Prime Minister Pierre Trudeau has dropped the writ. I'm not running again. Would you be interested in representing my Davenport riding? I would be pleased to make the introductions."

Despite the fact that I had caught the political bug, I said, "Walter, my children are still in school. I'm enjoying what I'm doing. It would be better in about two years."

He replied sagely, "There's never a good time, Alastair."

Cynthia was going off to McGill; Ian was in his last year at Upper Canada College; Diana had many interests and was close by UCC for Ian. Walter was right. If there ever was a time, this was it. I thought about his kind offer to introduce me to his former Davenport riding. But it was all wrong for me. It had become increasingly an Italian-Canadian riding, one where an Italian heritage would be helpful. And there was such a person, Charles Caccia, who had been a member of the St. Paul's executive with me. Charles did become the candidate and held the riding for an astonishing thirty-six years until the Paul Martin Liberals forced him out.

Fortunately for me, Bob Winters' decision to leave politics after his defeat in the leadership opened up the riding of Etobicoke, where I was, by happy coincidence, president of an electrical heating manufacturing company that employed a lot of people. This time I did not hesitate to throw my hat into the ring. I called Winters, met with the local executive, and they offered their support. After a contest, I won the nomination and thus became a part of the incredible wave of Trudeaumania of 1968. What followed was a blur.

After winning the nomination battle, the usual preliminaries to an election followed. First, there was a picture session with the leader at the Royal York Hotel in Toronto. Mr. Trudeau was sitting in a chair tossing green grapes into the air and catching them with a remarkably well co-ordinated mouth. We shook hands for a second time. It was still limp.

This was not a particularly exciting first encounter with my leader. The next one was somewhat better but still unusual. It was several days later.

"Mr. Trudeau is coming to Toronto," I was told. "He will be landing at Malton. Malton is in your riding. We have arranged for you to meet him." I was duly driven to the airport, escorted out onto the tarmac and placed at the foot of the stairway. The door opened. Out came the Pierre Trudeau with a huge bunch of roses clasped in his hand. Did he carefully walk down the steps? Not at all, he hitched himself up onto the handrail and slid down on his bottom, roses in hand. I was starting to wonder where politics was going to lead me. Some of my supporters who had backed Bob Winters muttered something like, "Well what would you expect from a philosopher king?" As a businessman who had had a little experience with groups, committees and boards of directors, I was curious about how this strange though charismatic man with the limp handshake would manage the group dynamics of a caucus and a Cabinet. There was no question he could handle large crowds. They adored him and "charisma" became the cliché of journalists. My doubts about Trudeau's abilities – and his handshake – began to dissipate.

My family did not share my concerns. I'm not sure whether Diana, Ian and Cynthia caught "Gillespie fever" but they became quickly infected with Trudeaumania in that wild 1968 campaign where Bob Stanfield and the Tories did not stand a chance. Diana and the children were out every day, as they were in all my campaigns, knocking on doors and working in the campaign rooms late into the night. Cynthia organized the Gillespie girls, who dressed in kilts and brought a touch of the sex appeal that surrounded my leader to my campaign. Never was an election campaign so easy; we had, as they say, caught the wave. On election night the Gillespie girls and hundreds of others cheered as we won almost every poll. My margin was 14,278, the largest I ever had. As I left the cheers of the crowd behind and left the party, I said to myself, "What the hell have I got myself into?"

My first important experience was in national caucus. It met every Wednesday at 10 a.m. after the Toronto and Ontario caucuses. The Toronto caucus started the day over breakfast at 8 a.m. We then proceeded to Ontario caucus at 9 a.m. During these preliminary caucuses we focused on items which had local as well as national interest. And then there was the national caucus. PET, as we called him, would sit at the middle of a long green beige table, his various ministers spread out on either side. These meetings were almost always of considerable interest – offering a considerable diversity of views. It was an opportunity I began to value. At times it was useful in letting off steam but also an opportunity to register one's ideas to one's fellow MPs and senators and ministers. There were almost always certain predictable performances. Phil Givens, a former popular mayor of Toronto, had his pet peeves about the lack of federal interest in and support for urban centres. He loved a fight. So did PET and Givens never became a minister and soon gave up politics. John Reid, the MP for north Ontario, always sat right in front of PET. He had an irascible style which subsequently helped him with his appointment, after his House of Commons and ministerial career, as Privacy Commissioner. There he continued as a burr under the government's saddle. Of course there were many other contrarians who come to mind: Lloyd Francis who later became Speaker; Ralph Stuart of Northern Ontario, Steve Otto from Toronto and Eugene Whelan before he joined the Cabinet. Inside the Cabinet, Gene pursued his own particular points of view with uncompromising vigour and fractured English, sometimes to the frustration of his colleagues. He had many hobby horses and when he saddled up there was no telling where the ride would end. Sometimes the PM found this helpful in running out the clock. Gene liked to talk about free speech as "carte lablanche."

There were many interesting people in the caucus. Martin O'Connell, a Ph.D. in political science, was always worth special attention. He was a quiet-spoken, thoughtful member who left his successful career in the financial sector for public service as a Member of Parliament. He was one of the "bright young men" retained by Walter Gordon as a contributor to Gordon's highly controversial and politically damaging budget. Barney Danson brought humour, compassion, focus and fire to our caucus meetings. He chaired a group of Toronto Liberal MPs which we called the Metpac, inspired by the recently announced Metropolitan Toronto's Planning Area Committee. Another Torontonian, John Roberts, also a Ph.D., combined a cool detachment with a sharp analytical mind and point of view influenced by his previous employment at the Department of External Affairs. One non-Torontonian who deserves special mention is Pat Mahoney, the Liberal member for Calgary South. Pat brought a desperately needed Alberta point of view to a Liberal caucus that was overloaded with Ontario and Quebec members. Despite my initial concerns about Trudeau, he managed his caucus masterfully. I was impressed with the way he reconciled often very emotionally charged proponents.

He would show enormous patience. He took notes and would occasionally call on a minister to address a particular issue. He had an uncanny ability to always grab the initiative, perhaps because he had the last word. More probably, it was his ability to turn the energy and thrust of a critic to his advantage, just as he did in the dojo as a black belt in judo.

Later when I jointed his cabinet I saw another side. Recall that as a younger man I had been a student of business and management practice. I was fascinated by the subject. I had read widely about the origins of scientific management, I knew many of the management consultants at Woods Gordon as well as a special visiting professor at the University of Toronto Business School, Colonel Lyndall Urwick, one of the founders of a leading British management consultancy. I had taught a course on marketing research and advertising at U of T's Institute of Business Administration, where I shared an office (part time with an old friend, Ed Ballon, a recent graduate of the Harvard Business School).

But this was also a time when I was a disciple of the management practices of the American Management Association (A.M.A.). With Gage Love, my boss at W.J. Gage, I would go to New York for conferences sponsored by the A.M.A. One piece of advice had imprinted itself on me; it was limiting the number of members of a board to seventeen to assure an interactive character. Over seventeen was ineffective, and twelve was the ideal number. All of these experiences affected my first response to cabinet government.

How could the PM chair and guide a cabinet with thirty-five or more disparate players – many with prima donna personalities? And each with his or her (after 1972) own power base? Ministers in a parliamentary system of government have a lot more power than those in a presidential system. Ministers in both systems have almost always tenure only for "good behaviour." Nothing more. They are there at the whim of their leader. But in Canada a minister fired by his PM still has a potentially useful political power base. He or she has a seat in the House of Commons – a platform to criticize – and a rallying point for the disaffected that might unseat a government.

The Canadian/U.K. system has a feudal origin. Ministers with constituencies are like barons. In the past this influence was reconciled by the king, the non-elected chief of the executive branch of government. Today, the head of the executive of a government in the U.S. or Canada is elected. In the U.S. a minister has no ongoing electoral platform. That belongs only to the president, the erstwhile king. In Canada, many ministers have a sway that challenges the authority of the prime minister. Think of John Turner in the seventies or Paul Martin in the nineties. Our system has its advantages and some profound disadvantages. It requires a prime minister with good judgement and personal authority to make the Canadian system work.

As chairman of Cabinet, Trudeau controlled the agenda. He encouraged participation from his ministers. He would give the presenting minister all the time he or she needed to put forward a recommendation, and he would then invite comment from others. Anyone was free to offer an opinion. But watch out. If an opinion was volunteered by a fellow minister, the PM would question that minister's argument with skill. If he found the comment without substance, shallow or superficial, he would say little but stare at the offender with a level, disapproving glare. That minister, the one offering the comment, (and the rest of us) would know that he or she would not likely be recognized again during that cabinet meeting. The English would say that the unfortunate one had been sent to Coventry.

I wondered how Trudeau would control his group of barons. It didn't take me long to find out. He started with several advantages. His intellect really knew no equal. He was always well prepared, which indirectly was probably one of the reasons for his failing marriage. He would spend Wednesday night with his briefing books to prepare for the Thursday cabinet meeting. The House had regular evening sessions on Monday, Tuesday and Thursday. Wednesday was considered by many as a time for play and relaxation. He loved to play, too, and so did Margaret. I was always impressed with his athletic flare on the dance floor – quite acrobatic if his partner was up to it. Ruth Macdonald, the pretty and vivacious wife of Donald, used to challenge his virtuosity. But never on Wednesday nights. Trudeau meant business.

Walter Gordon, a leading voice for Canadian nationalism.

CHAPTER SIX

A POLITICAL CAREER

Trudeaumania had swept the country in 1968 and new Liberal MPs arrived in Ottawa in large numbers, 155 from all parts of Canada. Even Alberta sent four Liberal members to Ottawa. There had been none in 1965 and have been very few since. In Ontario, the Liberals took 64 of 88 seats, which meant much rivalry for cabinet positions. Trudeau, unlike some prime ministers who have followed, offered his leadership rivals major portfolios. A few were kept for those who had supported him in the leadership campaign, notably E.J. Benson, who became his first finance minister. Bob Stanbury and Don Macdonald were two others. Mitchell Sharp, who threw in the towel early and endorsed Trudeau, got External Affairs. John Turner, whom I had supported, became the justice minister and continued the work that Trudeau began when he was justice minister of getting the state out of the bedrooms of the nation and breathing fresh air into our justice system.

I entered politics with the hope of becoming a minister because I knew that the "action" took place at the cabinet table. I also knew my chances were slim of gaining a place at that table in 1968. I was a little envious of the newly elected Jim Richardson of Winnipeg, who got the Defence portfolio. But I was geographically challenged being an MP from Ontario, where able Liberals were so numerous.

A new MP is truly an innocent. John Turner was helpful: he emphasized the importance of a good secretary, which I realized with Jeannine Enright. She proved to be first class —one of the best on the Hill. He also recommended that I concentrate on a few issues and build up a group of supporters, by which he meant supporters beyond my own constituency. But as a veteran politician, John knew the importance of looking after the constituency. I set out to be such a "constituency MP." Trudeau once said that backbenchers were nobodies when they left Parliament Hill, but he did more than any previous prime minister to improve the lot of the backbencher and make them more effective in Ottawa. Partly these improvements flowed naturally from his concept of participatory democracy, which I took to mean that voters should become involved in shaping a government's agenda. This meant that the MP's job was no longer a part-time occupation. In my case, it took all my energy for over a decade. In 1969 when still a backbencher, I wrote to a friend that I had never worked so hard in all my life.

The first thing I did was resign thirteen of the fourteen directorships I held, even though in those days there was no policy requiring resignations even for ministers, much less backbenchers. I kept one directorship at W. J. Gage, because I believed that because it was an educational publisher, there was no possible conflict of interest. Education was a provincial responsibility, not a federal government one. As it turned out, this directorship didn't last long.

One of my first actions which captured press attention was, in fact, my resignation from the board of directors of W. J. Gage Ltd. It contributed to my reputation as a Canadian nationalist. I had objected on nationalist grounds to a board decision of W. J. Gage to sell its educational division to the American publisher Scott Foresman. W. J. Gage was the major educational publisher in Canada. Its sale would reduce Canadian-owned publishing to 10 per cent of the market. Put another way, 90 per cent of all books used by students across Canada would be published by non-Canadian owners. Inevitably the research and the points of view would reflect U.S. values and culture rather than Canadian. As one closely tied to the "nuts and bolts" of the publishing industry, I knew what the sale of Gage meant for Canadian publishing and Canadian students.

At a seminar at Columbia University, considerable coverage was given to my statement that "what is shocking about it to me is that gradually, over the years, the process of developing strong Canadian strains and Canadian points of view which are subtly different from those of others, a pride in things Canadian, in a Canadian heritage, is going to be eroded inevitably." I continued that the dimensions of current Canadian nationalism took many forms. It was a deep felt conviction that if we were to build

A signed photograph of Pierre Trudeau in appreciation of election success.

a distinctive nationhood we must find ways of retaining independence in making our own decisions. Would Americans be comfortable if virtually all the textbooks used in their schools were published by Canadian publishers or British publishers? The answer was obvious.

My resignation from Gage focused public attention on this issue and on book publishing in Canada in general. There was a good deal of media coverage relating to my comments. I don't think it's an exaggeration to say my remarks helped to create the conditions which led the Federal government to create certain programs of assistance for Canadian publishers generally – part of the government's approach to protecting cultural sovereignty.

When I was appointed vice-chairman of the House of Commons committee on finance, trade and economic affairs I was very pleased. As a backbencher it would provide me with an opportunity to influence public policy. One of the first assignments of our committee was to review the White Paper on Tax Reform and to make recommendations. I decided then and there to avoid any conflict situation that might arise because of a perceived benefit that I might obtain for any investment that I owned. I put my financial interests into a blind trust, which piqued the interest of Michael Pitfield, then Secretary to the Cabinet and a major advisor to Trudeau. He asked if I would let him have a copy of my agreement. At that time there was no requirement for cabinet ministers or backbenchers to divulge what their assets were. Soon after, I learned that the government had decided to require all cabinet ministers to have blind trusts. This was a major change in government policy that I had accidentally triggered. I told Pitfield that I had decided to do it because I was determined to avoid any perception of any conflict of interest which might arise because of my previous business experience and the investments which I had made prior to entering the political arena.

Considering my early contribution to conflict-of-interest legislation, it is ironic that I would later become the target of Conservative innuendo in the eighties when the vitriolic Erik Nielsen launched a personal attack on me for "conflict of interest" for some activities of mine that occurred after I left government service. We will return to this question later.

When I went to Ottawa, a Member of Parliament made $12,000 per year and had an expense account of $6,000. There was no other money for constituency offices or for a residence in Ottawa. Some MPs slept in their offices, even though in some cases those offices were shared. I was luckier than all but a few because of my previous business success, yet my time in Ottawa certainly drained my accounts. I will be blunt and direct: I was worth approximately one million dollars in 1968. When I left politics just over a decade later, the amount was reduced by nearly a half, not accounting for inflation, which was high in the later seventies.

There were no funds in 1968 to support an MP's role outside of Ottawa. In the first months, however, I decided that I must have a constituency office, and I opened one at 4800 Dundas Street West in Etobicoke. Initially, I paid for it myself and was extremely fortunate to be able to hire Ruth Cruden, wife of long-time Liberal activist Joe Cruden, as my assistant. The office was open 1 to 4 p.m. each day and on Saturday mornings. An answering machine took calls at other times, and Ruth used her few spare moments to deal with them. I would set out for Ottawa every Monday morning and return on Friday. On Saturday morning, I would go to the constituency office or to other meetings that Ruth had arranged with constituents. Every other week I would write a column for the *Etobicoke Guardian*, which I used to publicize the constituency office and public meetings that Ruth organized where constituents, sometimes very vocally, expressed their views on government policy. She really was worth her weight in gold. When Ruth went on to become a Citizenship Court judge, I was very fortunate in recruiting Bea Yakimoff as her replacement.

In Ottawa, I had a small office with a sofa and two desks, one for me and one for my superb secretary, Jeannine Enright, who helped me throughout my eleven Ottawa years. Jeannine more than fulfilled John Turner's advice about getting a good secretary. (Later when Turner became prime minister, she joined his staff.) She developed her own network and even became a marriage broker. She actually was the inspiration for the marriage between my daughter Cynthia and my special assistant, Ian Webb. I was concerned about nepotism and that my son-in-law would be on my payroll. So I fired Ian Webb. Later, when I had the Science and Technology portfolio, I had Cynthia fired when I discovered that she had obtained a summer job at the Science Council, for which I was the responsible minister. I think she has finally forgiven me.

The office had a washbasin, which was important when MPs used their offices as a bedroom. I had it removed. I was located on the fifth floor of the Centre Block and had the good luck to be surrounded by a group of excellent MPs, most of whom had just arrived in Ottawa: Barney Danson, Ottawa's Gordon Blair, who later became a judge; the shrewd Martin O'Connell, later a Trudeau minister; Norm Cafik, who saved Pierre Trudeau from defeat by winning the Pickering seat in 1972; Colin Gibson, a Hamilton lawyer who made such a partisan racket in the House that he got the name "Hoot"; and Pat Mahoney from Calgary, who had been president of the Canadian Football League. In those days, in addition to sitting daily, the House sat Monday, Tuesday and Thursday nights; we would often go out and have a beer together after the session. We'd debate such things as how a particular minister answered a question in the House and assess his competency. Regrettably I must say "his" because the Liberal Cabinet of 1968 had no female members.

I had few illusions about the status of a backbencher. Shortly after my arrival, *Globe and Mail* journalist George Bain wrote a humorous column of "Advice to the New Boys." He warned, "Do not, on coming to Ottawa, look for much deference on the part of the natives due to you being an MP.... If, when you go to rent an apartment, you say, 'I am a member of Parliament,' the best you can expect is a look of glacial disinterest. On the other hand, you may be told, 'In that case, it will be two months rent in advance.'" No wonder MPs slept in their offices. I stayed at the much more friendly Juliana Apartments, about a mile away from the Hill, to which I walked each morning; I still recall how my shoes would squeak on the snow on the coldest winter days. I slept less than I had before I entered politics, but even so I found that I didn't have the time to handle all the issues that were before Parliament. I quickly realized that if you were to be effective, you had to confine yourself to a few major topics, and I did so.

I enjoyed the life, especially the committee work and debates in the House of Commons, yet I was troubled by the lack of support, which made an MP's life more difficult than it had to be. Less than a year after my arrival in Ottawa, I was bold enough to write to Trudeau to express my views. Already, Trudeau, to his great credit, was pressing forward with a commission that was examining the situation of the MP and comparing the MP's compensation with that in universities, business and elsewhere. I began my letter of February 18, 1969, brashly: "The future role of the Member of Parliament is one thing, making him more effective now is quite another. In my view, it is the latter question which should receive priority consideration. If there is a difference between the views expressed by the Members of Caucus and by you, it is here."

The letter followed a discussion we had in the House. I wrote:

In the very brief chat we had in the House on Tuesday at the end of Question Period, I tried to stress the importance which a lot of us attached to your recognition of the fact that we are being asked to do a job with a poor set of tools.

The rules' changes, with a new emphasis on the Standing Committee, provide a larger legislative role for the private member – a really significant advance in participatory democracy. But as a result we have less time in our offices, not more; and there is the additional time required in preparation if one is to participate actively. Let there be no mistake about this, we are not complaining about it. We're all for the change and want to make it work. But we're being asked to do a man-size job with a boy's tools. If we devote more time to the Committees, we have less time to handle our constituency affairs, less time to dictate our correspondence, less time to make telephone calls, less time in the office.

I went on to argue for better facilities, office expenses and "an extra Dictaphone and an extra telephone line."

Changes did come through as a result of this external commission, which provided an air of objectivity to the changes. The result was almost a doubling of MPs' salaries and an itemized office expense list and constituency offices. I don't know if I influenced the Prime Minister but my first Parliament saw major changes in the way MPs lived and worked in Ottawa.

My letter also acknowledged the enhanced role his government was giving to parliamentary committees. For example, the Finance, Trade and Economic Affairs Committee (on which I was vice-chair) was given the enormous task of assessing the historic Carter Report on Taxation. The Carter Commission was created during the Diefenbaker government and became enormously controversial after its report was released in 1966. The majority report of the Carter Commission, which had strong dissent from one of the six commissioners, argued strongly that the Canadian tax system was grossly inequitable and recommended fundamental changes to the system. The word "equity" was present throughout the report, and its argument that "a dollar was a dollar" whether received in income, dividends, capital gains or interest became the focus for the lively national debate that followed. What the commissioners proposed was that the base for taxation would be the increase in the amount of resources over which a person had command. In the report, equity was deemed a more important objective than simplicity of the law and ease of administration. Many of the special concessions such as mining depletion allowances, tax-free dividends and benefits on life insurance policies, and the catering profits of the Royal Canadian Legion would end. As one newspaper remarked, the vice-chair of the Finance Committee was on the "hot seat" and for an exciting twelve months I was.

THE WHITE PAPER — TAX REFORM

What made the "hot seat" the best seat for me were the rich policy debates that took place as the committee considered the Carter Report and the White Paper on Tax Reform. Committee work was more intimate, and we had an excellent committee. Most of the Liberal members of the committee later became cabinet ministers and close friends: Barney Danson, John Roberts, Martin O'Connell, Norm Cafik and Bob Kaplan. The White Paper gave an ambitious young member an opening because a Green Paper is a statement of government policy whereas a White Paper is for analysis, debate and recommendation. Trudeau's talk of "participatory democracy" also gave us an opening. My business background led me to insist that we hire a professional staff to help us since a technical subject like tax reform required strong accounting, legal and economic research assistance. We retained Ronald Robertson, who had headed up the Canadian Tax Foundation, and Marshall (Mickey) Cohen, later a deputy minister and head of Molson's, to help with legal matters. We agreed with the Conservatives that they should choose the accountants to assist us because we believed, correctly as it turned out, that it would give the Standing Committee a much more bipartisan or non-partisan character.

In my constituency and that of other MPs, the White Paper dominated public meetings and telephone calls. It became wildly controversial as special interests resisted the end or reduction of their privileges. In my Ottawa Report of January 30, 1969, I wrote: "Estate Tax Proposals! The White Paper seemed the most important topic of interest during the parliamentary recess. I received more mail, more calls and more visits on this matter than all others put together." Even on weekends when I went to our ski chalet near Collingwood, I could not escape. Diana became so frustrated by the way the White Paper was controlling our lives that she put a sign on the chalet door: "You're all welcome on the understanding that you will not mention the White Paper." This helped to provide a little peace but I soon was targeted on the chair lift. A good deal of shuffling occurred to get near me as people waited in line. Since the ride up on the chair lift gave the other two "seats" each ten minutes with me, I was their prisoner. Irritating though it sometimes was, my work on the Finance Committee on the White Paper helped me greatly in establishing my parliamentary reputation.

Because of my activities, I quickly attracted press attention. It sometimes seemed that every word was carefully monitored. The *Globe and Mail* reported on February 10, 1970, for example, that "Gillespie has reservations about White Paper." It reported my participation in a panel discussion at the annual convention of the Ontario Retail Lumber Dealers Association. My reservations were correctly reported to be: the distinctions between the taxation of closely held and widely held corporations; the proposal of taxes every five years on unrealized capital gains; capital gains on principal residences; and especially the impact some of the Carter proposals would have on small businesses and middle-income groups. I told the crowd that I was only a backbencher but that it would be the Finance Committee and not the government that would decide what recommendations would go forward. I'm not sure what finance minister Benson thought of this analysis, but we developed a good working relationship even if I sometimes seemed offside with his approach. The committee served as a valuable buffer for Benson given the strong public reaction. In June 1970, he wrote a public letter to the committee in which he pointed that since the White Paper was tabled on November 7, he had said that the tax reform would not result in an increase in taxes but, in his own words, he had "not succeeded in putting the fears of some taxpayers to rest." He gave an undertaking that the White Paper was "to reform the tax system, not to increase taxes" and that the committee would have free rein to listen to the public.

Listen we did. We held hearings in Ottawa and crossed the country holding hearings where local or regional interests could be heard. I took responsibility for the hearings in Western Canada. When the report was released on October 5, 1970, we had received 524 briefs, 1,093 letters and other submissions and held 146 meetings in Ottawa and elsewhere at which 820 witnesses gave testimony. The 98-page report recommended some of the White Paper proposals but rejected others or recommended many modifications. I reported to my constituents at the time that there were three principal recommendations:

1. The tax load borne by lower-income Canadians should be reduced and redistributed.
2. That in principle, capital gains should be taxed and that the revenue base should be expanded in other ways.
3. That preservation of an economic climate favourable to growth must be a central consideration of Canadian tax policy.

In my mind, the Standing Committee recommendations struck a proper balance between equity and economic growth. They also recognized the importance of small business to the Canadian economy. I told my constituents that the reservations I had earlier expressed about the White Paper were covered in the report.

The Carter Report had "scared the hell" out of many Canadians and the parliamentary process brought some reassurance. Carter and the White Paper dealt with a tax system that had grown like Topsy and had fundamental inequities. While inequities remained, the reform established the basis of how the Canadian taxation system dealt with fundamental questions such as capital gains, which were to be taxed at 50 per cent rather than the 100 per cent recommended by Carter; gifts and inheritance taxes; and whether the family should be taxed as a unit or whether husband and wife and children should be treated separately for tax purposes. I did not agree with critics, including the *Toronto Star*,, that our report chose growth over equity. In fact, there was a very high component of equity in what the committee recommended and in what the government accepted. According to journalist George Radwanski, our reforms "dropped about a million low-income Canadians from the tax rolls, reduced taxes for some 4.7 million others, and increased the bite for about 1.3 million at the top of the income scale."

Politics often leads to misunderstandings and misstatement. On May 22, 1970, the journalist Douglas Fisher wrote a column that was lavish in its praise for me, claiming that I radiated the "well-bred confidence you so often get from a private school, Anglican, ex-Navy background" and contrasting me, the vice-chair, with the committee chair, Gaston Clermont. He further claimed that a finance department adviser, when asked about Clermont, responded that the department was not worried because "Ben's counting on Alastair to handle the grief-mongers." Although I had good relations with "Ben" Benson, I was by no means his agent on the committee. Also, the comment was unfair to Clermont. He was an accountant whose skills were important and a very wise man. While he may not have had experience with large corporations, he was thoroughly professional and he recognized that the undertaking that we had been given was a huge one. He also recognized that he had a very strong committee, whose members could make a valuable contribution. I think he drew out the best of what he had and I know he had the respect of Liberal and Opposition members. He deserves much credit for what we achieved.

Although wrong about Clermont, Doug Fisher was correct in saying that on the committee I "zeroed in on the small business dilemma, the tax treatment of resource industries, the integration of personal and corporate income tax, the distinction between private and public companies, and the capital gains on homes and personal property." It is true, as Fisher argued, that the committee report did not reflect many of the Carter recommendation in that area. He was also correct to suggest that these were the areas where the Liberal caucus was most troubled by Carter. By limiting my focus, I think I did achieve real gains, but I did not perceive then or now that I was undermining the White Paper or Ben Benson. A white paper invites debates and changes, and the committee in general, and I personally, listened to people and urged changes. Ben Benson and the government accepted most of what we said. We made over 100 recommendations, of which the government accepted over 70 per cent – and I believe with some alacrity and relief. Whatever the gains, the process had a serious, negative political impact. We won no votes and probably lost many, particularly in the business community.

PARLIAMENTARY SECRETARY

I do believe that my work on the committee attracted the attention of those who make decisions about which MPs should move forward. Probably because of the work on the committee, I was made parliamentary secretary to Charles "Bud" Drury, the Secretary of the Treasury Board. Drury was an outstanding minister who greatly impressed me and, fortunately, Prime Minister Trudeau. His brother-in-law, Walter Gordon, probably recommended me to him. "Bud" was universally respected, had a distinguished war record and had worked for the UN after the war in Europe. He loved to debate and I enjoyed those debates but there was a problem when a decision had to be made. I found the best way I could get him to focus on an immediate problem was to debate with him on something that needed a decision far in the future. Then when the House of Commons bells began to ring at two o'clock, I'd say, "Bud, this is something we have to decide immediately." And he would decide because he could debate no longer.

The parliamentary secretary position is worthwhile when the minister gives him or her some real work and when the minister is strong. Some parliamentary secretaries never move up because their ministers are weak; others use them to carry forward important issues. Bud fell into the latter category and I learned a great deal about the operations of government in working with him, knowledge that was invaluable when I became a minister. My files reflect that I worked on the Science Council, the National Research Council and a variety of other issues, including the situation of francophones in the public service. On this last issue, the Royal Commission on Bilingualism and Biculturalism had reported that francophones were badly underrepresented in the public service and, prior to Trudeau, in the Cabinet. With Trudeau, Ottawa changed dramatically. The public service became increasingly able to work in French and English, as did the Cabinet. It was one of Trudeau's greatest legacies. His friends Gérard Pelletier and Jean Marchand were extremely impressive. Pelletier was intellectually sophisticated with strong views, but he did not try to force them on others. He clearly had the confidence of Trudeau. Marchand I adored. I would have chosen him ahead of Trudeau as leader, a secret I once confided to him. He was feisty, magnetic, with a wonderful personality that could move a crowd and charm a small group. He had his weaknesses, most of which came in glasses. He could be hilarious when he had too many drinks. Once in question period, an Opposition member asked him about some matter concerning the Department of Transport, and he replied that he could not answer the question because the department was a complete mess. No minister had ever said that before about his department and the result was shock on our side, and hilarity on the opposition benches. He was always good fun and great company.

In the case of the Science Council, the Canada Council, the Economic Council and the National Research Council, I eagerly took on responsibility to consider what they contributed to Canadian research capacity. The problem we faced was stated clearly in a cabinet memorandum on the role of the universities in research: "In recent years, the overall Canadian research effort has been characterized by a strong federal government component, an increasingly strong university component, a weak industrial component and an insufficient degree of interaction and collaboration among them." Moreover, Canadian research seemed especially weak in the social sciences and the humanities. Simultaneously, a special Senate committee under Senator Maurice Lamontagne was trying to develop a science policy for Canada, and his efforts were attracting much-deserved attention. While I agreed strongly about the weak capacity of industrial research, I was sceptical of moving too quickly to link the federal councils with industry. In response to a cabinet memorandum on July 15, 1971, that proposed a new industrial research centre that would link the National Research Council with industry through these centres, I told Bud Drury that the memorandum did not make the case "that industry would use the facilities," adding that industry has not asked for the centre and the NRC had not undertaken a study to see if there was industry interest in the subject.

I was also interested in the attempts by Trudeau, Michael Pitfield and others to introduce new "systems" approaches to government. At the request of the Privy Council, I attended a meeting at Montebello of the Club of Rome, which became famous, and in many quarters notorious, for the study *The Limits to Growth*. The emphasis on future studies and systems approaches, in my view, meant that far too much time was spent on analysis and review. It seemed to me in many cases that it resulted in avoidance of responsibility. Theory came to outweigh facts, and there were some terrible memoranda that Barney Danson and I made fun of by taking their highfalutin language and translating it into everyday English. Despite the doubts I had about the analysis and the language, I did think the Club of Rome's approach had merit in that it tried to raise the question as to how long our natural resources would last. I also agreed that it was important to govern with an eye to the future. While there were supporters of a "Futures" approach in the Privy Council, others were strong opponents. Later, when I held the Science portfolio, I remember a heated argument with Simon Reisman, the vociferous Deputy Minister of Finance, who declared that all of it was nonsense. He added, waving his finger and almost jumping across the table, "I hope, Minister, you don't believe it." I said that I believed there was some merit to the arguments for understanding the limits of resources. He snapped, "Ridiculous," and turned to another staff member and said that it was all a matter of price: "There's not a problem with respect to the world running out of resources. If the price is high enough, it's all solved." The other member of his staff shook his head indicating agreement with Simon and indicating his belief that I was naïve. There was a time when I wondered whether he was right. I know now he was wrong.

Simon's habitual insubordination reflected the tension that sometimes exists between civil servants and their supposed masters. The *Globe and Mail* columnist George Bain, in his amusing advice to new MPs, had warned how civil servants handled MPs in the fashion of the British show, "Yes, Minister." He said that ordinary MPs rarely encountered civil servants except for the messenger who fixes the Venetian blind in your office. If you did encounter one, he or (rarely) she would be "polite enough, if a little stand-offish and wary." However, beneath the surface "in every good civil servant, there lurks the belief (expressed to me in just these words by a retired civil servant the other day) that "The only time things get buggered up is when the politicians get involved." Some probably had that attitude; others did not. I had little experience with them until I became minister since backbenchers do not cross paths often with bureaucrats. My ministerial experiences are a different matter about which I will comment later.

My term as parliamentary secretary was surrounded by troubles and turmoil. In October just as I was appointed, James Cross was kidnapped by the FLQ and Canada confronted terrorism and violent separatism in Quebec. Trudeau used provisions of the War Measures Act to meet the challenge. I remember my first taste of this. Late at night I returned to my apartment, and as I exited the elevator I was confronted by a military man who shoved the muzzle of a submachine gun into my belly. "Who are you? Where are you going?" he asked. I only then realized that he had been sent to protect Arthur Laing, a minister from Vancouver, who occupied the room across the hall. My first concern was for Cynthia, my daughter, who was a student at McGill, where tensions were enormous. I called the RCMP and asked them to maintain surveillance of her. As the situation deteriorated and Quebec cabinet minister Pierre Laporte was kidnapped, all MPs became very troubled. We Liberals were supportive of Trudeau's decision to invoke the War Measures Act. I think, in retrospect, he was correct. He believed that once blood starts to get spilled, as Laporte's blood was in a ghastly assassination, a dangerous legacy is created. Ireland is a good example of what could occur. Terrorism ended in Canada in October 1970 and Trudeau's decisive action stopped the flow of blood. The country returned to normal activities.

One such activity was the highly complex issue of constitutional reform.

I did not take part in the debates on constitutional reform, but I shared the disappointment that came when the Victoria charter failed to be realized after long negotiations in 1971. I did, however, take a very active part in the debate about Canada's participation in NATO. Here I disagreed with Trudeau, who wanted Canada to withdraw its troops from Europe at the very least and perhaps withdraw from NATO entirely. I was a member of the Canadian delegation to the North Atlantic Assembly, which was the parliamentary wing of NATO, and in this capacity travelled regularly to Brussels.

The following extract from a speech summarized some of my views:

• I would like to deal with three points and to underline those three points. The first is that conditions are changing and that we must adapt to, indeed, anticipate change. More than that we should try to bring about the kind of change that we think is needed. We should not react passively, we should anticipate actively.

• The second is that NATO is not just a military alliance. It is a political alliance with political objectives. Similarly, Canada as a participant in NATO participates in more than just a military way. Membership gives our country political benefits, and resident membership in the club provides just that many more.

• Third, the decision to re-examine our nuclear role in Europe is timely and one which I hope will lead us to reject nuclear weapons as part of our armaments, after discussion with our allies.

I fear some of the things that the last speaker mentioned. I fear perhaps more than anything else miscalculation or accident. I fear misunderstanding and misunderstandings will develop if there is not a clear intention on the part of the western alliance.

In speaking to these three points, I think it is important that we recognize the foreign policy framework within which our NATO posture must operate. First, defence policy should be a servant and not the master. This debate should have taken place before now. It should have taken place at the time of the unification debate, at that time or before it. It is long overdue.

Second, we should see our foreign policy objectives as a whole, not as component parts. Too often there is a tendency to look at foreign policy in terms of military objectives, set aside from cultural or political objectives, or set aside from trade objectives. In my view, we should examine each of our foreign initiatives against each of these tests. For instance, how does NATO serve our political objectives? How does it meet the test of our cultural or national identity objectives, and our trade objectives? In my view, it meets them all and meets them well."

I became head of the delegation when Senator John Aird, who had also served in the navy, resigned from the Canadian leadership because Trudeau had raised the question of withdrawing our forces from Europe. I shared Aird's concerns but decided to see what influence I could bring to bear. What motivated Trudeau? I think he never had much respect for the military. Military budgets seemed large and to him it appeared they always wanted more. He was never convinced by the argument that Canada's voice would be more influential if it had a stronger presence in Europe, something he wanted very much. I thought then and still believe now that he was wrong about NATO. Our forces were reduced, and I believe we lost influence. However, on foreign soil, I always defended the government. On one occasion, a Dutch representative lectured us about withdrawing from Europe. I responded by saying that NATO in Europe has a huge responsibility from Norway to Turkey, but its common border with the Soviets is not as great as Canada's border with the Soviets which Canada defends alone. "None of you are there," I declared. That ended the Dutchman's complaints quickly.

FOREIGN OWNERSHIP ISSUES

The other issue where I gained attention was foreign ownership of Canadian industry, which in many ways coincided with the responsibilities I had for the various research councils. I believed, very simply, that foreign-controlled companies do little research in Canada. In the seventies, the automobile industry was our largest industry, but it did no research in Canada. There were many other examples. I was, of course, associated with Walter Gordon, who was the patron saint of the Canadian nationalist movement. Like him, I was a member of the Committee for an Independent Canada (CIC) along with diverse individuals such as my former student Peter Newman, future Conservative External Affairs minister Flora MacDonald, future NDP leader Ed Broadbent and Edmonton publisher Mel Hurtig. I wrote some articles for the *Toronto Star*, very much a nationalist paper closely linked with Gordon, where I argued that foreign ownership had value where it supported projects that Canadians themselves would not undertake. I went on to argue, however, that Canadians should have a greater share in the future development of their resources. I suggested in March 1970 in the *Toronto Star* that we consider limiting foreign investment in the resource sector to a 50 per cent equity interest, with the remaining 50 per cent to be taken by Canadian private investors or, if necessary, a Canadian Development Corporation. I also argued that the multinational corporation was a permanent feature of the international economy, but foreign ownership limited the capacity for Canadian firms to become multinational themselves. A commentator summed up my arguments in the *Winnipeg Free Press* on July 27, 1970: "Mr. Gillespie begins with two general propositions. We need an industrial policy which is expansionary, entrepreneurial, outward-looking, future-oriented, research supported and which recognizes the multi-national corporation as a principal agent for this kind of economic activity. Secondly, future prosperity will depend on the development of our natural resources, their processing and the competitiveness of our other manufacturing industries." It was a good summary.

Some more extreme nationalists made me a hero in October 1970 when I resigned as a director of W.J. Gage because Gage had sold its textbook division to American interests. I criticized the provincial government for not blocking the sale but said that the federal government had also been insensitive to the special needs of the textbook industry. Some of my new fans were disappointed when I said I was not anti-American but pro-Canadian. I added that there was a place for foreign investment but that it should be used more effectively. At the same time, Walter Gordon was moving away from this attitude and told me that he thought he would have to support the NDP in the next election because the Liberals had let him down. We continued to share some concerns, but Walter's views had hardened into frequent anti-Americanism, not only on foreign investment but also on NATO. I came to believe that some of Walter's policies tended to be inward-looking, not outward-looking. My own belief is that we should protect our interests but always look outward. A good example of our differences and agreement was the mining industry. Like him, I remained troubled that Canada was one of the leading mining countries in the world. But how much mining machinery did Canadians produce? Almost none. The answer was stronger research-based Canadian companies, not simply punitive action against foreign companies in Canada, which it seemed Walter supported.

He was not the only Liberal troubled with government policy. In late April 1971, Eric Kierans resigned from Cabinet, attacking government economic policies. Paul Hellyer also resigned and complained about the government's policies more generally. Immediately, the *Globe and Mail* speculated that I was the "leading candidate" to succeed Kierans as Minister of Communications. The article pointed out that I had been previously rumoured to be a candidate for a new Ministry of Science and that I had attracted attention with the concern I had shown (as had Kierans) about foreign investment. My riding association was overjoyed upon hearing these rumours. On June 20, 1971, it held a meeting where, minutes record, they agreed that the association would hold a reception "to personally honour and congratulate Alastair within four weeks of the appointment." On the Saturday or Monday following the appointment, the executive said that they would meet with me and share two bottles of champagne. But the champagne remained on ice as the association and I had to wait several tantalizing weeks. On August 12, 1971, I finally entered the cabinet as Minister of State for Science and Technology, and we broke out the champagne.

PARTICIPATORY DEMOCRACY

As I look back on my tenure as a backbencher, I recall many trying moments, very little sleep and a huge amount of personal satisfaction. It was a robust time – one that excited young and old alike. I made a point of trying to engage young students in Pierre Trudeau's appeal for "participatory democracy." A number had already helped me in my campaign and some had worked in Bob Winters' campaign in the recent leadership contest. A group appointed themselves as the Young Liberals Club of Etobicoke. On one outing, we set out in rubber boots and running shoes to clean up the visible pollution of Etobicoke Creek, under the leadership of an active young Liberal, Paul Watson. This was in addition to our regular meetings on Saturday mornings in someone's basement. The word got around. Interested students contacted Paul Watson for information. On one occasion, a curious young man joined us from Richview Collegiate. He said he was interested in finding out about politics. His name was Stephen Harper – yes, the future Prime Minister of Canada. He became a young Liberal and an interested participant in some of our Saturday morning basement meetings.

Pierre Trudeau's charisma had captivated and stimulated a new generation of Canadians, even those like Stephen Harper, who later attacked him and his legacy. Schoolrooms debated public policy. I remember one letter which went something like this:

"Dear Mr. Gillespie: I am twelve years old and a student at Richview Collegiate. My teacher has been talking to our class about politics. There's so much poverty and crime and violence, people are being killed. How did it all start and what are you going to do about it?"

I can't recall my answer, but this type of letter fortified my commitment to public life. I don't know whether Prime Minister Harper's later successes owed much to the meetings in Etobicoke. What I do know is that my first years in politics were lively, contentious and fundamentally rewarding.

CHAPTER SEVEN

MINISTER AT LAST

I n August 1971, Diana and I were living it up in the Bordeaux wine district. We had enrolled in a French language school at an attractive seaside village, Royan. It was to be a three-week course. About halfway through, I got a call from the Prime Minister. He said that he was making some appointments and wondered whether I would like to join his cabinet. He was about to create a new Ministry of State for Science and Technology, and he knew of my interest in the field. I very happily agreed. I don't know whether he was impressed to find me studying French. He never tested me. I do know that I was thrilled by his call. Any serious politician wants to be a cabinet minister, and we were overjoyed.

The government was already in its third year. I knew the next year would be intense with its preparations for an election, which in majority governments normally occurs in the fourth year. Would a new minister and a new department of government resonate with my electorate as a new and positive innovation? Trudeau had soared in popularity following the October Crisis in 1970, but since then the polls showed a steady erosion of that popularity. I had become concerned in the spring of 1971 with the government's declining position. After a lunch with Torrance Wylie, the national director of the Liberal Party, I reflected on our discussion:

"I think that we have got to do more than hope that the mood of the country, now rather sour, will turn 'round of its own accord. We've got to seize every opportunity to project an optimistic, positive posture" – I was gung-ho. In the upcoming budget, the government needed to reinforce "a new positive, optimistic posture. I would like to see us talk more about our opportunities as a nation and less about our difficulties. The future is something which we should anticipate with confidence and not apprehension." I sent a copy to Barney Danson, who shared my beliefs and fears.

Privately, many of us worried that the government's message was unclear and lacked electoral appeal.

My ministry was new, and the position of minister of state was an innovation borrowed in 1971 from British practice. In Canada, a minister of state is a cabinet minister appointed to assist another cabinet minister with his or her portfolio or to undertake specific responsibilities assigned by the prime minister. A minister of state is a peer, not a subordinate, of the portfolio cabinet minister. Ministers of state are full members of cabinet and bound by cabinet confidentiality and cabinet solidarity. For that reason, the Prime Minister was careful to outline what responsibilities a science ministry would have. The Order-in-Council establishing the position said that the minister "shall formulate and develop policies with respect to the application and development of science and technology in Canada as well as the coordination of government policies in that area." In his confidential letter to me, he set out in more detail what was different about the ministry. He said that he wanted to "nurture" the concept of ministers of state to encourage innovation in government. Specifically, he asked that I regard "as a primary task" advice to the government "on the priorities that it should set for expenditures and the use of manpower in the development and application of science and technology in the national interest." Of course, this would mean defining what our national interests actually were. He asked me to submit as soon as possible a memorandum outlining "proposed national objectives in science and technology and on the ways and means" by which those objectives might be achieved. This memorandum, he continued, would allow "for the assessment of programs against an agreed policy background". He added that "the task of being influential with our colleagues without having general overriding authority for implementing program responsibilities is indeed difficult." He urged me to create a strong secretariat and to be selective in what we suggested as national objectives.

After speaking about the relationship with other departments, he indicated that the Science Council would now report to me, not to Treasury Board. He asked me to consider Quebec's concern about federal grants to universities and to consider how Canada can contribute to "the area of international science," which he said was a personal concern. Finally, he asked the ministry to assess the Gendron Report on the organization of scientific activities within government. It was an impressive letter, an indication of Trudeau's attention to detail and, less positively, his focus on the "systems approach to government" and theoretical obsessions. Most press comment on my appointment and the creation of the new ministry was favourable. However, the *Globe and Mail* while supportive of my entry in cabinet was critical of the terms of reference for my ministry. It claimed that the terms were unclear about what I was supposed to do and how I could do it. It correctly said that the new ministry was a response to a long litany of criticism of Canadian science policy, culminating in the Lamontagne Senate Committee's report of December 1970. Deploring the generalities in the Order-in-Council creating the ministry, it said that I would have "the duty of pursuing what is undefined with ambiguous powers in a manner vaguely described. No wonder that Mr. Gillespie talks about the low profile that will characterize his operations in the new ministry."

The journalist Warner Troyer sounded the same tune in a mock letter to me that he published: "I know, sir, that your job is a difficult one. When the cabinet, in its sagacity, made you minister without giving you control over the various scientific and research agencies of the government departments, they certainly provided you with a challenge. It's about as silly as though the order-in-council had appointed you police chief of Ulster."

The critics had a point. One memorandum from the Privy Council was a hopeless jumble about "conceptual frameworks" and confused prose such as "if science and technology is to more effectively serve as a handmaiden for economic growth, harmonious natural environmental and quality of life, then policies must be chosen to support Canadian secondary industry through research development and, at the same time, science and technology must be used to negate to the greatest extent possible the effects of the environment, while enriching important human values". I had a challenge before me; this rubbish drove me crazy. Sometime I had a feeling that some policy wonks were more interested in writing stuff which wouldn't involve them in any sort of responsibility for the written word; that would be someone else's problem. I soon discovered I was not alone. In October 13-14, 1971, I attended a meeting of ministers of science of OECD countries in Paris. Other governments had also created ministries of science and they shared the problems that I faced.

EARLY MINISTERIAL MEETINGS

On the way to the Paris meeting, I called on my British counterpart, Margaret Thatcher. She was then Minister of Education and Science. She shared her views and convictions, which sometimes coincided with mine. She was irrepressible – and she exhausted me after a couple of hours of discussion. She displayed all the energy of a fighter plane warming up just prior to take-off. How different she was from her predecessor, Edward Heath, when she became prime minister. I had an opportunity in my next cabinet post as Minister of Industry, Trade and Commerce to size him up on a visit a couple of years later. It was at 10 Downing Street. He was particularly interested in getting a Canadian "take" on President Richard Nixon's government. Europe was worried by what they regarded as the overreaching attitudes of the Americans. The French author Jean-Jacques Servan-Schreiber had captured this concern in his book *Le Défi américain*. "Gillespie," Heath said, "it's now 6 o'clock. Would you join me for a Scotch?" Jake Warren, the very able Canadian High Commissioner, was with me as we settled down in front of his fire. I know Jake felt it was an open and useful exchange of views. Prime Minister Heath volunteered some negative comments about Nixon.

When I returned home, I was blunt in an interview with the *Globe and Mail*. I told them that I was "a little disappointed" with the OECD meeting of ministers because it was full of generalities. "There was," I said, "an almost total lack of 'for instances.' There were some great statements about the importance of science policy for the quality of life. But I kept thinking, what are people actually talking about?" I told them that I was determined to question assumptions and, above all, to be pragmatic. Of the meeting, I said, "There seemed to be a singular lack of understanding that if science policy is to have any meaning for people, you've got to be able to articulate it and implement something."

The cabinet position brought major changes to our life. Our kids were at school, and Diana, who was a strong supporter of the government with our often-critical friends, was able to come to Ottawa, where we rented a house. We went on ministerial trips together and she loved the experience. The Trudeau government understandably worried about the impact of political life on marriages, and encouraged travel together. Together, we got to know other ministerial couples such as Don and Ruth Macdonald, Jean and Aline Chrétien, Barney and Isabel Danson and formed close relationships that endured far beyond eventual political defeat.

Of course, cabinet members were bound together by cabinet secrecy and the common experience of being at the cabinet table. My first experience at the cabinet table was memorable for me and my colleagues. I had not expected to speak but did. The first cabinet meeting was not in the traditional cabinet room in the Centre Block but in the East Block because of renovations. The room was elegant and intimate but very small.

I was nervous and I did not expect or want to participate. However, tax reform matters lingered on, and the Prime Minister turned to me and asked what I thought of the decision to remove succession duties. I answered that I thought the government was wrong. Succession duties represented a significant resource that would not affect the living, only their inheritors. Moreover, succession duties had been a part of Canadian life for a long time. Edgar (Ben) Benson, the Minister of Finance, quickly intervened and said, "Well, I think we have looked after that with the capital gains tax that will require the estate to be valued on death and those elements that have grown during the life of the deceased will be taxed at higher rates." Since I had not been in cabinet when that decision had been made, I backed off but did say that I was pleased that he had recognized that important point. I think it was a bit of a shock to the more senior ministers that the "new boy" had spoken out.

Although I may have shocked my cabinet colleagues, I was reassured by the warmth with which they welcomed me to the cabinet and enthusiastically went off to develop science policy for Canada. I did not have a large staff. There were only seven or eight senior people, who were drawn from the Privy Council staff, and about twenty staff. They formed a secretariat that was headed by Rennie Whitehead, who acted as the secretary, equivalent to the function of deputy minister. He had a plan for the ministry that focused on three items: the first was basic research, the second applied research and the third "manpower." I asked him whom he had to cover applied research. It became clear quickly that the person responsible had no knowledge of business and the essential link between such research and business. I said to Rennie that we had to find someone else, and we did most successfully when we hired L.R. "Red" Wilson on a contract basis. He was a breath of fresh air and he immediately understood what I wanted. He later became an Ontario deputy minister and, after working in the banking sector, joined Bell Canada and became its CEO.

Wilson recognized immediately the problems identified in the press and also in the letter Trudeau sent to me when I was appointed. The science ministry was to approach problems horizontally whereas most of the departments of government have vertical responsibilities in a particular and defined policy area. Science policy, in other words, cut across these other departments. How, then, do you rationally integrate a horizontally-based policy department with these vertical departments with more specialized responsibilities? Let me give an example. I took responsibility for putting forward a plan to "contract out" research. I believed that the government of Canada should de-emphasize in-house research, which was funded and directed by departments for their own purposes. It could be sourced out to universities and private institutions in a way that built capability outside the government. Eventually, cabinet adopted a policy that permitted such contracting out, but at every step towards integration of science activities in government there was resistance.

That resistance was understandable because some departments had extensive research operations. Agriculture was an excellent example with experimental farms throughout Canada. Not surprisingly, the department and its officials were nervous about this new unknown minister with his notions of "contracting out." And they had reason to be nervous because it would affect jobs and create a new kind of scrutiny of their work by affecting the pecking order within the department. In my conversation with Thatcher, she made the point strongly that you never knew what was going on in a department because of the intricate relationships within it. She was not always wrong.

As mentioned above, science as an issue became increasingly important within society and in Parliament because of the personal interest of Trudeau and some of his advisers and because of the Senate committee's report that was so strongly critical of the disorder of Canadian science policy, and in particular of the weak links between academic research and what was termed applied research.

In the 1960s, protecting the environment and the effect upon it of human activity also had become a major political issue in much of the Western world. The role of industry in causing environmental damage became a major public policy concern. Pierre Trudeau created one, if not the first, ministry of the environment in '68 with Jack Davis, another B.C. Rhodes scholar, as minister. I don't recall any previous government with such a department. The possibility of scientific solutions to environmental degradation further enhanced the importance of science. In my remarks at the OECD, I tried to reflect these broader concerns that meant that the time was long past when government's sole obligation was to provide funding for basic research. At the time, there were even some speakers who were, because of concern about the environment or human overcrowding, calling for an end to growth. This view was probably shared by many in the Club of Rome, which had nurtured such thoughts in the widely acclaimed and criticized and debated book *The Limits to Growth.*

I believed that "economic growth by itself is by no means our only important objective." We needed to focus on the quality of life by recognizing that health depended on maintaining and improving the quality of our natural and man-made environment. I referred to recent comments by Prime Minister Trudeau that warned that technology, despite its enormous benefits for society, can become a Frankenstein monster. He asked why we "worshipped at the altar of GNP," adding, "Isn't it time we paid heed to resource exhaustion, to environmental deterioration, to the social costs of overcrowding, to the amount of solid waste disposal? Shouldn't we, in short, be replacing our reliance on GNP with a much more revealing figure, a new statistic which might be called Net Human Benefit?"

Trudeau was, of course, ahead of his time, and I followed his lead in urging the development of new social indicators. His remarks also reflected the report on Science, Growth and Society carried out by Harvard engineering dean Harvey Brooks for the OECD. It emphasized that the understanding of science in society had changed dramatically in the 1960s from a time when there was a high degree of public faith in science – the time of Sputnik and the American response to it – to a period of disenchantment in the later 1960s. Brooks had written: "Scientific research became associated in the minds of many with war and with the environmental and social deterioration resulting from the large-scale application of technology. For the first time in many years, the steady and occasionally spectacular growth of R & D began to falter, and scientists, whether deservedly or not, lost some of their influence and credibility in government and before the public."

In that same month, October 1971, that I discussed Brooks' analysis in Paris, I responded to the ambiguity of scientific discovery when I spoke out strongly against the American decision to test an underground nuclear device on Amchitka Island as a "mistake of gigantic proportions." My sensitivity to the Pacific coast environment undoubtedly was fostered by my background on Vancouver Island.

Yet negativism was not the answer. I announced in Paris that the government was supporting the creation of a new Institute for Research on Public Policy, which would be a think tank and a new type of "futures operation." At the end of the speech, I returned to the role of the international firm and to the importance of understanding their effects and actions.

After acquiring staff and meeting with them, we began the task of deciding what this our new ministry would do. Our first task was to produce a submission to the cabinet committee on Priorities and Planning on "Proposed National Objectives in Science and Technology," which would begin with a definition of the national interest and would fit the role of science into that definition. As in all things, I told the staff that we had to emphasize the need to make choices, to focus. The basic questions seemed to me: how do we make choices between medical, social and physical science support; what is the appropriate emphasis between fundamental research, applied research, and development and innovation; where should research be carried out – the private sector, universities, institutes or industry? And, finally, the perpetual Canadian question, the role of the provinces and the federal government. An initial task was to collect information about science and research that was scattered throughout thousands of different places in government, universities and the private sector. In a memorandum I wrote to myself, I thought selectivity was a key to going forward. In this respect, the Science Ministry, which came to be called MOSST, did not function as a priority-setting body. It had an influence but its real heft came from Treasury Board, where I had experience as the parliamentary secretary to Bud Drury, its minister.

The *Toronto Star* was a strong supporter of my appointment and especially, in one of its reporters' words, my businessman's belief in "harnessing scientific energy to bolster the country's economic independence." It was correct that I worried about these questions. In September 1971, I wrote to Dr. Aurèle Beaulnes, our newly recruited secretary expressing my concern about science policy and industrial policy. I told him that many thoughtful business leaders were deeply concerned about the federal government's lack of leadership in articulating an industrial strategy. It was true that the government had worked on the instruments of such a strategy, the Canada Development Corporation being an excellent example. Moreover, it was developing a foreign investment strategy. However, this approach meant that the instruments came before strategy, which was not the best way to proceed. Moreover, many government statements were simply confusing matters. Some said we should concentrate on industries of the future. "Okay," I wrote, "but which ones?" To the claim that we should focus on those areas where we had comparative advantage, I again asked, which ones? Did this mean we should simply ship more raw materials to the United States and Japan because we had a comparative advantage – in natural resources? Should we simply say, "To hell with conservation?" It was said that Canada should encourage secondary industry. Okay again, but did this include processing of our raw materials? Finally, I asked the politically charged question of how making Canadian industry internationally competitive could ever be reconciled with regional expansion programs.

THE MISSING LINK — ARE THERE LIMITS TO GROWTH?

The questions we asked then seem so relevant to our lives in the twenty-first century. Why did we do so badly in the last part of the century in dealing with them? When I asked them in the early seventies, it seemed to me that in each of these questions we were already at a crossroads. And I don't think we took the right turn very often.

We had to assess the costs and benefits of economic growth, of environmental emissions, of the expansion of industry. But we tended to shy away when confronted directly with the questions. The proliferation of multinational corporations increased the need for a comprehensive national strategy. Multinational corporations had become the most important economic agents in the world of the 1970s but we had not decided what rules Canada, as a host country, should impose upon them, nor had we decided how government policy could contribute to the creation of effective Canadian multinationals. I concluded a memorandum written in 1971:

"In my view, we need an industrial development strategy. We have been looking for one. The Department of Industry, Trade and Commerce has done some work in this area, but we still haven't got one. Only through an industrial strategy will we be able to answer the kinds of questions posed above. Only with an industrial strategy will we be able to set forth policies for the use of science and technology in support of the economic prosperity of our country and its individual citizens. We have a joint interest with the Department of Industry, Trade and Commerce in developing such an industrial strategy and in working out policies to encourage innovation, to improve the R&D capabilities of industry, and to facilitate the technology transfer, be it from abroad, be it from government sources, be it from the universities or from Canadian domestic industry."

Reading these documents and others of this time, I am always struck by how many problems and issues have endured while others have changed. The debates about the place of science, the role of computers, the general role of science and society are much the same. To be sure other issues have changed and some have completely disappeared. In my interview, the *Toronto Star* reporter quoted my concern and the Science Council's concerns about the effects of a drop of 2 to 3 per cent in the surface temperature of the globe which would "set the great glaciers again marching across our land." On the other hand, a small rise in temperature could melt the icecaps and cause an overwhelming rise in sea level. "Both," the Science Council and I stated, "have occurred before in the earth's history. Either could occur again." We know today the latter is occurring in the form of global warming; the former is not. In the early 1970s, we did not know which way it might go, although the bets seem to have been on cooling rather than warming. And they were soon to be lost. I shared some of Simon Reisman's objections to *The Limits to Growth*. For example, the doom and gloom predictions about overpopulation, which were made in the book and by many other futurists who simply projected current trends into the future, proved to be mistaken, although concerns about world hunger and poverty persist.

Troubled by a world where the environment was clearly threatened, inequalities abounded and the future was uncertain, I wrote a memorandum to myself in August 1971. René Whitehead, Michael Pitfield, and others were involved with the Club of Rome and with "systems approaches" and futurist ideas. My own impression of the book *The Limits to Growth*, which was inspired but not authorized by the club of Rome, was that it was provocative, particularly in its assessment of future change. Its argument that there would have to be a great shift from the wealthy to the less-developed nations in the distribution of the world's goods was one that I accepted. I have mentioned my reservations about their overestimates of population growth. I also thought the book ignored energy, which was to soon become the cause of a great international crisis with the founding of OPEC, nor did it deal sufficiently or well with such factors as "peace and social stability, education and employment, changing values and different values in different parts of the world." The section on the impact of DDT was absolutely convincing and remains so.

The Club of Rome was also correct in stressing that certain problems – they mentioned the nuclear arms race, racial tensions and unemployment – have no technological solutions. The book's point was, I said, "that even if technological progress fulfils all expectations it may create a whole series of social side effects of a negative character." In conclusion, I wrote,

"The study does not claim to be the last word. Far from it. A very crude first attempt – a direction and an imperfect technique which the authors hope others will improve upon." My work in the science ministry opened my mind to the wonderful blessings and future promises of science, but it also made me aware of new challenges we faced.

INTERNATIONAL INFLUENCES

When I took the office of Minister of State for Science and Technology, people were talking about "future shock," the title of another overheated book of those times. Governments everywhere were trying to understand what it all meant. The Cold War, which had seemed to be moving towards détente, took a turn for the worse after the Soviets stamped out the liberal ideas that developed in Prague and elsewhere in 1968. In Asia, things were going badly as the conflict in Vietnam was a proxy war, communism vs. the West, and tragically spread to Cambodia and Laos. The Chinese were embroiled in their mad cultural revolution. Never a cold warrior, Pierre Trudeau was looking ahead and he wanted to engage the Soviets in dialogue. He was greatly assisted by the Canadian ambassador, Robert Ford, the dean of the diplomatic corps. Ford spoke Russian fluently, translated Russian poets, overcame a difficult physical handicap and was much respected by many well-placed Soviets. To break the ice with Moscow, Trudeau decided to send me to head a trade mission of Canadian businessmen. This was only a few months after my appointment as the first science minister in 1971. It was the precursor for his later trip to meet with the Soviet leaders, some time ahead of President Nixon's first visit. He repeated the process with China and established Canadian recognition before the historic visit of Kissinger and Nixon to China. These were troubled times, but they were also times for action.

In Russia, I discovered that, despite great differences in our systems, many problems were the same. It was essentially a trade mission, not a science mission, but I later had the Soviet Minister of Science to my home in Ottawa. I think such exchanges helped in breaking down differences between our peoples and systems, and the kind of experience the Soviet minister had in Ottawa, in my home, showed him how we lived and what

The newly appointed science minister takes a trade mission to Moscow in 1971. Diana and I are pictured here with Canada's ambassador, Robert Ford (right), and our Russian hosts.

an open society could offer. Indeed, the Russian ambassador to Canada, Alexander Yakovlev, dean of the Ottawa diplomatic corps was an important influence on Mikhail Gorbachev. We now know that Yakovlev's experience in Canada, his understanding of our agriculture and his close friendship with Trudeau and Eugene Whelan were important factors in developing the ideas of *glasnost* and *perestroika*, which altered the Soviet system irreversibly and from which the whole world benefited so much.

Meeting foreign politicians and scientists made clear that Canada was not alone in facing new complexity in the organization of research, science and society. I found discussions abroad very helpful, especially with Lord Rothschild, the British Science Advisor. I first encountered him at the OECD meeting in October 1971, where in contrast to the papers and many of the officials, he was "practical, succinct and pointed." The papers we got before the meeting, I wrote at the time, were "general, often vague; they avoided assiduously any reference to specific situations." Rothschild, by contrast, was far more concerned about technology than anyone else there.

Indeed, he said science policy for government was a misnomer; what most people are concerned about are policies for technology. His words had an impact on me and I sent my notes to Dr. Beaulnes. My final comment was intended to guide our approach: "One cannot expect scientists or engineers to produce a formula or a system which will make choices. We can ask them what are the consequences of this or that alternative. But politicians must make the judgment – this is where science policy and public policy merge."

When I met Rothschild later that year, he stressed that his primary concern was the management of science and technology in the government service. He believed the government R&D activities should be clearly and closely related to that of the British councils, which in some ways replicated our councils. They should be placed alongside the relevant departments and become granting institutions in the particular disciplines. My problem was that Canadian businesses, because so many were branch plants, did relatively little research. Moreover, government and universities carried out research that often had no impact on technological change. There was, of course, a need for continuing pure research, but a modern economy and society have a compelling need for a quick flow from scientific discovery to practical application. By the end of 1971, I was becoming aware of the broad sweep of my ministry's interests and I was troubled. "Quite frankly," I wrote in November 1971, "I am exasperated by the number of organization charts that have been submitted, revised, approved." There was also an abundance of proposals that came forward, went on the shelf and stayed there. At the end of the year, I warned Dr. Beaulnes that we had little time left. It was an election year and there would be only about eight weeks of 1972, I thought, where Cabinet would be able to deal effectively with major issues. Our main concern was a statement of national objectives on science policy. We had to develop a tighter office and a shorter response time. I reiterated, as always, that we had to be more selective and asked for a clear setting of priorities.

The minister of state position was an experiment but it has endured. The need for horizontal approaches across the vertical departments is now largely met by the ministry of state positions. The *Globe's* scepticism about whether such ministries could work was unjustified, and I hope that their prediction that I would find the task impossible was also untrue. I believe I accomplished some important things, such as a government policy on "contracting out," and we also managed to focus councils (Science, National Research, Humanities, Economics, Medical Research) on the need for outreach. The cabinet agreed in May 1972 that, as a general principle, departments should be required to demonstrate why R & D should not or could not be done in industry rather than within government.

The National Research Council, in those days, was an enclosed world, and we began to open it to closer relationships with business. In 1972 we persuaded External Affairs to join with us in a policy that would expand and coordinate Canada's international scientific collaboration policies. MOSST was designated as the Canadian government's representative to the international think tank, the International Institute of Applied Systems Analysis (IIASA) in Vienna. IIASA was a fascinating initiative. Created by Soviet and American scientists who recognized that there were many common problems where Cold War tension need not bar cooperation, IIASA brought together scientists from around the world to focus on global issues, such as the impact of airborne pollution. For the first time, scholars from the West could get to know scientists from the Soviet Union. It was in this sense a useful listening post and an organ for debating issues of mutual interest.

In the case of university research and the councils, we tried to emphasize the linkage between research and applied application. In a meeting with Dr. Omond Solandt of the Science Council, we agreed that the federal government should take on the major responsibility for research support in universities rather than leaving it to the provinces. We also agreed that we should take a "centres of excellence" approach that would focus on particular strengths and schools. Reading the press today, I sense that there still seems to be to be too much of a gap between the universities and the business world and entrepreneurship, although the University of Waterloo has had some an impact with its cooperative program and links to high-tech industries. So, too, is the promise of the exciting MARS venture in Toronto and its chair, Dr. John Evans. Nevertheless, the problem of company research remains. The foreign corporation has never seen its branch plant as a place where research can be done, and the automobile industry remains the prime example now as it was then. It's frustrating to read how we still cannot commercialize research in Canada, that most of our companies do little research, and that the universities and the world beyond still seem too far apart.

One of my satisfactions of office has always been my early recognition of the future importance of hydrogen and directing government financial support to it. This occurred because John Polanyi, a future Nobel laureate in chemistry, and Alexander (Sandy) Stuart came to see me. Sandy had inherited an enthusiasm for electrolysis from his father, an early specialist in the science. Sandy has devoted his life to the practical production of hydrogen by electrolysing water into its two components, oxygen and hydrogen. He has supplied hydrogen generating units to over 120 countries. He has become recognized as Mr. Hydrogen by scientists all over the world. As a scientist with vision he was ahead of his time – so often the inventor's solace. But one thing seems certain, future generations will be his beneficiaries.

IN THE SHADOWS OF A GENERAL ELECTION

Just after I was appointed to the Ministry of State for Science and Technology in August 1971, Canadian unemployment reached its highest level in a decade: 7.1 per cent. The Americans, facing a large trade deficit, had gone off the gold standard and adopted trade restrictions. Nixon's move sent shock waves around the world. These actions were particularly damaging to their trading partners, the largest of course being Canada, although President Nixon seemed to be unaware of it when he publicly declared that Japan was the largest partner.

Nixon's move was a response to the irresponsible policies of American administrations during the Vietnam War. A decade of stagflation began in 1970, when inflation and unemployment, previously thought to be incompatible, bedevilled politicians throughout North America. The Canadian economy had moved from a pattern of continuous growth to one of uncertainty. Not surprisingly, there was increasing criticism of Trudeau's leadership. George Radwanski wrote that Trudeau "failed to deliver not the little he has expressly promised, but the very much he had implicitly offered: an inspirational style of leadership that would challenge the nation with the boldness of its initiatives and unite Canadians in a shared sense of purpose and involvement." There seemed to be too much talk and too little action. Again, Radwanski says that the pursuit of "efficiency in government was regarded as cold and somehow vaguely anti-democratic; planning was equated with procrastination."

Interestingly, my own notes from the time indicate that I shared some of these views. I told an official who interviewed me that I thought the cabinet was much too large and inefficient. Departments should be combined. I also said that committees were "robbing Ministers of too much of their discretionary time. Material which did not need to go to Cabinet was being sent there. Generally speaking, the Government had tried to accomplish too much without spending sufficient time on implementation. Cabinet was too concerned with the specifics of policy decisions rather than the overall posture or stance of government."

Still, no one thought we would lose the 1972 election, not even the Conservative journalists or the party's leader, the decent but often beleaguered Bob Stanfield, but we knew we would have troubles. In my case, one local issue – the decision to build a second airport in the Toronto area – caused me problems but unexpectedly brought a political opportunity. I had strongly fought a proposal by Paul Hellyer, the Minister of Transport, for the limited expansion of Malton in the early years of the Trudeau government. That view, of course, reflected fully the views of my Etobicoke constituents, who didn't want more planes and more noise at an already congested airport. A group of constituents formed a lobbying organization, the Society for Aircraft Noise Abatement (SANA), which did its homework. The members tabulated the time and frequency of flights and recorded the noise ratings in decibels. I had many a meeting with them and passed on my recommendations to the transport minister.

If the Department of Transport's projections and analyses were to be believed, the existing set-up was just not going to be adequate. Failing an expansion, Toronto like London, England, would need a second airport.

This became the rallying cry for those opposed to the major expansion of Malton. SANA's efforts were a good example of Pierre Trudeau's "participatory democracy at work." The government got the message and decided that a second airport would solve the problem and set about negotiating a plan for an alternative site with Ontario's Premier Bill Davis. But the proposal for a second airport solved one problem but it soon created another.

The federal government's first move was to choose a site west of Toronto. After all, the argument went, that's where the greater population lived and worked. Industry was expanding. A site near Brampton would be ideal, Ottawa thought, but Bill Davis had other ideas. Brampton, after all, was the heart of his own constituency. What the provincial government said they wanted was a location east of Toronto, a "magnet" for more balanced industrial growth in the province. The new federal minister, Don Jamieson, negotiated a deal with the provincial government's Darcy McKeough. The provincial government would provide the services – the federal government would provide the land through expropriation.

The alternative site was to be east of Toronto near the town of Pickering. When the site was announced in cabinet, Mitchell Sharp said it was close to a little place named Claremont, which nobody had ever heard of. Except for me. It was close to my farm – a quiet sanctuary in the country and the week-end family retreat. The Liberals may not have known about my farm, but David Lewis of the New Democrats did. He soon rose in the house and asked Trudeau if he was aware that one of his ministers had a conflict of interest on the airport location, all the while pointing his finger at me. Trudeau, who had been briefed, answered crisply, denying there was any question of conflict since I had acquired the property ten years before, long before I had become an MP. That was the end of that so far as Trudeau was concerned.

Unfortunately, the affair was not over, and it cost me the friendship of some very good people in the Claremont area. The airport land, 18,000 acres, was acquired through expropriation. The land was acquired in the seventies but no airport has emerged to this date. There was an immediate uproar and yet another citizens group, "People vs. Planes," was formed to combat the choice. As in Etobicoke, they were very effective. Whether an airport will be needed in the future seems unlikely given the expansion of Pearson and the wishes of groups in Hamilton for the expansion of their airport. I did learn the lessons of airport politics, which have proven dangerous to politicians from Toronto through London to Tokyo. At least we did not have riots and tear gas as happened in Tokyo and elsewhere.

With the 1968 sweep, Toronto MPs had formed Metpac to deal with Toronto area issues, of which there were many, like the airport. We worried about such things as the future of the waterfront and similar urban issues that are important today. Apart from the growing disillusionment with the government's economic policies, some of its social policies caused troubles with some of my constituents. I was a firm opponent of capital punishment and, unlike some of my Liberal colleagues, had no doubt that the state should move out of the bedrooms of the nation. The more liberal policies on abortion, homosexuality and divorce upset some of my constituents but did not trouble me. When Trudeau called the election for the fall of 1972, I knew it would be a difficult campaign, partly because of these "social" issues. And it was, far more than anyone expected.

HARBOURFRONT

A few months before the expected date of the 1972 general election, I was approached by a colleague, Bob Andras, who had been designated by Pierre Trudeau as the campaign chairman for Ontario. "We have an opportunity to secure and preserve the waterfront of Toronto. It will be part of our campaign 'goodies.'" He made the point that public access to the waterfront was likely to be cut off by a "concrete curtain" of apartment buildings. He mentioned far-sighted decisions by other cities (particularly citing Vancouver's Stanley Park), which had preserved their waterfronts for public enjoyment. He pointed out that the owners of the land in question were the Toronto Harbour Commission (centrally located) and several private companies such as Direct Winters, a transport company. Would I oversee the negotiation of the purchase of these properties so an announcement could be made as part of our election strategy?

I was happy to do so. There was, however, little time – the approach to Direct Winters (a U.S.-controlled corporation) had run into difficulties

He's best for Etobicoke

We hit the campaign trail once again in the election of 1972.

even before the writ was dropped. It was not until a week before election day that the properties were secured for an announcement. Do we go ahead? If we do, it would look like a desperate last-minute attempt to bribe the voters of Toronto. I recommended against it. I thought it would backfire. The Toronto candidates caucused. One old hand said it would be insane not to go public, even at this late date. He added that if we stayed silent, the Tories would announce it and get full credit. His view prevailed. It was announced. But it did not do us very much good.

The party slogan, "The Land is Strong," quickly seemed ridiculous in a situation where unemployment was rising and inflation problematical. Trudeau did not campaign strongly and critics attacked his apparent disinterest and weak responses to criticism. The Gillespie team in Etobicoke compensated for the weakness at the national level with a strong campaign. We responded to the criticisms and pointed out that Etobicoke had a minister in an exciting new portfolio that had a strong future. On October 30, 1972, election night, my team quickly learned that we had won the riding again with a significantly reduced majority, but the national result was far worse than expected. Into the morning, it was unclear who would be the next prime minister since Liberals and Conservatives appeared to be virtually tied. One seat, Pickering, near Oshawa, where my friend Norm Cafik was the member, was the closest with only a few votes separating him and Frank McGee, the Tory candidate. It would all come down to the recount. McGee, in one of the stupidest moves by a politician I have ever heard of, did not show up for the recount. Norm did. I'm sure his presence had an effect on the officials as they decided whether this or that ballot counted. In the end, Norm won. Four votes saved him, Pierre Trudeau and my chance to be a cabinet minister again. It was a close call that profoundly affected Canadian history. All because of four votes.

CHAPTER EIGHT

MINORITY GOVERNMENT

The final tally was 109 seats for the Liberals, 107 seats for the Progressive Conservatives, 31 seats for the New Democratic Party, 15 seats for the Social Credit Party and 1 seat for an Independent, Roch LaSalle, who was elected in 1968 as a Progressive Conservative and won re-election as an Independent in 1972. With his political life saved by four votes Pierre Trudeau remained at 24 Sussex Drive, and I returned to Ottawa uncertain of my future. So many of my colleagues had lost, and I knew how much they would be missed, that there was a vacuum and that this might bring new opportunities. The government needed to respond, on the one hand, to its weakness in the business community and the West and, on the other hand, to the need to maintain the support of the New Democrats to retain office in Ottawa and of the nationalist *Toronto Star* to win votes in Ontario. As a Westerner by birth, an Ontario MP, a businessman by profession and a Canadian nationalist by inclination, I knew that I had advantages when it came time for Pierre to create his cabinet. That time came quickly. Without a formal meeting, Pierre called me and asked me to become the Minister of Industry, Trade and Commerce – ITC, as it was usually dubbed. It was a senior ministry, and I was delighted not least because trade was in my blood. My Canadian ancestors had made their mark as traders over 150 years earlier as partners in the North West Company operating out of Montreal and Michilimackinac. Their efforts along those of others had built a trading empire which Canada inherited when it became a nation. Now it was my turn to help guide their successors.

Despite my business experience and trading genes, I had a hard act to follow. Jean-Luc Pepin was a lively and popular minister and a gifted orator. In question period, he would rise and charm the opposition members by creating apparent empathy for their concerns while actually turning the subject totally to his benefit. He was known in some circles as the Laughing Cavalier. He was highly independent, and while he knew Trudeau well, he was not part of his set. He marched to his own drummer as he demonstrated when, at the end of the 1970s, he co-chaired the Pepin-Robarts Commission on the constitution and brought forward recommendations which contradicted Trudeau's own beliefs. He was an excellent salesman, and I recognized and respected the enormous talent he had brought to the position. It would prove to be a very exciting time in my life. I never travelled as much as during the years in ITC as I tried to sell Canadian nuclear reactors, airplanes and countless other Canadian goods in all corners of the world. But that came later. My first task was to set out my goals in the new department and to evaluate my fellow ministers and the public servants who reported to me in a very large department.

There were some important additions to cabinet, notably Marc Lalonde, who had served in Pearson's and Trudeau's office. He was an exceptionally strong minister. Although he might have been seen as arrogant by many of the English-speaking ministers, he advanced Quebec interests ably. Jean Marchand was much more popular. He was wonderfully passionate and, broadly speaking, personally attractive. I had told him earlier that if he ran for the leadership I would support him. He didn't, but the memory of the earlier comment may partially explain why we got along so well. He had been a fine minister in the innovative Department of Regional Economic Expansion, but in the shuffle Trudeau moved him to Transport. It turned out to be a bad decision. The Toronto representation in the cabinet was especially strong with Donald Macdonald as the Minister of Energy, Mines and Resources, and Mitchell Sharp as Deputy Prime Minister and Minister of External Affairs. Overall, it was a good cabinet with several (Jack Davis, Otto Lang, John Turner) fellow Rhodes scholars.

Trudeau realized that his office, which contained many friends and some highly intelligent thinkers, had been politically out of touch. Although his aides talked about issues impressively, their reasoning didn't resonate with the public. I recall one moment when I took part in a discussion about the importance of "crisis management" and the need to develop a system to manage crises. I soon realized that the nebulous logic and approach I heard would never convince the Canadian public. Trudeau's charisma faded after

1970, and his sense of direction, even his commitment, seemed to have deserted him. Many thought that Trudeau had become so captivated by the process of government that he had lost sight of its goals. After the election, Trudeau turned to political veterans, notably the wily Keith Davey and Jim Coutts, Pearson's appointments secretary and one of the cleverest political operators of our time, and others who had long been immersed in politics and quickly recognized the issues that were important to Canadians. As for the rest of us, we realized that Trudeaumania had its limits and that we could no longer expect charisma to carry the day. And yet I cannot recall a single MP or minister uttering a word about a change of leadership.

As ITC minister I moved into the West Block of the Parliament Buildings and furnished my office at my own expense with early Canadian pine furniture. Colleagues thought I was crazy to do it, but the pieces were functional, thoroughly Canadian and bore a message. My coffee table, for example, was a former chopping block, and one side showed the knife cuts while the other side showed where a hatchet had been used. With some of my guests, I would ask, "Now which side do you want?" It certainly broke the ice for conversations. These pieces now sit comfortably at my farm in Claremont.

My deputy minister, Jim Grandy (another Rhodes scholar), was an extraordinarily effective individual. He came to my office every morning at 8:30 to discuss current problems, and I knew he had spent the previous evening preparing for the meeting by poring over reams of documents in the massive department that we ran. My responsibilities included the numerous industry sectors within the department as well as Crown agencies such as the Trade Commissioner Service and the Export Development Agency. A fundamental strength of ITC was the Trade Commissioner Service. These trade commissioners were respected for their knowledge of foreign markets and for their knack of identifying business opportunities. I often received comments from executives of American companies who told me that they were putting export business through their Canadian subsidiary. Why? Because the Canadian Trade Commissioner Service was much more competent and professional than its American counterpart.

Despite its success or perhaps because of its success, External Affairs constantly complained about Trade usurping their responsibilities and de-

The federal presence with Prince Philip at the Queen's Plate in 1973. Premier Bill Davis of Ontario looks on.

manded that the Trade section of ITC be transferred to them. Many might have considered such a coupling as natural. We saw the inherent dangers of such integration, where the political and commercial were merged. Grandy and I fought them off successfully but Joe Clark gave in to the pressures when he became prime minister in 1979. The service has since been shuttled around, and the confusion has damaged morale and effectiveness.

I had known Grandy slightly when we were at Oxford together and had formed a high opinion of him as I followed his rise in government service. He worked hard and well but, to my disappointment, he decided to leave the government as he and some other public servants, notably Simon Reisman of Finance, had become disenchanted with government policies. Although they claimed at the time that their departure was caused by favourable pension benefit changes, I wasn't convinced. They had difficulty with, among other items, the minority government's approach to economic policy, including foreign investment and FIRA, which was an area of my responsibility. And I suspect they believed they could make more money as consultants, and I'm sure they did. (The professional lobbyist came to Ottawa in this period and the country is worse for it.) Fortunately, Gerry Stoner replaced Grandy and brought the same professionalism and expertise to the position.

My appointment seemed to meet with general approval. The eminent journalist Bruce Hutchison wrote in the *Victoria Times* on Valentine's Day 1973 that his fellow Victorian "has everything it takes to succeed – the lean handsome face, neither too old nor too young; the folksy manner and colloquial idiom with a nuance of modest scholarship to intrigue the groundlings; the air of sweet reasonableness but, in the background, an aura of ruthless power when needed." He continued in the spirit of Valentine's Day: "Clearly such a man can solve any problem." Although I barely knew Hutchison, he thought well of my Island ancestors and reflected his respect for my genes. I'm not sure I shared his optimism about my ability to "solve any problem" nor his belief that "an aura of ruthless power" surrounded me. I suspect it brought a few smiles.

Troubled by the election results and wary of the narrow minority, we realized quickly that things were not as bad as we feared. The Conservative Party seemed essentially a collection of dissidents. It was not a unified party under Bob Stanfield and it often seemed both in the House and outside that regional differences outweighed party solidarity. David Lewis, who led the NDP, ran a good campaign in 1972 and was a fine orator, but he did not impress me greatly. I had known him before I entered politics because he had been a labour lawyer who often appeared before arbitration boards. He was involved in one arbitration involving W.J. Gage, for which I was then responsible. I engaged Willard "Bud" Estey as our lawyer to oppose Lewis. Bud, who later became an eminent Supreme Court Justice, said to me, "Don't worry about this one, Alastair, I'm going to win it." I said, "How can you be so sure?" "Because David Lewis never does his homework. I've beaten him every time." We won the case.

As it happened, we had to beat him again in the next election after relying on his party's support in the minority government. And the times became ever more difficult. While I was ITC minister, we weathered the shock of the protectionist measures President Richard Nixon took. The first shock was when he broke the connection between the American dollar and gold, which destabilized international financial markets. These shocks were compounded by the formation of OPEC and the oil crisis of 1973. Moreover, a well planned and strategic Russian purchase of largely American and Canadian wheat created a world food crisis as prices soared. As a wheat and oil producer, Canada gained some benefits but the turmoil created great regional dissension, especially in Western Canada after Peter Lougheed became premier of Alberta in the fall of 1971.

Further complicating the general economic situation was the entry of Britain into the European Economic Community. Canada was to lose the preferential trade arrangement enjoyed by Commonwealth members but Trudeau sought to offset this problem through a new European trade initiative. The "Third Option" represented this determination to elbow his way into the European market. This was to prove more difficult than we first thought it would be. It was, in my view, a rather forlorn hope that we could find new markets in Europe given the momentum of the thriving European Economic Community. "What about Asia?" I would ask. I knew we must try to find markets everywhere because there were and are too many dangers in over-reliance on the American market.

These events coincided with the end of the postwar boom. Growth rates in the west declined, and government budgets fell into deficits as costs soared. "Stagflation," as this combination was called, challenged the Keynesian consensus and made economic governance difficult throughout the western world. Finally, the United States, our major trading partner and investor, was passing through the horrors and embarrassment of Vietnam and Watergate. The Americans, therefore, were less predictable in their policies and attitudes, especially as Nixon's impeachment hearings proceeded to their dramatic end.

Despite these troubles, I began my tenure at ITC quietly optimistic about Canada and its future. Canada still had a trade surplus – $1.1 billion in the first ten months of 1972. Moreover, ITC gave me the opportunity to act upon the strong convictions that I had long held. First, I believed that Canada had been and would continue to be a great source of raw materials for the expanding resource needs of the rest of the world. Second, those resources were not controlled by Canadians but by foreign interests who were less interested in Canadian well-being than in how they would convert the raw materials into a profit. In short, when value was to be added, they would add it in their own countries, notably the United States. I believed that this situation had to change as Canada became more economically mature. Third, we Canadians ignored the lessons from the United States. If, for example, one examined the petrochemical industries, one would observe that the United States had long before introduced measures to ensure that the primary interest of the industries would be in the United States and that the raw materials of other countries would serve their interests by providing the feedstock for the petrochemical plants. American measures made it highly attractive to upgrade in the United States while simultaneously protecting that upgraded product from foreign imports. Nickel was another excellent example. Canada, at the time the world's greatest producer of nickel, exported the raw material to the United States, where it was converted into coinage and various other end products. Why couldn't that coinage be made in Canada? We began to take measures that would assure that at least some of it would be Canadian made.

THE FOREIGN INVESTMENT ISSUE

Finally, my personal interests coincided with the government's ambitions after the 1972 election. Before the election, I had thought that Trudeau and the government had not realized the powerful influence of the foreign investment issue in Ontario and, particularly, in Toronto where the *Toronto Star* had supported the NDP during the election campaign. Almost every day, the *Star* led the charge with articles and editorials on foreign investment and foreign ownership and control. Trudeau himself was suspicious of the issue and was open about that suspicion. He said to me, "You know I'm not a nationalist and this is a form of nationalism, which I find suspect." I pointed out to him that the issue was control, something that did not arise with debt investment. Trudeau did come to recognize the political and economic significance of the issue in vote-rich Ontario and, at the insistence of the NDP and many members of our own caucus, his minority government created the Foreign Investment Review Act

(FIRA). I had the responsibility of putting this act through Parliament and implementing it, and it made my portfolio a focus of press attention and some controversy. The topic remains controversial and later Conservative governments attacked FIRA, but I remain convinced that the rhetoric attacking FIRA, which often ridiculously claimed its intention was to close Canada to "business," ignored its important real purposes which I set out above. It responded to real concerns of Canadians. At the time, F1RA was an important factor not only in maintaining the minority government but also in the election of a Liberal majority government in 1974. It allowed the Liberals to resist the calls for much stronger action from the NDP. It deserves a much better reputation than it has.

As noted above, foreign investment and Canadian control of Canadian industries had become a major Canadian issue in the 1960s. Walter Gordon compelled the Pearson government to study the issue and the result was a report by University of Toronto economist Mel Watkins on foreign investment that appeared in January 1968. Gordon promoted the report widely, as did the *Toronto Star*, and their activities had a real impact in defining the issue. On my copy of the report, I have underlined what I then perceived as its most important recommendations:

1. At the core of Canadian policy must lie a determination to recognize the existence of the multi-national corporation, the opportunities it creates and the constraints it imposes. Where the foreign corporation is not truly multi-national but defers to the authority of a foreign government, then Canadian policy must be directed toward compelling adherence to Canadian law and policy in its Canadian operations....

2. There must be more information on the operations of foreign corporations.

3. There is a need to ensure Canadian participation in the benefits of foreign direct investment and a Canadian presence in the decision-making of multi-national corporations.

4. Licensing agreements, which were of great significance for technology transfer, must assure that Canadian interests are protected.

Although I shared many of the concerns expressed in the report, I wrote in my copy that I thought it overlooked the role of education in preventing misuse of foreign investment and that protecting Crown corporations from political domination had been ignored. Without adequate education, I wrote, "Why would one expect to see a distinctive Canadian point of view presented?"

The impetus from Watkins and other nationalist efforts led to the creation of the Committee for an Independent Canada, which, as I mentioned earlier, I joined as a charter member, and to the report on foreign investment tabled in Parliament by Herb Gray in 1972 just before the election that year. Although I was a member of the CIC, I quickly realized that some activists, like Mel Hurtig, were obsessed with the subject and unreasonably hostile to foreign investment. I also became fed up with the *Toronto Star,* which criticized me for not doing enough. At times it seemed to be urging me to promote restrictive foreign investment policies that would have been destructive to Canada's economic interests. In the 1972 election, my fears were realized when the *Toronto Star,* Walter Gordon *and* Mel Watkins supported the NDP. Watkins, in fact, became one of the founders of the radical "Waffle" group that challenged the NDP leadership while calling for massive nationalization. While no socialist, Gordon was sowing seeds of discontent within the Liberal Party. In my view, they had become unreasonable and even irrational. I thought the *Toronto Star* was like a carnivore that was devouring its young when it came to foreign investment.

These defections irritated me and my colleagues. For his part, Trudeau worried about nationalism but he was also deeply concerned about the impact of American control over Canadian resources and, especially, the impact of extraterritoriality. Contrary to public belief and journalistic impression, he was not difficult to serve provided one did one's homework. As his minister, I never felt constrained or believed that I should not take some action because it was too sensitive or because I would face cabinet opposition. When I brought FIRA forward, there were two parts. The first dealt with takeovers of existing Canadian businesses. In this case, there was little controversy or opposition. The second part dealt with the approval of new foreign investments, particularly in the resource industries.

In this case, I had a fight with officials and some cabinet colleagues, particularly Mitchell Sharp. Trudeau backed me, and the others relented when it became clear that I was prepared to resign unless the second element was incorporated in FIRA.

FIRA was passed in 1973 but it did not come into operation until 1974. In the meantime, I produced the so-called Gillespie Guidelines that sought to clarify for businesses the government's concerns and policies. They presented the concept of "significant benefit to Canada," one that some criticized as being too subjective. My answer was: "You make the case that the foreign investment provides significant benefit to Canada, and then I'll let you know whether it's a good case." Of course, there were real tests. The guidelines (see Appendix 2) set out five criteria whereby "significant benefit" could be assessed: the number of jobs generated; the extent of Canadian participation in the management; the overall effects of the takeover in terms of competition; the potential for development of new technology in Canada; and, finally, the consistency of the takeover or investment with federal and provincial economic policies. The guidelines were actually welcomed by many American firms. For years, I received letters of appreciation from American businessmen, who would tell me long after I left office, "You know we still go by those Gillespie Guidelines." It helped them to frame their takeover bid not only for governmental approval but also for the support of the Canadian public.

The guidelines also strengthened the hand of the Canadian boss in a foreign-owned subsidiary. These Canadian managers could point to the guidelines and tell their head offices that their approach to Canada was wrong. The guidelines were a temporary measure that eventually formed the mandate of FIRA on its start-up in 1974. I recruited Richard "Dick" Murray, a talented former chairman of the Hudson's Bay Company, who had brought the head office of the oldest company in North America from London to Canada, to be its head. He had excellent experience, a good personality and a sense of humour. He said, memorably, that Laurier had said that the twentieth century would belong to Canada, not that Canada should belong to the United States. Later, when the Conservatives changed "significant benefit" to "net" benefit, the purposes of FIRA became thoroughly confused. I recall shouting across the House floor when they talked about "net" benefit in the seventies: "What accountant will you find to define "net"? It was a far more elusive concept than significant benefit. I never got a good answer from the Conservative critics.

As I write, the world has entered another recession. The Stelco plant in Hamilton has laid off almost all its employees, even though it is probably the most efficient in the U.S. Steel operation. Management in Pittsburgh, however, decided to "bring the jobs home," which is certainly a "net benefit" to the American economy but it makes no economic sense. Nortel was our great technology leader. At one time it conducted almost half the private sector research in Canada, and its market capitalization far exceeded that of any other Canadian company. It is now a bankrupt shell, and the government is permitting its invaluable parts to pass to foreign owners with no objection even though Canadian taxpayers through subsidy and tax breaks paid for much of it.

Today our great nickel mines in Sudbury are subject to distant head offices, as are Stelco and Dofasco. We have failed to build multinationals as we dreamed of doing, and that failure reflects in part the emasculation of FIRA, which sought to establish a level playing field with other countries that used subsidy and protectionism to create their own multinationals. American military spending was a massive and barely hidden subsidy to Boeing, Lockheed, the automobile industry and so many other American multinationals, while Europeans often did not even bother to hide the restrictive practices that protected their own firms. Had we more businesspeople in government and fewer theoreticians and free market ideologues, Canadian business would stand on stronger feet today.

My business experience and Murray's was enormously helpful in developing FIRA. We understood the files quickly but there were few with that kind of experience and understanding in government at the time. Later, some of my successors were slow in giving responses because of their lack of understanding of business, and the delays brought strong criticism and weakened support for FIRA. Of course, there was American criticism but I found it easy to counter. I would say to American friends, "Well now, tell me, if the Japanese were to buy control of General Motors, wouldn't you have a view on that? If a German company were to take over Boeing or any other major institution, wouldn't you have a view on that?" Of course, they did then and do now. Witness the way a Chinese take-over of a major U.S. oil corporation (Unocal) was thwarted. In the early eighties, the Americans fought off a "Japanese" takeover of their film industry, and "national security" is a shield they bring out whenever a takeover becomes politically unpopular. Thus, although Dubai Ports runs many of the ports of the world and the United Arab Emirates are a major American ally, "national security" was invoked to keep Dubai Ports from the United States.

Was FIRA successful? It's not easy to answer the question, but I know that at the time it did change the attitude of Canadians and others, particularly where resource investments were concerned. It asserted the Canadian interest in a way that was not seen before, and it had a real impact. I recall a visiting German delegation of which an obnoxious member bitterly complained that investment review was dreadful and that Canada should get rid of it. I asked him, "Why does it concern you?" He responded, "Well, we have a 25 per cent ownership in Algoma steel and we'd like to broaden it." I said that he should have no worries if he could show significant benefit to Canada, and if he could, it would surely also be a benefit to him and his investor colleagues. He blew up. Within forty-eight hours, he sold off his 25 per cent ownership. I told him I was very pleased because eager Canadian investors bought it quickly.

It is true that FIRA was not particularly popular in the West, particularly Alberta, although differences on energy policy were more serious there. I also heard some criticism from the Maritimes that had more merit. I recall Premier Gerry Regan of Nova Scotia saying to me once, "Well, FIRA may be fine for Ontario but where do you think all the investment that we have received in this part of world has come from? It hasn't come from Toronto but from foreign investors through direct foreign investment." I took the point and recognized that we had to modify the process of assessing "significant benefit" to Canada. We knew we must recognize that regional issues were important and that we should not discourage foreign investment when it was to the advantage of a particular area.

In 1974 I said that my two major goals were in developing Canadian multi-national markets in the emerging countries and converting more raw materials into processed products. In the latter case, I focused on the question of control of an industry. These priorities were reflected in the amendments that I undertook in the Export and Import Permits Act. Walter Gordon and others had talked about ownership, but my business experience had taught me that control was more important. You could have a controlling interest with a 25 per cent interest. With that interest, policies could be set on such subjects as licensing agreements. I discussed this question with the Mexicans and the French. I was very concerned that one of the reasons why Canadian firms were not more outward-looking was that they were basing their manufacturing on license agreements with foreign companies. The central nature of a licensing agreement was that you would have the exclusive right in Canada to employ the technology to produce whatever product or process was involved. For this, you paid a license fee. If, however, you improved the technology and wanted to export it, the agreements normally prevented both actions. You'd have to turn it over to the licensor free and you would have no international marketing rights. I wanted to introduce legislation which would have required all license agreements to be registered in Canada in order to know better what the true nature of the license was. I discovered quickly from Jim Grandy that the Finance Department and other bureaucrats were "scared stiff" of the proposal. It didn't go forward because, as I said earlier, the cabinet did not have much business background and did not understand my arguments. My good friend Barney Danson did understand and Charles "Bud" Drury also understood, although he would have worried about interference with the market. I still regret we did nothing in this area.

AN INDUSTRIAL STRATEGY

With the NDP, there were few complaints about our legislation, but there was an incessant demand for an industrial strategy. I was a skeptic. Here again my business experience was useful in making me understand that there was no "cookie cutter" which fitted all industries. A so-called "departmental insider" told the press that in contrast to Jean-Luc Pepin, who had talked about an industrial strategy, "Gillespie is a more pragmatic person. He's interested in an industry sector approach but the department must begin to establish some priorities and this is very difficult." This change represented a fundamental reorientation of a whole department. I tried to establish priorities and believe I did so in several areas. In the case of the aircraft industry, I successfully advocated the purchase of de Havilland and Canadair. The former, a subsidiary of the British firm Hawker-Siddeley, was being closed down with the manufacturing activities moving to the United Kingdom. The latter, which had major military importance, was up for sale. I thought that we should purchase the companies, preserve many jobs and operate them until future buyers were found. De Havilland's Beaver aircraft provided historical linkages in the Canadian north, where its versatility and reliability made it invaluable. De Havilland also produced the Twin Otter, a twin-engine aircraft, and later the short take-off and landing (STOL) Dash 7 planes for inter-city traffic.

To let these two companies pack up and leave because their foreign parents wanted to rationalize their operations was unthinkable to me. They were part of the industrial fabric of the country and, in many respects, ambassadors for a new Canadian industrial competence. I recommended their purchase by the federal government. The government through ITC would hold them until another buyer who would ensure their continuance and growth in Canada could be found. There were critics, such as my former colleague Paul Hellyer, who denounced the move as "preposterous and disastrous." However, we took the initiative and this "incubation" by the federal government preserved a major Canadian industry as de Havilland thrived and Dash 7s and 8s flew around the world. In Montreal, Bombardier became the owner of Canadair's operations and the world leader in the production of corporate and smaller jets, notably the famous Challenger. If we had followed the path taken by the market force ideologues, Bombardier would not be a major international player and we would not have an aircraft industry that is one of the best and biggest in the world.

In the case of the automobile industry, there was already a sector strategy, the Auto Pact. The Auto Pact demonstrates that industrial strategy cannot be a monolith but should have different components. Each industry had different needs. The Auto Pact dealt with the question of how to ensure production in Canada, which was approximately 10 per cent of the North American market for automobiles. The pact established production sharing equivalent to market share in Canada, but I was aware and told the Economic Club of Detroit that Canada had almost no share of the research done within the automobile sector. The speech had a surprisingly good reception. The Auto Pact was a conditional agreement for a particular sector. In this respect, it was very dissimilar to the Free Trade Agreement negotiated by the Brian Mulroney government in the late eighties. The Auto Pact was a conditional agreement, which had measures that could be brought to bear if certain things did not occur. These were lacking in Mulroney's trade agreement and the result has been highly damaging to Canadian interests, as, for example, in the softwood lumber case. Canada has had no way to challenge Congress's ability to change rules or ignore agreements with an attitude too much like "Heads I win, tails you lose."

One great concern of Trudeau and of ITC was the American application of extra-territoriality, a concept that is now very familiar because of the Helms-Burton legislation of the 1990s, which penalizes foreigners who do business with Cuba. It's been a consistent problem because Canada continued to recognize and export to Cuba. During my tenure at ITC, I argued strenuously that American laws stopped at the border, but a Montreal company, MLW-Worthington, wanted to sell thirty locomotives to Cuba. The company, however, had American directors who declared that they would not authorize the sale as they'd go to jail because of American law on trading with the enemy. I was outraged and declared that there was a simple solution: the directors should resign if, as directors of a company in Canada, they feared American law. I heard external affairs minister Mitchell Sharp gasp. He thought I had lost my marbles, but it was important that a strong stand be made even if it annoyed Washington. We used the Competition Act to limit extra-territoriality.

EXPORT AND IMPORT PERMITS ACT

There was also some opposition when, in March 1974, I introduced an amendment to the Export and Import Permits Act to give Ottawa more control over export of renewable and non-renewable resources. Clause 1,

A social occasion with Governor General Roland Michener and his wife, Norah.

the proposed new paragraph, would permit the Governor-in-Council to restrict the exportation of any article that is a product of a natural resource of Canada where national policy requires the further processing of that product in Canada. I argued that we should negotiate an end to tariff structures that favoured the sale of Canadian raw materials rather than processed projects and urged that we take these arguments to the GATT negotiations. I told the *Financial Post* that "What we are really saying is that the days are over when Canadians would rather haul rocks and logs for other countries' manufacturers." I also established a modest fund for upgrading processing facilities here. The article correctly suggested that what "Gillespie is really doing is changing the rules of the game."

On February 11, 1974, in my address to the Economic Club of Detroit, I tried to spell out what we were hoping to achieve by our policies. I specifically addressed the question so often asked by some Americans and Canadians: "Are Canadian policy initiatives un-American activities?" The remarks indicate the growing crisis in the western economies after the

Arab oil embargo and the troubling rise of inflation and the decline of economic growth. In this context, I concentrated on three policy areas: energy policy, industry policy for resource upgrading prior to export, and foreign investment. I began by illustrating how quickly the North American world had changed:

"It was only two years ago that you, the U.S., were restricting your purchases of oil from us – our exports to you. Now we've had to limit our oil sales to you – your imports from us. Would it make sense for Canada to be importing nearly half its oil needs at world prices while exporting an equivalent amount of domestic production at less than world prices [these had increased from US$4 a barrel to US$12 a barrel?] We have continued to ship oil and natural gas to you at prices no higher than the prices we must pay for our own imports. In spite of this, we were accused last month by one U.S. Senator of being 'un-American.'"

I continued in the same vein on foreign investment policy. I argued that it should be seen as an important adjunct of our industrial policy. "Canada," I pointed out, "has paid a high price for the high degree of foreign ownership in our economy. Part of this crisis has been that Canadians have become too accustomed to expecting others to do our research, product innovation and market development, and too accustomed to expecting others to tell us what we might do.... In too many cases, the senior officers of our leading firms – subsidiaries of foreign parents – do not have the freedom to choose where to source the components for their products, what product to make or where it will be ultimately sold." In this case I was referring specifically to the problem of extra-territoriality – trading with Cuba or with China, for example – and to the broader problem of the lack of research in Canadian industry.

The Canadian-American relationship, of course, was critical and, in the seventies, ever more difficult. I ended my remarks with the observation that "important subjects such as energy and the health of our respective automotive industries are just two examples of the importance of working together and understanding one another. We are each other's largest customers." I then ended the speech with a strong expression of the beliefs I held then and continue to believe now: "Respect for each other's priorities and understanding of each other's needs are essential to the growing maturity of our relationship. I have always worried less about disagreements than about misunderstandings. Nothing can be quite as dangerous as a misunderstanding between friends. If we are to avoid these misunderstandings, it is essential that we consult with another, both on day-to-day problems and also longer-term initiatives."

When choices have to be made, should Canada always acquiesce to the U.S. point of view and act as a cheerleader? Is it being anti-American to criticize U.S. policies or practices such as their stand on softwood lumber, where numerous rulings are simply rejected? Was it wrong to keep American mortgage lenders, who were responsible for the sub-prime mess, out of Canada and to prohibit Canada's banks from risky activities? Why are Canadians criticized when they criticize American government action when their criticisms echo those made by American Democrats? When a person is promoting Canadian interests, why should he or she be mocked as anti-American?

Americans fight forcefully and effectively for their interests. My government experience tells me that we should never be reluctant to defend our interests. Americans respect others who can clearly define their own interests, so long as they are treated fairly. In all my debates with the Americans and, even more, with the wilder Canadian nationalists, I insisted upon fairness and respect. FIRA defended our interests, but those Americans who knew Canada best – for example, Treasury Secretary George Shultz, who was a straight shooter – understood that FIRA responded to Canadian concerns and did not threaten American interests. We've not always defended our interests well, but it's not the Americans' fault. It is our own.

CHAPTER NINE

MAJORITY GOVERNMENT AGAIN

The campaign of '74 was a tough one in tough times. The country was suffering from the twin evils of high inflation and very slow growth – stagflation. I was much in demand from constituencies all over the country to support their Liberal candidates. My approach seemed to have registered positively with a large part of the public. I was able to do it because of the help from friends and family, who beat the bushes for me in my own riding. We were all ready for a holiday when it was all over.

The speech in Detroit on Canada's economic interests occurred only a few months before the minority government fell and we faced another election, which took place on July 8, 1974. As a high-profile minister, I had major responsibilities in Ontario, which was the major battleground for the election. Conservative leader Robert Stanfield campaigned on a program of a wage and price freezes in response to rising inflation. Trudeau mocked the program, saying, "Zap, you're frozen." His appeal and a very effective campaign in which Margaret Trudeau took a major part resulted in a majority government, with the New Democratic Party taking most of the losses. The Tories fell from 106 seats to 95, the New Democrats from 31 to 16. We rose from 109 to 141 seats, not a large majority but the base for a government that lasted almost five years.

Things initially went well. Dick Murray brought enthusiasm, business expertise, and a sense of humour to his job as head of FIRA. We shared the same concerns about the need to slow the sale of our resource companies. Far from the stereotypical bureaucrat himself, Murray was supported by an able professional civil servant, Garth Howard, who took the top job when Murray retired. I also recruited a bright young personal assistant, Allan Lutfy, who later had a very successful career in the public service and is now an eminent jurist as Chief Justice of the Federal Court of Canada.

While I was minister there were many demands from the opposition

Campaigning with Pierre and Margaret Trudeau in the 1974 election.

and even from some government members for the establishment of an "industrial strategy for Canada" as the solution to our problems. They argued it would provide simple answers to the regions of Canada and would be a public document that would act as a blueprint for industrial development while providing some certainty. Although the *Toronto Star* continued to trumpet the need for such a strategy, I remained steadfast in the belief that strategies should be designed that would best serve a particular industry and that an all-encompassing industrial strategy was a reach too far. I approached the various industrial sectors, such as automotive, electrical manufacturers, electronics, shipbuilding and aircraft, and asked each to propose a strategy for their individual industries. The exercise quickly proved useful and allowed policy-makers to better understand industrial interests. The Auto Pact set out the rules for that industry and as mentioned above, we proved successful in creating a policy focus in the aircraft industry.

METRIC CONVERSION

One of the interesting responsibilities I acquired was that of metric conversion – the conversion of our measurement systems for temperature (Fahrenheit to Celsius), distance (from miles, etc. to kilometres, etc.), from pounds to kilograms, etc. Most of the world outside the U.S. and the U.K. was already on metric measurement. Canada was an exporting nation and its customers, apart from the U.S., largely used metric. The automobile industry had already adopted metric for sizing its parts and the U.S. itself was thought to be flirting with a wider conversion. I obtained my colleagues' agreement and then had the responsibility for getting the matter through Parliament. I spoke to my Conservative Opposition critic along these lines, "You are comfortable with feet and inches, I know, but the future is in metric." It is the measurement of science and it is international in usage.

There was always resistance. Canada had established a Metric Commission Canada in 1971 to act upon a 1970 white paper that had recommended adoption of the system in Canada. The British Commonwealth was adopting it, the automobile sector already used it and scientists spoke only in metric units. Trudeau was strongly behind it, partly because he thought it was a way where we could be separated from the American identity. Just as we had two languages not one, we would be able to talk about "Celsius" to differentiate ourselves from the United States, where Fahrenheit was cherished on the weather forecasts. Unfortunately, the American scientific community could not counter the strong opposition the metric system faced there, which proved fatal. The conservative American opposition lent force to the opponents on the Conservative benches in Canada. Here we were, foolishly ignoring our largest trading partner and flirting with a system that no one over the age of twenty-one would understand. My opposition critic, my friend "Gorgeous George" Hees, was resisting the early passage of a resolution facilitating the adoption of metric. I went over and spoke to him privately: "You know, George, you always thought of an attractive woman as being 36-24-36. You've got a reputation of having a great eye for that." He smiled as I told him, "Just think, she'd now be 90-60-90, and I offered him a pin-up with those numbers underneath her." Then, I added the clincher: "George, what do you think half a foot would be? You've always thought of it as 6 inches. Now you'll have 15 centimetres." His opposition weakened immediately.

And so metric was introduced and endures today. With the help of Grandy and other officials, we also strengthened the Federal Business Development Bank and tried to provide more management expertise to small business through the use of retired businessmen with the Counseling Advice for Small Enterprises (CASE) program. I believed that even more than financing, management skills were the major problem for small business. The scheme has worked and has been expanded. We also provided equity financing to small business. In general, ITC under my direction tried to expand services for small business, especially in the area of skills training. We also expanded the Export Development Corporation (EDC), Canada's trade financing agency, which until the seventies was considerably weaker than the U.S. agency, the Export/Import Bank (EXIM). Some have criticized the EDC for taking business away from the banks, but the charge is unfair. The Canadian banks did not possess the confidence, competence or taste for export risks. They did, however, participate as secondary lenders.

EXIM received massive government grants for "loss make up." I am particularly proud of the strengthening of EDC and its further development by my son, Ian, who worked for the bank for over twenty-five years and was its very "hands on" CEO for seven years. By 2004, EDC financings had amounted to $60 billion, a doubling over a period of seven years. Moreover, EDC received no government grants. His achievement was exemplary.

During my tenure Statistics Canada strengthened its position as the pre-eminent statistics agency among Western democracies. Sylvia Ostry was its head and she had an outstanding international reputation, one that was crowned when she became the chief economist of the OECD. Her husband, Bernie, was the deputy to my good friend John Roberts. Bernie was often controversial and sometimes drove John crazy with his schemes. Sylvia, however, was an insistent but always interesting public servant. She came to my office every fortnight and smoked almost an entire package of cigarettes during the meeting. Sylvia always asked for more resources because she argued that business needed more information to make informed decisions. I was regularly a sceptic, asking, "How much more information, what kind of information?" I would argue that many businesses don't make decisions, not because they don't have information, but because they don't like making decisions. She seemed to blow smoke my way whenever I didn't show any enthusiasm for her argument. My own experience in the business world was often a great advantage in government.

As mentioned above, my predecessor Jean-Luc Pepin had a deserved reputation as a superb salesman. One of my responsibilities was to promote Canadian products and it was one of the fascinating parts of the ITC position. My period as ITC minister in '73, '74 and '75 coincided with the energy crisis, and as a result I travelled to several countries where energy was a major concern. I shared these responsibilities with my good friend energy minister Don Macdonald, whose department sometimes complained that I was treading upon his territory. He never complained himself. One of the major Canadian sales efforts was made in support of the sale of the CANDU nuclear reactor. It was a period of intense competition – the Americans were the world leaders with two companies, General Electric and Westinghouse, which produced light water reactors. The

CANDU was a heavy water reactor. It was my responsibility to market the CANDU and it took me to unusual places, where I met interesting but not always scrupulous people. One of my journeys (1974) was to Romania where I met its notorious leader Nicolae Ceausescu. He told me that they were interested in CANDU because they didn't want the Soviet reactor. They wanted to be independent of the Soviet Union but purchasing the American system would cause difficulties with other members of the East bloc. He told me that he understood the CANDU system was excellent and that he had consulted other countries – he mentioned the Chinese, the Albanians and the Iranians – who were also interested in the system. They all wanted to stand outside the American and Soviet empires!

While the Shah of Iran was interested, he knew little about the distinctions between heavy and light water reactors. I ended up giving him a short chemistry lesson. The interest remained in a later trip he arranged for his prime minister to visit Canada where we continued the dialogue. I had discovered that the Shah of Iran was interested in the CANDU in 1974 when I took what I described as a "hard sell trip to the Middle East," which was then awash in petrodollars. We landed first in Beirut and then flew on to Riyadh and Jeddah in Saudi Arabia. There we met King Faisal, who was very imperial and imperious. From there we travelled to Baghdad, which charmed me with the historic and beautiful Euphrates that wound through its centre and with its splendid residential quarters that seemed very European. I still recall, but now with great sadness, the chestnut braziers on the Euphrates banks and the night club with a beautiful belly dancer who gratefully and graciously accepted folded dollar bills in her bodice.

Iran fascinated us, as did the Shah himself. As we approached Tehran from the airport, we quickly realized that we were not in a democracy when our police escort forced all cars off the road as our cavalcade proceeded to the palace at high speed. There Empress Farah Diba received Diana and showed her the exquisite and abundant crown jewels. We managed to make numerous deals in a country that was suddenly very rich from oil. It was fascinating to speak with the Shah about his ambition to industrialize and modernize the country. He had heard about the Niagara Peninsula and how a steel industry and a food industry existed side by side.

Meeting the Shah of Iran in Tehran and (below) King Faisal of Saudi Arabia in Riyadh on our trade mission to the Middle East in 1974.

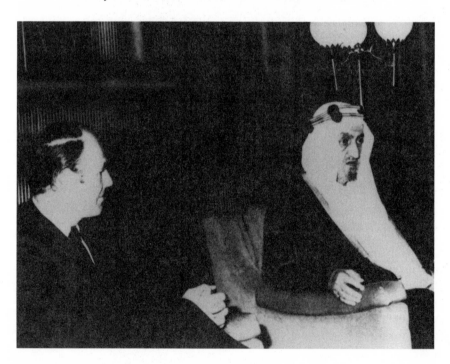

He thought of Iran, where agriculture was still the occupation of most of the population, and wondered how heavy industry and agriculture could co-exist. He sent his prime minister, Amir Abbas Hoveida, to Canada to study the nuclear business and also to see the nuclear power plant at Pickering. A highly cultivated man, he wore a boutonnière in his lapel, carried a cane, dressed elegantly and spoke superb English; he was my guest while in Canada. Given the apparent stability of the country at that time, we did not suspect that someday Iran would wish to build a nuclear bomb.

Of course, the Shah's dreams disintegrated. In 1979, the Shah, in an ill-judged attempt to appease the revolutionaries, had Hoveida arrested. Unable to escape, Hoveida was shot immediately after the mullahs took control. It was a troubled time throughout the world. I believe about ten of the various heads of states or their senior ministers that I met as ITC minister were shot or assassinated. King Faisal was assassinated, as was Hoveida, and Ceausescu was killed by a mob. Elsewhere, Indira Gandhi of India and South Korea's Park Chung Hee were also assassinated while Pakistan's Zulfikar Ali Bhutto was executed. I recall saying after I left the portfolio that not everyone recognized the advantage of a democracy like Canada, where the normal punishment of our electoral process is retirement.

The trade mission to the Middle East identified a billion dollars of sales potential for Canadian industries. I felt a personal sense of accomplishment. My pleasure was cut short upon my return to Canada. My assistant, Mike Gillan, met the plane to inform me that my mother had had a stroke and was close to death in Victoria. I boarded the next flight and thankfully I was able to spend the last days of her life with her. Her parting instructions to me had to do with my Uncle Dugald. He had intended to travel to Scotland to his old school Loretto to inform the students about the nature of Canada. She told me to stop him at all costs because "he knows nothing about Canada and would talk nonsense to them." It was very sad and difficult to say good-bye to her as she had been an enormous influence throughout my life. Years later I received a box of letters from Victoria. My mother had carefully collected every letter I had ever written to her. I treasure them to this day.

Upon my return to Ottawa, I had to prepare for my next trade mission to Mexico. Like the Middle East, Mexico became a more significant Canadian interest because of the oil crisis. I went there twice, in 1973 and 1974, and had fascinating conversations that in many ways foretold our future relationship within NAFTA. I discovered how our absence of Spanish language skills affected our access to South American markets and began a support program at the University of Western Ontario business school to teach Canadian business students to speak Spanish. Of course, most Mexican leaders I met could speak English, a reflection of their close but ambivalent relationship with the United States. President Luis Echeverria had a strong interest in Canada, particularly in the CANDU and railway equipment. Diana became Diana de Gillespie and charmed all she met. In my conversations I was struck by how leery of the United States Mexican ministers were. I recall specifically how Foreign Minister Emilio Rabasa spoke with scorn of Nixon and his administration, emphatically declaring, "We don't want to do business with those fuckers!" Echeverria himself said, "Are you the slightest bit interested in a free trade agreement with the United States?" I said, "No, not on the basis of anything I've heard to date." He replied, "I'm not either." NAFTA remained a generation away.

On my departure, the president gave me a magnificent Mexican silver-embossed ceremonial saddle with a sword on which was an inscription declaring steadfast friendship. It would have required an enormous horse and, though beautiful, was impractical. It's now in the Museum of Civilization in Ottawa. I had my own problems with official gifts. On the trip to the Middle East, I was determined to give Canadian gifts, not the normal trinkets like embossed Ronson lighters. I therefore decided to give them Hudson Bay blankets, to the considerable consternation of my staff. I told them that the days were hot in the Middle East but the nights cold. Grudgingly, they bought the blankets. Somewhere over the Mediterranean as we were approaching Beirut, one of the senior departmental officials came to me and said, "We've got a problem." On the label of the blankets was the statement "Made in Scotland." We considered cutting off the labels but decided not to and left the blankets at the embassy in Beirut, where our diplomats, I suppose, still use them on cool Lebanese nights.

Not all visits or relationships were easy. Britain's entry to the European

(Above) Inspecting the oversize ceremonial saddle that was our present from President Echeverria of Mexico.

I didn't buy Christopher Soames' proposals

Common Market and the compensation for Canada was a difficult problem made unpleasant by the British negotiator Christopher Soames, who was Winston Churchill's son-in-law and a member of the British cabinet. He came to Canada and offered the same deal Britain proposed to give to the United States, even though the United States lost nothing but Canada lost a great deal because of traditional imperial preferences. I had dealt with Soames in Britain and found him difficult, pompous and arrogant. I recalled Churchill's comment when asked whom he most admired, Hitler or Mussolini. Without hesitation, he answered, "Mussolini, of course. He's the one who had the guts to have his son-in-law executed." I suspect he was thinking of Soames.

Soames, who later became the industry minister in the European Economic Community, was once my host in Paris at a so-called working lunch, which meant that there were seven courses and about seven different wines. Every so often he would shout and wave, *"Encore du vin! Encore du vin!"* and a waiter would rush forth with another expensive vintage. As the "working" lunch extended into the afternoon, someone came up to him and said, "Mr. Soames, the Japanese delegation is waiting. You were supposed to meet them at 2 p.m. What will I tell them?" Soames dismissed him saying, "Tell them to hang their goddamn cameras on the peg and wait for me."

My time in ITC gave me the opportunity to develop and act upon my beliefs. I had written at the beginning of the decade that "an appropriate economic policy for Canada should emphasize our opportunities alongside the largest market in the world; it should concentrate far more on adapting to the multinational form of corporate organization than resisting it; it should be concerned with converting Canadian entrepreneurs from a rather inward-looking group to an outward-looking group. It should commit resources to the building of Canada rather than buying it back. It should place primary emphasis on new technology." Critics of FIRA and other attempts to stress the Canadian national interest, as the Americans did with EXIM and military spending and as the British did when they entered the European Community, missed the point. I wrote in 1971 that we must have more Canadian multinationals: "The Canadian spirit will only thrive if we look outwards." We needed to develop our own

Greeting Fidel Castro at the Canadian embassy in Havana. My visit in March 1975 was the first by a Canadian cabinet minister and paved the way for Pierre Trudeau's visit in 1976, which raised eyebrows in Washington.

technologies, our own multinationals and our own professional business schools. In my years in ITC these were my central aims. Unfortunately, they remain our aims today because we still lack Canadian multinationals and have not often enough commercialized research successfully. I have argued that an activist government aware of Canadian interests can play a large part in building an outward focus for Canadian business. I'm not an interventionist but I do believe that the failure to consider whether "significant benefit" mattered was a significant loss to Canada.

My tenure at ITC came quickly to an unexpected end when John Turner, who was increasingly upset with Trudeau, resigned as finance minister in September 1975. Trudeau asked me if I wanted to take over Finance. I said I preferred Energy, where my ITC work had given me a strong base. Trudeau agreed, and I became Minister of Energy, Mines, and Resources on September 26, 1975, and Don Macdonald became finance minister, with the challenge of dealing with wage and price controls. Energy was a hot spot in the seventies, and I accepted the challenge with alacrity. And what a challenge it proved to be!

CHAPTER TEN

MINISTER OF ENERGY

I n 1975 I finally moved to Ottawa, buying a home on John Street in the New Edinburgh area, not far from the prime minister's residence at 24 Sussex Drive. It was a renovated worker's house and perfect for us. It became our centre of operations. Cynthia was married and living in Toronto. Ian was finishing at Queen's University. We rented our Toronto house to the British Consul General. I continued to return to my constituency but more and more I faced the need to satisfy other demands. The propinquity to Pierre Trudeau attracted Diana and me less than the charm of the home and the numerous mature trees, which gave the area a country feel in the heart of the city.

I became Minister of Energy, Mines, and Resources at a difficult moment for the government. Turner had been a powerful minister, and rumours soon swept Bay Street and the Liberal Party that Trudeau had forced him out. I had supported John for the leadership in 1968, and he had always recognized me as a member of the "club of 195," who were the core upon which he would build a future bid for leadership. Not surprisingly, John talked to me confidentially and personally at this time. When he saw that he was not going to get the cooperation of the organized labour movement, he told Trudeau that he wanted a change – External Affairs. Trudeau had only a few months before appointed Allan J. MacEachen to that post. It wasn't available. John told me Trudeau could offer him a seat in the Senate, which he took as an insult and promptly resigned. We sat in the garden of 78 John Street as all of this was revealed – a sad story.

THE BROADER CONTEXT OF ENERGY POLICY

Under the terms of the British North America Act, the provinces were the owners of their natural resources, not the federal government, as was the case under the U.S. Constitution.[1] This was not the intention of the Fathers of Confederation, but, after judicial and political debate, it became the fact after a referral to the Privy Council (the Law Lords of the United Kingdom) in 1934. That was their decision. It changed the whole dynamics of natural resource development in Canada. Forty years later, this issue became a central issue for the Canadian federal government in meeting the energy crisis. The issue became manifest in terms of national security and the broader national interest. How does the federal government manage the development of an essential resource (oil) over which it has only limited jurisdiction and control? How does it establish the pace of development of key resources "owned" by the provinces and managed by foreign oil companies? Should the federal government consider invoking the ultimate federal power to protect peace, order and good government? How do you balance the interests of the consuming provinces and the producing provinces?

Cheap energy came abruptly to an end in the early 1970s, and the Canadian energy minister faced the challenges of radical change. The previous minister, my friend Don Macdonald, warned me that a few minefields awaited me in the path ahead. My experience at ITC had prepared me for some of the dangers, but others appeared in unexpected places. The strong dislike Macdonald had taken to Alberta premier Peter Lougheed was reciprocated. As a westerner and a newcomer, I had some hope of repairing the relationship with Alberta, but the divide on the issues was deep and conflict almost inevitable. Most Albertans, I imagine, thought the energy minister should be an Albertan but, unfortunately, there were no Alberta Liberal MPs.[2] Alberta and its premier seemed to believe that Ontario had

---

1. The exception was the Northwest Territories which became the provinces of Alberta and Saskatchewan. When the two provinces were created in 1905, the federal government retained control of natural resources. The result was an understandable sense of discrimination. Control of resources became a political issue and the Conservatives under R.B. Bennett, a Calgary lawyer, pledged to give responsibility to the provinces. They did so when they came to power in 1930. Of course, the overwhelming bulk of oil and gas resources are in those two provinces, but the extent of the natural wealth and the importance of oil in the modern world were not realized in the thirties, when both provinces suffered greatly in the Depression.

2. The Liberals won only five seats on the Prairies in 1974, which was two more than in 1972. But none in Alberta.

too much influence and that central Canadian politicians had increased costs for Albertans over the year through high tariffs. In fact, Canadian energy policy in the sixties had favoured Alberta through the creation of an arbitrary dividing line, drawn roughly on the Quebec/Ontario border. Those to the west of the borderline had to buy oil from Alberta rather than the cheaper Middle Eastern imports. By the time I became minister that policy, which had assisted enormously Alberta's energy development, was not even a dim memory for the Albertans with whom I negotiated. But despite the importance of the relationship with Alberta, there were many other issues that preoccupied me in a portfolio that seemed to expand constantly.

The period is badly misunderstood. The oil crisis affected all parts of government, all Canadian governments and all governments of the world. Runaway inflation, partly the product of the oil crisis, had become a major threat. The rapid increase in oil prices that marked the post-OPEC world presented new challenges and cleavages in Canadian confederation. In Canada, central Canadian manufacturing interests faced much higher costs while Alberta's boom created higher inflation. As finance minister John Turner wrestled with the pressures, wage and price increases continued and his policy of voluntary restraints failed to work. After Turner left, the cabinet reluctantly but unanimously came to the decision that we should adopt wage and price controls. The reversal from the 1974 election pledge meant that there would be a huge political cost, and the next few years were ones of sudden upheaval and surprises.

Two weeks after the imposition of the controls, *Maclean's* (November 3, 1975) wrote that the policy "was running into serious trouble … and threatening to split the country." The political costs were higher than we had anticipated. By August 1976, the Tory lead over the Liberals was fully eighteen points (47 to 29), a reflection not so much of the Tories' new leader, the Albertan Joe Clark, as disillusionment with the government itself.

The problems could have been seen as insuperable. Fossil fuels were concentrated in Alberta, population and manufacturing in Ontario and Quebec, and francophones overwhelmingly in Quebec. Alberta under Lougheed took the position that the natural resources belonged to the provinces and that it should have exclusive control over their exploitation and sale. Ontario and Quebec, however, were greatly affected by the cost of oil and their residents could not understand why Canadians should pay the higher world price when their country had abundant reserves within its boundaries. Alberta, of course, had just over 10 per cent of the population while Ontario and Quebec had roughly six times as many people. For any democratic government, that voter imbalance must matter, and it did. Finally, to complicate matters more, on November 15, 1976, Quebec elected a separatist government that challenged the basic principles of Canadian federalism.

As a government, we used the federal constitutional authority over trade and commerce to shield Canadian consumers and businesses from the escalating international price for oil. It was a new game with new rules. After the first OPEC crisis in 1973, Canada developed a two-price system, i.e. a world price for exports and a lower price for Canadian consumers. The Americans paid a higher price than Canadians in the two-price policy adopted and kept asking Canada to reduce its consumption so that more could be exported to the U.S. This international tension was mirrored within Canada. As Robert Bothwell and Jack Granatstein suggest in their analysis of Canadian foreign policy at the time, "Lougheed thought in a continental context. Since Trudeau did not, there were the makings of a clash."[1] I would be on the front lines of that historic clash.

In my first months as energy minister in the fall of 1975, my experience as ITC minister proved an advantage because I had dealt with foreign investment and economic matters more generally. It seemed clear that the era of cheap oil was over and I explained this unpopular truth at every opportunity. The principal issue was the maintenance of the two-price system which Canada had adopted after the 1973 oil crisis. The *Globe and Mail* commented shortly after my appointment that "the 53-year-old former Toronto businessman was a key proponent of keeping oil and natural gas prices lower in Canada following the sharp increases in world levels two years ago." However, I also shared the government's view that

---

1. J.L. Granatstein and Robert Bothwell, *Pirouette: Pierre Trudeau and Canadian Foreign Policy* (Toronto, 1990), 88.

sound economics meant that our prices should rise to world levels, and in this respect I was in agreement with the petroleum industry and Alberta, although they were in a much greater hurry to raise prices than I was. In choosing me, Trudeau perhaps hoped for an easing of tensions. The *Financial Times* (September 29, 1975) commented: "Easy-going, Mr. Gillespie will represent a definite change in style from the aggressive Mr. Macdonald, but the needs of the portfolio are changing as well. From a period when it was necessary to ram through a variety of unpopular measures, the job is entering a phase in which the emphasis will be on more subtle negotiations with the provinces and with the U.S. on energy matters." While the report exaggerated my placid nature, it fairly described the tasks ahead.

With the Americans, the task was to manage our decision to reduce exports at a time of shortage. In November 1975, I announced that Canada would cut oil exports to the United States by one-third in 1976. This announcement would reduce oil revenue by about one billion dollars and would increase the need to raise the domestic price, which was then $8 per barrel. The Americans had already expressed their upset with our pricing and export policies in the case of natural gas, and the result was a continuous set of negotiations with the Ford and later the Carter administration on energy questions. For Canadians, there was some irony in the situation since for many years Americans had restricted our exports to them because they wanted to promote their own oil and petrochemical industry. Moreover, American companies dominated in the oil patch, and the Americans naturally supported their own companies, who wanted to open the spigots to the United States. Those companies were not always helpful in my view and in the view of the government. In a memorandum to file I noted the problems we faced when I was appointed:

SOME UNPLEASANT FACTS:

1. The world price for oil had increased from $2.20/ barrel to $11.50 – a four times increase.
2. The subsidy to Eastern consumers was $4.60/barrel. The Alberta Government wanted world price.

3. Our crude reserves were declining for oil and natural gas.
4. Canada imported more than it exported.
5. There were disappointing drilling results and the Syncrude [oil sands] project was proving to be very costly.
6. No assurance of import supply – reference the Arab-Israeli boycott. Further, all the major oil companies were foreign-owned and subject to their own government's influence – Imperial, Gulf, Texaco, Shell, Chevron, as well as BP, Phillips, Conoco, Petrofina, Global, etc.
7. Who determines (and how) the pace of development? In a supply crisis, whom do you support? The consumer or the producer?
8. There were options to reduce growth in oil consumption by substitution – e.g. renewables, and or:
   – Conservation
   – Upgrade discovered reserves to recoverable
   – Increase exploration activity
   – Rationing
   – Research to improve efficiency

As a government, we had a full plate upon which we had heaped even more since the first months of the crisis.

A POLICY INSTRUMENT — PETRO-CANADA

Today Stephen Harper talks about Canada as an energy superpower and encourages rapid development of the oil sands to serve the American market. In light of Mr. Harper's free market beliefs, it is ironic that government intervention and policy in the 1970s allowed him to make this claim that would have seemed ludicrous earlier. The whole oil sands development almost collapsed just as I became minister when Atlantic Richfield withdrew from its 30 per cent share in Syncrude, the pioneering firm developing the oil sands. The federal government scrambled to save Syncrude, which appeared about to collapse. Through Petro-Canada, which we had created during the minority government years, Ottawa purchased one half of the Atlantic Richfield (ARCO's) shares. Alberta and, surprisingly, Ontario came in to purchase the other 15 per cent. We also agreed that Syncrude royalties to the Alberta government could be deducted from income for federal taxes. It worked. Those oil patch people who claimed that Petro-Canada never got things right and that governments can't make good choices conveniently forget this critical intervention, which Alberta energy minister Don Getty praised highly at the time. Without it Canada would not have been the energy power it has become, much less hope to be a superpower.

Petro-Canada was a central part of the energy strategy that we developed in those times. We knew that there were large reserves in the North and on federal lands in the Territories, and we encouraged Petro-Canada to move into those virgin lands. There were also reserves in the Atlantic where Nova Scotia and Newfoundland made claims that went far beyond what was recognized in international law. The international companies were reluctant to exploit these resources, and at a time of energy insecurity Canadians did not want these potentially rich claims to be hostage to international whims. One of my greatest concerns was how to affect the pace of change when the industry was private, reluctant and mostly foreign. The only avenue was an instrument such as Petro-Canada or subsidies, and we used both. Our policies therefore required 25 per cent Canadian participation in the offshore and on the frontiers; if needed Petro-Canada, with its $1.5 billion capitalization and its access to loans on a privileged basis as an agency of the Crown, was available to become the Canadian partner. Moreover, the North and the offshore drilling brought sensitive environmental considerations to the fore and Petro-Canada, because of its public ownership, could be a model of corporate responsibility as well as subject to direction through its independent board chosen by the government.[1]

Petro-Canada was the product of the minority government years, when the NDP had called for the nationalization of the oil industry. We needed

---

1. Petro-Canada was given one year to acquire as much of the federally owned land under lease that its budget allowed; for seven years, it would obtain 25 per cent of all lands, returning to the Crown, when existing leases expire; and where no prior discoveries were made, Petro-Canada would have the opportunity to obtain 25 per cent interest in any exploration interest when up for renewal. With these provisions, Petro-Canada gained a strong position in future development.

their support and responded with the proposal for a state-owned oil company, which finally was launched in January 1976. Petro-Canada with its headquarters in Calgary was not popular with the Alberta government. It was greeted with a barely disguised hostility, and suspicion greeted its every move. Peter Foster (author of *The Blue-eyed Sheiks*) said that the walls of the Petroleum Club in Calgary "resounded with indignation at the thought that a 'window' should be needed on their activities. The oil community's more general regurgitation of its favourite philosophy – free enterprise good, government bad – intoned with about as much critical analysis as – 'four legs good two legs bad' of the animals on George Orwell's farm – was now given a particular, and all-too-close, example against which to rail."[1]

But the Petroleum Club critics ignored that fact that Petro-Canada's creation reflected similar actions in other countries, where governments established or used state-owned corporations as a "window" on the critical and turbulent energy world. Why Canadians distrusted the large national companies who controlled the international marketing of oil became clear in 1979 when Imperial Oil faced a cut of one-quarter of its supplies because of the decision of its international parent (Exxon). I was angry and said so: "Imperial gets oil from Venezuela, which hasn't cut back at all. Why should Canada suffer shortfalls when there's been no restriction from Venezuela?" Exxon played God, and Canada was not a favoured land in Exxon head offices.[2] I angrily referred to the double cross in the Exxon name. It was symbolic of their behaviour?

In terms of federal management it seemed important to set forth a

---

1. Peter Foster, *The Blue-Eyed Sheiks: The Canadian Oil Establishment* (Toronto, 1979), 150.

2. Quoted in ibid., 64. Foster says that "Imperial winced as they realized the opportunity had been presented to Donald Macdonald's much more politically-inclined successor, Alastair Gillespie, to score some points in the run up to a national election in the spring of 1979. Conservative leader Joe Clark had been taking pot-shots at the Liberal creation, Petro-Canada, so here was Gillespie's chance to belabor big, foreign-owned oil." However, Foster, who generally is unsympathetic to state intervention, agrees that "The key issue, perhaps, is whether a company like federally-owned Petrocan, can, in a more nationalistic world oil environment, secure Canada's imported supply needs better than the multinationals." For Canadian consumers, there was no doubt that they trusted Petro-Canada more than Exxon and its sisters. Quotations, 64-5.

With the newly appointed president of Petro-Canada, Bill Hopper, and my very able executive assistant, Jamie Deacey.

number of targets aimed at balancing the needs of consumers and the expectations we, the government, had for performance by the oil companies. I had several priorities: first, a pricing policy that would shelter Eastern consumers from world (read the OPEC cartel) prices; second, a policy that would help to support giving an advantage to Canadian industry, including petrochemical industries; and third, a policy which recognized that prices would advance to world prices.

At another level, I promoted a course of action which, in regional terms, could be described as doing what you're best suited for. For instance, P.E.I. became a chosen instrument for conservation leadership.

There were also conservation policies, such as the one I announced in February 1976, which required average fuel efficiency in automobiles to rise from 18 miles to the gallon to 24 in 1980 and 33 in 1985. The announcement stunned the automobile industry but they adapted. The government also offered support to alternative energy initiatives, although I emphasized that I did not expect solar, wind and other alternatives to offer much relief in the short run. In the short run conservation was more effective than the alternatives: one study claimed that if everyone lowered the thermostat 2.5 degrees Fahrenheit, we would need $40 billion less in capital investment. Yet we hoped that future generations would have cleaner and renewable energy. Richard Gwyn, a strong critic of the Trudeau government, nevertheless praised the energy department for its 1978 renewable program and even suggested, "Probably, if Gillespie had his way everyone would have a windmill above their garage and a nuclear reactor in their basement." (*Ottawa Journal*, July 3, 1978). Not quite, but believing that children needed to learn more about alternatives, I had a demonstration project set up where the Rideau Falls meets the Ottawa River, an ideal location to demonstrate hydro-electricity, solar power, wind power and even biomass. School buses packed with students came regularly. They got a sense of what alternatives might be. But on one occasion when driving to work, I noticed that the windmill was rotating madly. There was, however, no wind on that calm summer day. I called the National Research Council, which had responsibility for the site, and exclaimed, "What the hell's going on? There's no wind and the windmill is buzzing."

"Oh Minister, we thought it would be a good way for you to explain what a windmill looked like when children came."

I replied, "The last thing I could ever explain is how a windmill could rotate with no wind. Stop it now."

AN ENERGY STRATEGY

Some of the measures I pushed were stonewalled by the provincial governments or their agencies. Speed limits for example. The faster the speed, the greater the consumption of gasoline. The Americans, who had long line-ups at gasoline stations in the mid-seventies, pioneered this approach with their 55 mph limit. I opened the challenge to the provinces that had jurisdiction to lower their speed limits. This was resented though ultimately, and I think somewhat reluctantly, accepted in some provinces.

"Time of day" pricing of electrical energy was another measure. This had been adopted successfully in various foreign jurisdictions. Ontario Hydro, the Ontario government's energy Crown corporation and supplier

The Seven Sisters. One cartoonist's view of Canada playing catch-up.

would not, however, comply. Today, at least thirty years later, they have started to examine the practice. Then there was the Energuide program, which continues to this day, requiring electrical appliances to indicate the electrical consumption required to operate them. But the history of these years is one of too many missed opportunities for conservation and long-term common sense.

Until 1976 the government had largely responded to the unexpected. I decided to try to get ahead of events, and with that purpose in mind in April 1976 I released *An Energy Strategy for Canada: Policies for Self-Reliance,* setting out our central concerns. I was convinced that "self-reliance" was a far more meaningful objective than the Opposition's call for "self-sufficiency." I put forward the argument in the strategy document.

"While our proved reserves of oil and low-cost natural gas continue to decline, Canadian demands for these energy forms continue to increase. The growing gap between our energy demands and our ability to supply them from domestic reserves suggest that we could become increasingly dependent on the rest of the world, and the Organization of Petroleum Exporting Countries in particular, for our future oil supplies. This prospect carries with it economic and political risks which the Government of Canada views with concern."[1]

At the time the development of the oil sands wealth lay far in the future, frontier drilling had been disappointing and the OPEC threat continued to appear ominous for North America. The Americans were already hostage to foreign oil; we were determined we would not be.

The strategy emphasized the need to accept higher prices to encourage new development while adopting policies that encouraged conservation. Canada, it pointed out, no longer produced as much crude oil as it consumed, and there was little hope that the situation would soon change. We envisaged investments of $180 billion dollars over the next fifteen years to develop the oil sands and the Mackenzie Delta–Beaufort areas and to build the pipelines that would carry the oil and natural gas to consumers. There were five specific targets:

1. To move domestic oil prices towards international levels; and to move domestic prices for natural gas to an appropriate competitive relationship with oil over the next 2–4 years.
2. To reduce the average rate of growth of energy use in Canada, over the next ten years, to less than 3.5per cent per year.
3. To reduce our net dependence on imported oil in 1985 to one third of our total oil demands.
4. To maintain our self-reliance in natural gas until such time as northern resources can be brought to market under acceptable conditions.
5. To double, at a minimum, exploration and development activity in the frontier regions of Canada over the next three years, under acceptable social and economic conditions.

At the time Alberta was friendlier than Ontario to our ambitions because the latter did not want to move towards world price and was reluctant to accept some of the conservation measures we discussed. The *Calgary Herald* even declared the report to be "a level-headed document,

---

1. Energy, Mines and Resources, *An Energy Strategy for Canada: Policies for Self-Reliance* (Ottawa, 1976), iii.

giving a balanced view of the responsibilities and risks the nation faces if it is to bring its production and intake of energy into a rough equilibrium over the next 15 years."[1]

In Washington, James R. Schlesinger, de facto energy minister and assistant to the President, welcomed it too. At a joint press conference in Washington, Dr. Schlesinger waved our strategy book at the TV cameras and said, "I might mention in passing that we are seeking to emulate Canada, in that Canada has one of the few comprehensive energy plans and, within a matter of some months, the United States will emulate Canada by publishing its own comprehensive plan."

Although Alberta grumbled about some of our tax and lease policies, I managed to work out a direct relationship with Don Getty that calmed some of the angry words between Macdonald and Trudeau on one side and Lougheed on the other. After 1976 pricing questions for oil were not matters of dispute between Trudeau and Lougheed at federal-provincial gatherings but rather the product of detailed negotiations between me and Getty. My major problems often came from Liberals, elected or not. When I agreed to take Energy, Trudeau told me that I must make Petro-Canada a national policy instrument. He then said, "Would you have any difficulty if Maurice Strong was appointed president?"

I knew immediately that Trudeau had given Strong the job. I replied, "I've got three questions: How long would he serve as president? What would his role be? And who would appoint the board?"

He responded: "Well, he would be there in an organizing capacity, maybe nine months or so."

I continued, "Full time or part time?"

"Part time," Trudeau responded.

Then, crucially, "Who appoints the board?"

"You do."

That was all I needed. I chose the board and told them to keep a close eye on Strong.

Strong irritated the oil patch, and we had a poor relationship. After six months, I moved that he should be terminated or be made a non-executive

---

1. Ibid. 147-8.

chair. I put this forward in cabinet, and Trudeau looked around the room, expecting some other ministers to object. None spoke up, and Trudeau turned to the veteran Mitchell Sharp. "What's going on, Mitchell?"

"Well," Mitchell slowly replied, "I think it's this way, sir. Maurice has a reputation for starting things but then leaving them in a hell of a mess."

That ended my relationship with Strong until in 1979 when he decided he would enter politics as a Liberal candidate. There was a large fundraiser and, as senior Toronto minister, I sat beside him in his capacity as chair of the events. He introduced the sitting Liberal members and mixed up nearly all of them since he did not know most of them. He would say a name and look in the wrong direction as the MP stood. Other names he mispronounced. He then launched into a long introduction of Trudeau that went on and on, all by the way of introducing Trudeau. Finally, he introduced Trudeau.

Trudeau rose and said, "Well, Ladies and Gentlemen, I haven't come here to make a speech. I think I will thank the speaker."

Strong turned to me and said, "I'm not sure I'm cut out for this business." Within a couple of weeks, he had resigned as a candidate and announced that a political life was not for him.

SOME ATLANTIC CANADA CONCERNS

Strong was not the only Liberal who caused me troubles. Premier Gerry Regan of Nova Scotia was especially difficult. He did play a reluctant role in developing the Canadian Home Insulation Program, which we began in Nova Scotia and then expanded successfully across Canada. However, he and I fought regularly over Cape Breton coal, which he wanted to develop with large federal subsidies. Gerry had a problem because Nova Scotia's electrical generating plants were oil fired. The price of oil was raising electricity prices to the consumer. He wanted federal subsidies to support the Cape Breton coal mines as future sources of energy for his power plants. We also had tough negotiations over offshore oil and gas in the Atlantic. Regan loved to take shots at me. Provincial premiers often regard federal ministers as fair game. Although the law was on our side, we agreed that Sable Island revenues belonged to the province and that the federal government stake in other offshore resources was 25 per cent.

Nevertheless, Regan persisted, claiming that I was unwilling even to speak with him about coal subsidies. John Buchanan, Nova Scotia's Leader of the Opposition, declared that he didn't believe Regan. He flew to Ottawa, came to my office without an appointment and asked to see me. I was tied up in cabinet but he waited outside Parliament's Centre Block on a curb. When I emerged, he walked up to me and we had a good talk. He returned to Nova Scotia and declared that what Regan had said about my elusiveness was nonsense; he had no trouble meeting me and we had a good discussion. So much of provincial–federal interaction is simply bluster, and some of the players blustered more than others. John Buchanan subsequently became Premier of Nova Scotia. He was particularly helpful in my post-parliamentary, career which focused on the revitalization of the Point Tupper refinery properties.

I also had interesting negotiations with the Newfoundland government about the export of hydroelectric power and with Premier Richard Hatfield of New Brunswick, who wanted to harness the Bay of Fundy's tides to produce energy. In the case of Newfoundland I faced Brian Peckford, then the energy minister and a personality so emotional that it was difficult to have a conversation with him. In the House, the ebullient John Crosbie also reflected Newfoundland's strong sense of ownership and identity. I was a regular target of Maritime premiers and journalists who called for an energy subsidy for the poor provinces. One group even threatened to take over my riding association in Etobicoke by calling on Maritimers in the riding to join the Liberal Association to defeat me. Stimulated by this attack on me, the *Etobicoke Gazette* called my patient, politically wise and excellent assistant Ruth Cruden, who killed the story by simply pointing out that the only association member from the Maritimes was on holidays in Ireland and could not comment.

Two initiatives (disappointments) are worth mentioning. The first was the plan to harness the lower Churchill Falls power potential, often referred to as the Gull Island project. There was quite an extraordinary amount of unharnessed power going to waste. The Newfoundland government wanted to develop it but lacked the resources. I had a fight on my hands but I was able to persuade my colleagues that a corporation needed to be created in which the federal government would be only a 50 per cent shareholder.

The other project that I had great hopes for was a Maritime Energy Corporation. It was designed to rationalize electric power generation, including the Fundy tides, of the three provinces and transmission of power through a single corporation instead of the traditional three independent power companies. The plans for harnessing the valuable power potential of the four Atlantic Provinces were never realized, largely because the players changed with the election of the short-lived Joe Clark government of 1979.

I well remember a lunch when researching the tidal energy project in France – a project that later was realized in the Bay of Fundy. At the conclusion, the restaurateur presented me with a dusty bottle of that great French liqueur Calvados that was at least seventy years old, which he had hidden from the Germans during the occupation. "Please," he said, "I've kept this to honour the Canadians who came to our aid during the war."

I did have sympathy for Nova Scotia because New Brunswick exported Labrador power (which Quebec Hydro transmitted to New Brunswick) to the United States rather than to its Canadian neighbour. More controversial was the situation with Quebec and Newfoundland, which had to export its abundant Churchill Falls power through Quebec. The long-term contract continuing until 2040, which it signed with Quebec in 1969, was unfair at the time but the 3 mill per kilowatt hour rate became preposterous after 1973.[1] Frankly it is an outrageously unfair agreement that Newfoundlanders rightly resent. In July 1976 I warned after a meeting with Newfoundland ministers that "Quebec may have trouble arguing against the federal regulation of the free flow of hydro across provinces when it already benefits from a similar system of regulation for moving natural gas." I believed the federal government did have some capacity to act but it did not do so. The major factor was surely the sensitivity of Quebec politics during the 1970s and particularly after René Lévesque's government was elected in 1976.

---

1. Bruce Doern and Glen Toner, *The Politics of Energy: The Development and Implementation of the NEP* (Toronto, 1985), 88.

NUCLEAR ISSUES

Among the land mines which Don Macdonald had warned me about was Atomic Energy of Canada Limited (AECL), a Crown Corporation. Nuclear energy did not occupy a major part of the April 1976 *Energy Strategy* but nuclear matters did take up much of my time, not least because of the government's efforts to sell the CANDU reactor and Canada's key position as a major uranium producer. As ITC minister, I had some responsibility as a salesperson for the CANDU and got to know well this unique Canadian design and its very positive characteristics. As mentioned above, I tried to peddle the reactor to many countries while I was ITC minister with the full support of Trudeau, who told cabinet that the CANDU should be made available to other countries that needed energy.

The *Energy Strategy* I issued in 1976 did point out that, "The nuclear power stations existing, under construction and planned in Canada, employ the CANDU reactor developed in Canada. CANDU reactors use heavy water as a 'moderator', enabling them to use natural uranium as fuel. The design is such that over 90% of a CANDU nuclear power station can be built or supplied domestically." From a Canadian point of view, CANDU, therefore, offered many advantages, and the *Energy Strategy* suggested that nuclear could provide "about one third of new electrical generating capacity required by 1990 with plants built nearly entirely with Canadian materials and equipment and powered by Canadian uranium."[1]

While nuclear did become significant, particularly in Ontario, the analysis was too optimistic. The unique design was considered a "sleeping beauty" that one day would attract foreign sales, but there were never enough sales to generate economies of scale, as historian Robert Bothwell points out.[2] Unfortunately, building CANDU plants in Ontario proved expensive, heavy water was not always available at decent prices, and delays and cost overruns were constant. Still, we marketed our "sleeping beauty" energetically but had little success with western markets such as Australia, Italy or Britain. With other countries, the problems of nuclear

1. *An Energy Strategy for Canada,* 98, 103.

2. Robert Bothwell, *Nucleus: The History of Atomic Energy of Canada Limited* (Toronto, 1988), 426.

Henry Kissinger (left) meeting with me and my deputy minister Gordon McNabb post-Nixon to plead their case for access to Canadian energy supplies in their time of crisis.

energy became more meaningful. Trudeau and I were both insistent that we would not agree to any export unless there was a full undertaking on the part of the recipient country to respect the non-proliferation treaty and additional Canadian safeguards. Those standards were tough. German Chancellor Helmut Schmidt accused me of being totally unrealistic when I refused exports of uranium oxide to Germany. Despite our alliance with Germany, we would not bend unless the Germans gave the required undertakings.

But undertakings were not always enough and here the problems with nuclear become obvious. The Canadian nuclear relationship with India had been considered a great success, an example of technological transfer, and in 1971 India agreed to apply International Atomic Energy Agency standards to their project. Prime Minister Indira Gandhi personally assured Trudeau that her aims were peaceful. When the Indians exploded an atomic bomb on May 18, 1974, claiming it was for "peaceful" purposes, it shattered their credibility and outraged Trudeau, who never forgave Gandhi. They had betrayed us and damaged the cause of nuclear energy greatly. We took a lot of blame for "giving the Indians the bomb." Some was deserved, some was not and some was hypocritical. American complaints, for example, ignored the fact that the Americans were the ones who provided the crucial heavy water for the Indian reactor.

There was always a great deal of public ignorance about the subject of nuclear energy and nuclear safety. Amazingly, a poll in June 1976 by York University's Institute of Behavioural Research revealed that 44 per cent of Canadians over eighteen did not realize that "atomic science can be used to produce electricity in the first place." (Montreal *Gazette,* June 16, 1976). During this period, I often encountered protests at rail stations and other meeting places against nuclear power. These protests swelled in 1979 with the movie *The China Syndrome* and the meltdown of the nuclear plant at Three Mile Island in Pennsylvania. Various NGOs were strongly arrayed against nuclear power and there was no effective NGO that argued the case for nuclear as a means of dealing with the serious problems caused by fossil fuels. An effective voice favouring the "clean" nuclear option never emerged, as it has today with the dramatic evidence of the impact of carbon emissions on the atmosphere.

Nuclear energy, then, was a hard sell, especially for Atomic Energy Limited of Canada (AECL), which did not train its engineers to be salespersons. While the Americans and the French captured developed markets, we went after less-known but more controversial ones such as Romania. Shortly after I became energy minister, I learned that the sale to Argentina negotiated by the previous president had gone badly wrong. Costs had soared, and there had been little control by his successor. The Conservative critic, Allan Lawrence, began a sustained attack on our policies, an attack that was reinforced by the report of Auditor-General J.J. MacDonnell, which appeared in November 1976. With his report a crisis began. The result was a purge in AECL that resulted in the firing of five directors and a news story that continued for several years.

We discovered that not only had the Argentinean contract gone bad but also that AECL had engaged a shady Italian agent to conduct the sale. I was furious. It didn't help when one of the directors, Marcel Caron, who was involved in the original negotiations, was immediately appointed to the Royal Commission on Federal Financial Management. It was, as the *Toronto Star* declared at the time, a curious appointment. In my case, I was so angry that I told the *Star* (November 24, 1976) that I blamed AECL officials who, in my words at the time, "lacked judgment and foresight to protect us from the effects of inflation in Argentina and Canada. With hindsight, we can see that the protection they provided was minimal." I also blamed the former president, Lorne Gray, who had been involved in the original negotiations and the hiring of agents to sell the reactors to South Korea and Argentina.[1] His successor was an excellent engineer named John Foster, who informed me not long after I took the energy ministry that there was a problem with the Argentine contract.

When I first asked Foster how great the problem was he said, "About $20 million."

"Well," I replied, "would you find out exactly what the figure is?"

Rumours began to spread about the troubles, but I thought that I should get the facts before acting and speaking. The core of the financial problem was the failure by AECL to hedge against Argentina's inflation, which in the mid-1970s was disastrous. Foster then told me that AECL did not really know what the loss would be. First, he said $40 million but soon after said, "It could be lots more."

I sensed trouble. "What kind of system of cost controls do you have? You never can tell me what the losses will be."

He claimed that they had the best accountants in the world. But they were not auditing the construction management. Foster was a fine man and an excellent engineer, but I had lost confidence in him and in July 1977 I dismissed him.

Upon learning of these problems shortly after I took office, I called Ross Campbell, a "get things done" person, who had been a commando in the war. Ross was awaiting a reappointment in Tokyo, having just completed four years as Canada's ambassador to Japan. I told him the challenge. I asked him to become chair and to clean up AECL's board and its contract with Argentina. "I'll be on the next plane," he said. He came back, looked at the books, flew to Buenos Aires to renegotiate the contract, and managed to hold our losses to "only" $25 million. Still, AECL required

---

1. In the case of South Korea, AECL hired Shaul Eisenberg, an Israeli, who took 5 per cent of the contract. Gray told the board that Eisenberg had great knowledge of the Korean market and that fees were often higher. In the case of Italy, AECL entered a partnership with Italimpianti, which asked for a received $2.5 for marketing from AECL. The Canadians agreed to "ask no questions." See Bothwell, *Nucleus,* 427.

total reorganization and the House of Commons Public Accounts Committee spent the session of 1976-7 concentrating on the "bribes" to the agents, the cost overruns and the apparent fact that the only countries to buy CANDUs were dictatorships who needed to be bribed to purchase the reactors. These events occurred just as the government's popularity was dropping and with the memory of the American Watergate scandal very much in the public mind. Voters demanded transparency and accountability, and it seemed, correctly, that AECL had not passed the test. Without doubt, there had been a cover-up, and Campbell, my ministry and the Privy Council Office knew we had to act. AECL could no longer be what journalist Mark Gayn called "a state within a state, carefully doling out what information it has and concealing whatever lapses of judgment it makes."

This bad news made nuclear energy and CANDU a much harder sell despite some real successes at Pickering and impressive reviews of the CANDU reactor by scientists. We did not have the marketing skills to compete with the French, the Americans and others, and after the Argentine fiasco we had to do business differently from others who continued to use "agents," which normally meant bribes, to encourage sales. My own challenge was dealing with demands that I recover the fees, which Campbell did partially in the case of Argentina, and that I identify foreigners whom Canadian agents had bribed. It was an impossible task and the opposition knew it was, but it captured Canadian attention as yet another "cover-up" in the government, which was acquiring an increasingly bad reputation in the late 1970s.

Matters did not improve when an American legal case made public an attempt to develop a uranium cartel in 1972. An American Congressional committee in the spring of 1978 demanded that Gulf Oil produce documents that would reveal the existence of a uranium marketing cartel that sought to fix a price for uranium exports. American congressmen, blissfully unaware that Canada was a separate country, demanded full documentation for the trial of Gulf on the charge of engaging in a cartel to raise prices. The growing anti-nuclear mood combined with the anti-government mood to make the issue a major one in the summer of 1977.

Personally, I thought the attempt by my predecessor Don Macdonald and Jack Austin, then the Deputy Minister of Energy, Mines and Resources, to create a uranium cartel was an appropriate response to a serious problem in 1972. What had been forgotten by 1977 was that the Americans had used "national security" to justify their limits on imports of uranium at a time when the American market took 70 per cent of the world's uranium production. This decision, of course, had helped American producers, who competed for the remaining 30 per cent. The cartel was a response to American protectionism, the only one we had at the time. Canadian mines were threatened with closure as the market for uranium dried up in the late sixties and early seventies before OPEC emerged and governments turned once more to the nuclear option.

Canada had approached other producers, Australia, France and South Africa, about forming a marketing consortium – much like OPEC – to prevent mines closing and prices collapsing as Americans, assured of their domestic market, competed ferociously in foreign markets. Gulf Minerals Canada had participated in the creation of the cartel but when hauled before Congress had sought exoneration by complaining that it had been forced into the marketing arrangements by the Canadian government. To prove its case, it gave the House commerce committee the documents describing the creation of the marketing scheme. I was outraged, as was the government. I told a *Globe and Mail* reporter that Gulf's transfer of the documents might lead one to "wonder about how good a Canadian citizen" Gulf Minerals Canada was. Sensible Americans understood our argument. Senator Albert Gore of Tennessee, the father of Al Gore, backed our case and told the press that "The role of the Canadian government in coercing Gulf has been vastly over-stated by Gulf" (*Montreal Gazette*, August 16, 1977). The purposes of FIRA never seemed so well proven.

In any case, the argument was about the past. In the late seventies, there was a much different situation, one of scarcity. It was a situation where I thought there was an opportunity to use uranium shortages as a lever to secure long-term peaceful ends. The Carter administration was friendly to us, and I had a particularly good relationship with Walter "Fritz"

In Washington in May 1977 with energy secretary James Schlesinger and Vice-President Walter Mondale strategizing on Canadian-American energy policy.

Mondale, the vice-president, who was a friend of Canada and knew us well. On one of my visits to Washington, he said to me, "Let's join the president for lunch." We were in the White House, next door to Jimmy Carter's dining room. He was having lunch with George Meany, the labour leader. I noticed that there were no wine glasses, which was unusual at lunch in those days. Whether Carter drank or not I know not, but his guests at the luncheon table were offered no choice. Even without liquid stimulant, the mood was amiable. Fritz told me early on, "Call me anytime you want." I often did and was put through immediately.

I once visited Fritz in Washington and told him about my trip to Australia, where I had discussed the uranium supply situation. I told him that if the Australians joined together with the Canadians and Americans, the consortium would control 70 per cent of the world's uranium supply. They could establish rules on the export of uranium. We would have enormous power to extract undertakings for safeguards and non-proliferation. The Australians had said they would be with us in such a "cartel," although they didn't call it that. When I returned to Ottawa, I told Trudeau that here was an initiative that he should raise with Carter. He had given an important speech to the United Nations where he called for nuclear suffocation, and such an initiative had a place in such an approach. He raised the issue with Carter in his next meeting. The press ignored this approach, which promised to have such beneficial effects. Nuclear had become tainted, and it seemed in the seventies no good could come from anything that bore its mark.

NUCLEAR WASTE DISPOSAL

Nuclear waste disposal was perhaps one of the most sensitive and controversial energy policy matters to be dealt with. How should the spent fuel be disposed? The answer from some was to fire it into outer space or perhaps into the sun. Others, of course, would argue the simplest solution was not to create it in the first place. Several U.K. Labour government ministers, notably the radical Anthony Wedgwood Benn and Peter Shore, even argued that as Canadians were providing a great deal of the raw material, uranium, they should accept responsibility of its disposal. They wanted to ship their waste to Canada.

AECL had not been idle, looking at this problem and the various options, particularly in the case of Ontario, where all but one of the domestic

With U.K energy minister Anthony Wedgwood Benn in the second half of the 1970s.

CANDU plants was built. After a good deal of careful research, their scientists had concluded that the safest solution was to bury the waste. "Spent" fuel rods encased in cement would be lowered 2,000 to 3,000 feet down into the solid rock of the Canadian Shield. There were naysayers who argued that such a solution could risk the purity of underground fresh water streams. I was convinced that of all the options offered to me by AECL scientists, this was the best one: "to put it back where it came from". The Ontario government's energy minister, Dennis Timbrell, accepted the need for an Ontario solution. One Saturday morning he and I came to an agreement, a memorandum of understanding, which committed our two governments to work on such a scheme.

It's never been very clear to me why Ontario Premier Bill Davis should want to spike this far-seeing solution but he did. He moved Dennis Timbrell to the health portfolio and appointed Jim Taylor as his replacement. Taylor had had little if any experience in this field. But he represented a constituency in the Canadian Shield, and he stalled and fussed about our agreement. This, in my judgment, was one of the most glaring examples of the NIMBY – Not In My Back Yard – syndrome. There is of course a risk. But does anyone know of a solution with a lower level of risk? Ontario was going nuclear and it had to accept the responsibility.

While the reputation of government suffered during these debates, non-governmental groups grew both in number and influence. Accountability became a watchword of government, and this mood meant that major projects and corporations faced a higher degree of scrutiny than ever before. People were suspicious of multinational energy companies, and I responded to the complaints with the creation of a Petroleum Monitoring Act that required companies operating in Canada to report on whether their profits or cash flow derived from the increasing price of oil were being used to finance more exploration. It was a useful lever with respect to the pace of development issue. I argued the need to increase exploration in order to increase future oil supply. Public scepticism also affected development far more in the seventies than it ever had before. Environmental assessments, which were unknown twenty years earlier, became essential before any large developments took place. The environmental movement had developed quickly in the sixties and grew ever stronger in the seventies. On my native West Coast, there were deep and justified concerns about the rapid development of Alaskan oil and the tanker traffic that could threaten the sensitive environment of the Pacific Coast. In February 1977 I refused to let a Kitimat Pipeline go ahead until a full environmental assessment was made.

My cousin David Anderson, an MP and then B.C. Liberal leader, became an environmental consultant after 1976. He played a major role in the insistence on high environmental standards on the coast that he and I both cherished. The fact that the B.C. coast lacks the oil rigs that one finds on the Atlantic is partly the result of his activism and that of others who argued for the particular sensitivity of the region. And of course the tanker accident that Anderson feared eventually happened: the *Exxon Valdez* poured 11 million gallons of oil onto Pacific shores in 1989. Anderson became active federally again in 1993 and served as Minister of the Environment in Jean Chrétien's and Paul Martin's governments from 1999 to 2006,

ISSUES OF PIPELINES

Pipelines were a constant concern during the energy crisis of the seventies. There were not enough pipelines to carry Western natural gas and oil to Eastern Canadian markets. Moreover, the rich resources believed to exist in the Yukon and the Northwest Territories could only reach the market through the construction of pipelines. The terms of a natural gas pipeline agreement with the U.S. were handled by my colleague, external affairs minister Allan MacEachen, who negotiated with the American energy secretary James Schlesinger. I myself worked often with Schlesinger, whom I admired and respected as a direct and able public servant. Although I believed that President Carter had a tendency to micromanage, the Canadian government had excellent working relationships with his administration. Carter and Schlesinger personally thanked us for offering to halt our plan to reduce exports when shortages occurred in particular American locations. The Americans, for their part, encouraged Canadian pipeline development because they came to believe that the Canadian North, like Alaska, offered huge recoverable reserves of oil and gas, which would do much to quench the American thirst for energy.

The Americans were divided on the best route for Alaska gas. Some favoured a plan for shipping gas from Alaska through Saskatchewan to eastern markets and through British Columbia to West Coast markets. Other U.S. Federal Power Commission members favoured the Alaskan Arctic Gas Pipeline's proposed single pipeline into Alberta, where it would split into two with one leg going to Montana, the other to Illinois. The major debate during my period in office concerned the Mackenzie Valley Pipeline. Discussion of a pipeline from the Mackenzie Delta first began in the late sixties but accelerated dramatically when the oil crisis occurred. Immediately, there were calls for a pipeline but equally loud demands that proper environmental and land claim interests be considered. In 1974, Trudeau, then leading a minority government dependent on NDP support, appointed B.C. Justice Thomas Berger, a former leader of the B.C. NDP, to lead an inquiry on the Mackenzie Valley pipeline. Obviously the Berger appointment reflected our reliance on NDP support in the minority government situation. Berger took three years to report, during which time he heard numerous demands for resolutions of land claims before construction. Environmental groups insisted that no pipeline be built on the sensitive northern tundra. In the meantime, there were frequent discoveries of natural gas in the Mackenzie River delta. My son Ian had a summer job working on a drilling platform in the area when one of the discoveries occurred in 1971. The force of the escaping gas was fearsome. There was no doubt about the possibilities but there was considerable doubt about the route and the outcome.

Two consortia were involved, one headed by my old friend Bill Wilder. Bob Blair, a brilliant entrepreneur, quickly sensed the way things were going and presented an alternative, a pipeline along the Alaska Highway to move gas south. In spring 1977, Berger finally presented his report, which called for a ten-year moratorium on a Mackenzie Valley pipeline until native land claims were resolved and a total ban on pipelines across the Arctic coasts of the northern Yukon. The report infuriated me. After speaking with many native leaders in the region, I said on CTV Question Period:

"I think there are a lot of people in the Mackenzie Valley who are very uncertain about his finding and I'm not just talking about white people. I'm talking about our native people, particularly young people. It has come across to me that a lot of young people in the Mackenzie Valley feel a little bitter that they weren't asked for their views, that they weren't heard, and they're asking the question, 'What's going to happen to us?'" It was a good question.

Earlier, I had said that the resolution of land claims was desirable but not essential (Montreal *Gazette*, February 5, 1977). Some younger aboriginals spoke out to the press and said that the Berger inquiry had not listened to younger people in the community. They wanted the economic benefits a pipeline would bring, and they did not get them. Berger never considered that loss. He listened to seniors and elders who were opposed because the construction of a pipeline would interfere with their traditional hunting, fishing and trapping activities. Faced with Berger's report, the government said that the National Energy Board would decide. The Americans, through their ambassador, Thomas Enders, complained about the Canadian indecision. In the end, Foothills Pipeline and Bob Blair carried the day, but no pipeline was ever built. Interestingly, there is now new consideration being given to building a Mackenzie Valley pipeline, but the cost today will be many billions more than it would have been thirty years ago. We missed our best chance.

Today the bitterness between Lougheed and Trudeau after the oil crisis and later during the National Energy Program, in which I had no part, is well remembered. The same applies to Canadian-American relations in energy with memories of American attacks on our two-price policy and their hostile reaction to the National Energy Program of the early 1980s. If the Liberals had not returned to government in the eighties, I suspect the memory might have been different. While I was minister, the government was committed to the move towards world price, and Alberta was generally supportive. Joe Clark attacked Petro-Canada with ferocity in the House, but Petro-Canada took risks multinationals would not take. By 1979, it had $3.3 billion in assets and was the largest Canadian oil company, second only to Imperial Oil, which had $4.7 billion in assets. Joe Clark called for

Toaasting the new pipeline from the Arctic with my colleagues Jack Horner and
Allan MacEachen and (right) Bob Blair, the winner of the contest.

Petro-Canada's abolition but when he took power he soon discovered he
could not do it. In the case of the Americans, the relationship was excellent, so much so that one newspaper headline in 1978 declared "Canada,
U.S. cozy up under energy blanket." The article correctly argued that we
had established mutual respect for policies that assured both countries of
what I termed "security of supply" (*Ottawa Journal*, February 3, 1978). In
many ways, the most difficult dealings I had with any government during
my period as minister were with Ontario, which resisted the move towards
world prices and whose officials and ministers did not make effective contributions to the debate. However, the period when I was the minister was
a relative calm between the storms of the OPEC crisis in 1973 and Marc
Lalonde's National Energy Program in the early eighties.

Diana and I with OPEC leader Zaki Yamani and his wife, Tammam, at Banff Springs.
We had a snowball fight for the cameras, despite the near-absence of snow.

The energy portfolio was an exciting place to be. Many vignettes come to mind. One that I won't forget was the visit of Ahmed Zaki Yamani, the Saudi Arabian oil minister and the acknowledged leader within OPEC. I had come to know him slightly in Paris at an energy conference shortly before he was kidnapped and held as a hostage by North African dissidents. I asked Zaki and his wife, Tammam, to come for a visit – to Alberta, the home of the world's second largest (after Saudi Arabia) oil reserves. Deputy minister Mickey Cohen and his attractive wife, Judy, were Jewish, but this never once caused a problem despite the earlier Arab boycott directed at Israel. They got on famously. Zaki and his wife arrived with an official taster, who did a lot of shopping in Banff. But what was of particular interest to him was the snow and the mountain goats we saw way up on the mountain. We had a memorable snowball fight for the photographers.

Federal Energy Initiatives across Canada

Newfoundland	Lower Churchill Falls for the Gulf Island power project.
Maritimes	Maritime Energy Corporation – rationalization of transmission and power for the three Maritime provinces.
Prince Edward Island	Renewable Energy Centre
Nova Scotia	Home Insulation Program, later extended to all of Canada
	Heavy water plants in Cape Breton Funding tidal power demonstration project – Bay of Fundy
New Brunswick	Point Lepreau Nuclear Plant
Quebec	Installation of wind energy demonstration project in the Magdalen Islands. Extension of interprovincial pipeline to Montreal
Ontario	Eldorado Uranium Refining Company, Port Hope Renewable demonstration project – Ottawa AECL nuclear power plants Uranium mines
Manitoba	High-voltage electrical power connections AECL Research Station, Whiteshell, Manitoba
Saskatchewan	Heavy oil recovery projects
Alberta	Syncrude – tar sands project Natural gas pricing Creation of Petro-Canada
Yukon & Northwest Territories	Projected natural gas pipeline – Mackenzie River and Foothills Exploration drilling in the Mackenzie River Delta and the Beaufort Sea Pan Arctic natural gas discovery wells Oil and gas regulations for northern exploration and development
British Columbia	Regulation of Trans-Mountain Pipeline to Vancouver from Alberta

TROUBLES ACCUMULATE

Normally, majority governments go to the polls in their fourth year. In the winter of 1978 I knew I had a decision to make. I had promised Diana that I would devote ten years to politics, and my time was up in 1978. Trudeau knew about my commitment and asked me to lunch, something that very solitary prime minister had never done before. "Alastair," he said, "I think you're doing a great job as the energy minister, and I want you to run again. I've heard rumours that you're not going to run. If you do and we win, you'll have the energy portfolio again." Suddenly, my resolve weakened, as did Diana's when confronted with my desire to stay on.

On June 14, 1978, I was nominated once again, this time for the riding of Etobicoke Centre. Joe Clark had already announced they had targeted me and had recruited investment banker Michael Wilson, later the finance minister, as my opponent. Etobicoke's population had swollen and two ridings had been formed: Etobicoke Centre, which stretched north from Dundas Street West and Bloor to Highway 401, while Etobicoke North took in the entire borough north of Etobicoke Centre. I had a choice to make. I chose Etobicoke Centre not because it was the best Liberal riding – it wasn't. Etobicoke North had a much stronger Liberal voting record. But I knew that we would not form a government if I did not win Etobicoke Centre. In fact, Joe Clark himself had publicly declared that he could not form a government if the Tories did not defeat me in Etobicoke Centre. Frankly, I did not want to serve in opposition and chose Etobicoke Centre, where I would do better than any other Liberal but would not survive if there was a Tory sweep.

In the end, Trudeau decided not to call an election in 1978 even though we were ten points ahead in the polls. Instead, he called fifteen by-elections for October 16, 1978. It was a disastrous decision. The Tories won ten, the NDP two, the Social Credit one and we took only two seats, both in Quebec. We lost all Ontario seats, and many star candidates lost, including a good friend, University of Toronto president John Evans.[1] It appeared that the support for Trudeau and our government, which had been strong

---

1. R.B. Byers and John Saywell, eds., *Canadian Annual Review of Politics and Public Affairs 1978* (Toronto, 1980), 40-1.

after the election of René Lévesque in 1976, had waned. The mood had shifted in Ontario and in English Canada more generally. There was the dispute about the use of French in the air, where anti-French elements argued that English was the language of the air, an attitude that offended francophones in Quebec.

In my constituency, I, like others, tried to educate voters about the nature of the threat to Confederation and why it had occurred. I said on February 9, 1977 (*Etobicoke Advertiser-Guardian*) that Lévesque was a "threat" to Canada because he managed to "project from the heart" and took a "reasonable, even humble approach" to divide English Canadians. He was trying to lower their "level of concern." I told a constituency meeting that "The job of English-speaking Canadians in keeping the country united is to ensure equal rights for French-speaking people [who I claimed] had to learn English in order to get ahead. The reverse isn't true for English-speaking people." I reminded the audience that "four million Quebecois speak no English" and before Trudeau, "they couldn't deal with federal institutions in their own language." I admitted there had been some "weaknesses" in the implementation of official bilingualism but argued strongly in favour "in order to ensure French-speaking Canada enjoys a first-class citizen status, and to keep them in Confederation."

I told my constituents that Quebec was our greatest issue and it occupied most of our time in Ottawa. The "threat" from Lévesque seemed to diminish after 1977, and our policies faced increasing resistance in 1978 and 1979. Trudeau had recovered popularity in the immediate aftermath of the separatist victory in 1976 but by 1978 we were running far behind Joe Clark's Conservatives in the polls. The attitude towards Quebec and its demands was often paradoxical. People seemed willing to accept that improvement was needed. Wise parents enrolled their children in French immersion classes, notably in Alberta. I too took up the study of French, although French was rarely used in cabinet discussions. Occasionally, Marc Lalonde would speak to Trudeau in French, but few others used the second official language. However, Quebec language legislation, particularly Bill C-101, which made French the official language of Quebec and did not recognize bilingualism within the province, gave the anti-French forces a target.[1] The controversies around this legislation and the departure of many anglophones from Quebec fuelled opposition to official bilingualism and hurt the Liberal Party federally, even though the Conservatives under Clark and Stanfield officially supported our policies.

I always feared that Lévesque's excellent communication skills could carry the day if intemperate anglophones made statements he could use to inflame francophones in Quebec. I had an encounter that revealed Lévesque's charm and his passion. We were attending a state dinner at Rideau Hall. Diana sat beside René when a plate arrived with a pastry in the form of a colourful map of Canada. He picked up a spoon and broke it into little pieces. Diana said, "You're breaking up my country." He immediately said, "Let's dance and we'll talk about it." But there was no conversation. It did not occur because he was so short and Diana so tall that his nose was buried in her cleavage. But he charmed her as he did so many others.

The issues surrounding Quebec and Canada became a source of weakness rather than of strength for the Liberals as we came closer to the election in 1979. Other problems also arose with our relationship to the business community in Ontario. There had been problems with the Alberta business community for decades, but the Liberals had enjoyed considerable support on Bay Street and among industrialists in Ontario. I was evidence of that support, although I often heard talk that I was the only businessperson in the Trudeau cabinet in the late 1970s. There were some others, notably my good friend Barney Danson, who had business experience and a business sense, but it was true that the Trudeau cabinet was predominantly lawyers, intellectuals and others who lacked business experience. Moreover, the crises of the seventies made us an interventionist government as it did many others at the time. Capitalism seemed under threat, and there was much talk about a New International Economic Or-

---

1. In Bill C-86 the National Assembly of Quebec created the Charter of the French Language, which expanded upon the 1974 Official Language Act. Both were the product of the Commission of Inquiry on the Situation of the French Language and Linguistic Rights in Quebec (the Gendron Commission). The Charter gave the state the power to intervene in many sectors and the place of work to require the use of French. Legal battles continue today dealing with the Charter although recent studies have shown that the legislation is now generally accepted in Quebec.

der. It was in this context that Trudeau's year-end interview in 1975 created a great uproar. The economy had turned bad with the "discomfort index" (inflation plus unemployment) in 1975-76 the worst since the great depression, and our international balance of payments had gone into a deficit for the first time since 1961.[1] Also, John Turner had been considered a friend of business and his sudden departure and the subsequent imposition of wage and price controls caused a great stir in Toronto. When Trudeau said on December 28, 1975, that changes in the world meant that government was "going to take a larger role in running institutions" and that American liberal economist John Kenneth Galbraith had influenced him, the business community demanded explanations. There were advertisements in newspapers denouncing Trudeau, and I received many phone calls from disturbed friends.

I met some leading businessmen at the Toronto Club on January 12, 1976, to discuss the situation. Harold Corrigan, the president of the Canadian Manufacturers Association, who had responded cautiously and even helpfully to Trudeau's remarks, organized the meeting. Among those present were several corporation presidents, including Roy Bennett of Ford, Guy French of American Can, Dick Thomson of Toronto-Dominion Bank and Peter Gordon of Stelco. Bill Macdonald of the law firm McMillan Binch was among the attendees. Turner had joined the firm and became associated with newsletters that Macdonald wrote that were strongly critical of government. I was angered by John's association with these newsletters, which were increasingly right-wing and anti-Trudeau.

The group argued that Trudeau's approach was uncertain and Corrigan said many of his members were asking, "Is [Trudeau] trying to turn Canada into a socialist state using the powers of the Anti-Inflation Board?" After much discussion and criticism, I responded. My report on the meeting summarizes my remarks:

"I put forward the proposition that businessmen and their associations had a choice. They could react in a way which conveyed the impression to the public that the free enterprise system was designed for their benefit

---

1. Richard Gwyn, *The Northern Magus: Pierre Trudeau and Canadians* (Toronto, 1980), 162.

(or should at least be directed by them); that it is a static system for the benefit of vested interests; that it is unchanging and unchangeable. If they were to adopt those kinds of attitudes or to convey those sorts of attitudes in public statements, they would soon be branded as reactionaries without influence and painted into a corner. On the other hand, if they wanted to sustain the kind of activities which they have been working hard at in developing a better relationship with the Government, and with the public generally (and better relations with the Government in fact depend upon better relations with the public), then they should take the position that the free enterprise system is an evolving system, a resilient and dynamic system which had adjusted to change in the past, and would adjust to change in the future to meet the public interest – more than that, that the private enterprise system was not the preserve of any one group in society, but included all those elements of the system that is to say the general public, the community, the suppliers, employees, consumers, shareholders, and managers – all part of a Responsible Enterprise system."

I reported that the group agreed that the second option was the most appropriate but they did say they would seek greater clarification. Many, however, never lost their distrust of Trudeau and it grew in succeeding years. It haunted us in the election that finally came in 1979.

Japan – the ladies' program. Ruth Macdonald and Diana participating in the tea ceremony in the late '70s.

CHAPTER ELEVEN

NEW WORLDS FOR AN ENTREPRENEUR

With the Quebec issue giving way to economic concerns, the Liberals stumbled towards the election of 1979. I knew we had troubles as we postponed going to the polls. Although Trudeau remained a dominant figure and Joe Clark was not nearly so respected as a leader, Canadians were angry and they were ready to direct that anger against the Liberal government. Having opted for the challenging Etobicoke Centre riding, I decided I would help Roy MacLaren win the nomination for Etobicoke North. When friends asked why I took the more difficult riding, I was frank: "Well, if a minister can't win Etobicoke Centre, then the Liberals will be in opposition. If we win it, I will be a minister; if we lose it, I'll be able to return to private life where Diana wants me to be." It seemed the perfect solution, one that would satisfy both Pierre and Diana. Moreover, even if we lost the Liberals stood to gain an outstanding new MP in Roy MacLaren.

Whatever Diana's doubts about my return to politics, she and my family campaigned furiously for me. She was so committed that she did not easily take criticism. If someone gave her a hard time at the door, she responded in kind with a spirited defence of the MP, her husband. My son, Ian, and my daughter, Cynthia, and her husband were equally committed although perhaps a bit less vociferous if confronted by my opponents.

I knew that the campaign would be rough. In immigrant areas, where Trudeau remained very popular, the support was strong, but my riding had a major "English" population, which tilted ever more strongly towards the Tories. As I campaigned outside stores and on doorsteps, voters were friendly but I soon sensed that they were trying to prepare me for the defeat which they thought likely. On election night, the press was already speculating on my loss and network cameras arrived at the Old Mill Inn,

Getting ready to run again.

where we awaited the results. We quickly knew it was over when the first polls came in. My Conservative opponent, Michael Wilson, grabbed a lead and never lost it. Diana and I thanked our workers, congratulated Wilson, and went home and each had a double Scotch instead of champagne. My political career in the most turbulent decade of the postwar years came to the end. Pierre Trudeau, the most exciting politician of those years, finally lost an election.

The morning after, I mused about my fate and about my years in politics. Pierre Trudeau had dominated those times. I had few personal encounters with him even though our relations were warm and excellent. That was typical of his ministers because he was a surprisingly private and formal person in his relations with us. He was always "Prime Minister," not Pierre, and he avoided familiarity. Even Marc Lalonde, I believe, who worked so closely with him, was never invited to dinner at 24 Sussex Drive in the seventies. I did have one memorable encounter with him. Trudeau was not known as an animal lover, but Farley Mowat once gave Margaret and Pierre a black Labrador, which they named "Farley." He soon became a much-loved member of the family, and Trudeau's affection for the Lab was obvious to all who saw them together.

After Margaret and Pierre separated, Pierre became a single father with interesting consequences. One of the younger Trudeau children displayed a creative talent. He noticed that there were often a couple of saucers of assorted nuts on the dining room table. After dinner, when the grown-ups left the table, Sasha would move in and surreptitiously hide them under the cushions of the sofas and occasionally under the sofas themselves, like a squirrel storing nuts as the winter begins.

Trudeau often entertained foreign heads of state at 24 Sussex. On one occasion, he had an important dinner with the Pakistani foreign minister on the subject of nuclear non-proliferation and wanted me to be present. I came early and met Trudeau at the front door and he guided me towards the living room. As we entered, we immediately saw that Farley had left a large deposit of dog "moonies" on the centre of the carpet. Trudeau quickly rushed away and returned with a dustpan to clean it up. As he did so, he noticed that there was a large photograph of Indira Gandhi on a nearby table. He quickly put it into a nearby desk drawer. When he did so, he stepped on the nuts his son had stuffed into the cushions, and he quickly tried to pick them up before his eminent guest arrived. Having witnessed the stern prime ministerial demeanour, I recognized that there was an unknown domestic side to our "playboy" prime minister.

Trudeau took the defeat well. He was a man of enormous substance, whose piercing blue eyes were always fascinating. They refused to blink, which often troubled adversaries or even his associates. Richard Nixon, whose eyes darted in all directions, never liked Trudeau. I think he knew that Trudeau could see through him. In my years with him, I developed a deep respect for his intellect and fundamental honesty. After we lost the election, we were invited to the wedding of the daughter of American ambassador Thomas Enders and his charming wife, Gaytana. We picked up Trudeau to go to the wedding, and Diana said to him, "This may be a little difficult. There will be a lot of gloating Tories there." And we knew lots of them. "Well Diana," Pierre said, "We'll just stare them down, won't we." At the wedding, he stole the show as usual, dancing more elegantly than anyone else in the room and charming everyone in his orbit.

I left office proud of what I had achieved and proud of the government I had served. That we made mistakes was obvious and inevitable. With the energy crisis, stagflation, the loss of confidence in the United States after Vietnam and Watergate, and the election of René Lévesque in Quebec in 1976, we faced more crises than any Canadian peacetime government. There was much to criticize in what we did, but there was much accomplished which an alternative government would not have done. Frankly, I doubt Canada would have survived the Quebec separatist challenge without Pierre Trudeau, who brought "French power" to Ottawa and showed French-speaking Canadians they could work and lead in the nation's capital. He rightly resisted the strong forces of decentralization, which came not only from Quebec but also from Alberta. When Joe Clark took office, he soon discovered that Alberta's demands were incompatible with a democratic state where gross inequalities were unacceptable. A community of communities, Trudeau rightly said, would be no community at all. And we did so much more: the metric system; a science policy; bilingualism; enlightened immigration policies; reform of the criminal code; the abolition of capital punishment; parliamentary reform; and a more generous policy towards the poorest on the planet. Yes, I was proud to serve in the government of Pierre Trudeau.

Whatever the consolations of looking at what one has done, losing office is never easy. I needed some time to think about my future, and Diana and I took six months to consider what to do. Much of that time was spent at my beloved farm, Highwood, near the Pickering airport that we had never built. There were some offers that came in, such as becoming the head of the Canadian Chamber of Commerce, but I had no urge to be an administrator or lobbyist. Besides, the entrepreneurial spirit was stirring within me. Those urges intensified when I called the trustees of my stock portfolio. When I entered politics I had given them approximately one million to administer. Occasionally, I took sums to cover expenses that went beyond my government salary, but I thought, reasonably, that interest and dividends would more than cover them. To my disappointment and astonishment, I discovered that the portfolio was now worth only about half a million dollars. Poor returns, they said. Indeed they were; my "sabbatical" was shortened as my needs now increased.

Suddenly, another opportunity presented itself. On December 13, 1979, the Clark government suddenly fell and Canada faced another election. Trudeau, who had retired in November, returned as the leader and the polls indicated that the Liberals would win. Trudeau asked me to consider running again. However, my commitment to Diana remained, and I did not feel the urge to enter battle once again. The constituency was tough. Michael Wilson had won it by 31,498 votes to 23,141 for me, and the margin was large even if the Liberals regained much support. As a result, I decided to remain in private life and begin work as a consultant to businesses.

Michael Wilson did win and retained the constituency until 1993. That knowledge makes my decision seem wise, but it does cause me to reflect on what had occurred under the Clark government. Clark soon battled with Peter Lougheed, and the charge that the difficulties between Alberta and the federal government were a Liberal creation was proven completely false. In many ways, my relationship as energy minister with my Alberta counterparts was better than that enjoyed by the Conservatives in 1979. The central problem remained and remains: most of the Canadian population lives east of the Saskatchewan border, but virtually all oil and natural gas production is in the west. When Lougheed declared that he wanted international prices for Alberta's raw materials and that oil in the ground is a provincial resource to be regulated provincially, he inevitably caused a struggle with Ottawa. The perceived weakness of the federal power to prevent one oil-producing province from holding the rest of the country to ransom when there were serious national shortages became an obsession to many policy-makers – and not only Trudeau Liberals. We thought about how to deal with the assertions of Lougheed. Should the federal government use the declaratory power provided in the constitution but used mainly in wartime or should it invoke the peace, order and good government clause? The frustrations of the seventies in the negotiations with Alberta led to the National Energy Program of the eighties in which the federal government moved to regain its place in allocating the revenues from abundant wealth in the ground. My role in the seventies was to assure that the federal government's voice was heard and, in retrospect, I am proud that it was. As many colleagues remarked, my balanced approach of the late seventies contributed greatly to that strong voice.

THE SYNFUELS PROJECT

Even when one leaves politics, there remains a residue. I continued to benefit from my political experience and contacts as I embarked upon private life.

Towards the end of 1979 just a few months after my defeat and the defeat of Pierre Trudeau's Liberal government, I accepted an invitation to join a mission to South Africa. The delegates were drawn from four countries – the U.S., U.K. Germany and Canada. The central focus of the delegation was fact-finding and assessing the climate for some reconciliation of various interests. The Canadian members were myself, the Hon. Maurice Sauvé and Ian Macdonald, president of York University.

When initially approached to join the delegation, I was suspicious that this might be some sort of propaganda or publicity stunt aimed at whitewashing the apartheid regime of South Africa. Several inquiries put my mind to rest. The two Americans were both African-Americans, one a university president and the other a journalist with the *New York Times*. There were two members from Britain's respected Chatham House and one German from an independent public affairs organization. Our program in South Africa would involve meetings with a number of institutions, labour groups, business, public affairs, government and elected personnel.

On one occasion at a dinner with the nationalist Boer group the Broederbond, I received a call from Pierre Trudeau. He had decided being Leader of the Opposition was not what he wanted and had decided to resign. I remonstrated with him: "No, hang in." Several days later the Liberal caucus celebrating at their Christmas party helped to change his mind. Joe Clark had been defeated on a budget matter, largely through the lack of a "hands-on" approach. This meant that Donald Macdonald, who had asked me to be one of his leadership campaigners, was forced to withdraw.

I came away from South Africa with a sense that the democratic forces for change were seriously seeking peaceful transition. I also came away with an idea. As energy minister, I had become aware of the potential sources of oil through coal liquefaction. After all, this is what had fuelled the German war machine so successfully – the U-boats and the Panzers. After the Second World War, South Africa, fearing a boycott, adopted the German coal liquefaction approach with its plant at Sasol. Time and again I would ask senior African businessmen and government leaders about the Sasol project. Questions about the process, production, yields per ton of coal, were invariably met with a stony face. Then one South African government official quietly took me aside to say that if anyone were to answer my questions, they could wind up in jail. If I wanted information, he suggested I contact Fluor Corp., the engineering consultants in Irvine, California, who were responsible for process engineering.

A day or two later, several of us took a small plane to visit a gold mining operation. I asked the pilot if our flight plan would take us anywhere near the Sasol operation. He said yes and promptly altered course. What I saw as we circled the plant was an enormous industrial operation – one that dwarfed what I had seen at the Syncrude plant near Fort McMurray.

On my return to Canada, I discussed this experience with an old friend, Robert Shannon. He was a born innovator and had been active in hydrocarbon research. "Let's go to Irvine and find out what we can," he said. There we learned that Sasol was getting approximately 3.5 barrels of refined products per ton of coal processed.

In 1979, two of the major oil producing countries, Iran and Iraq, were at war, once again raising fears about security of supply for the import-dependent. The Maritime region of Canada was the most exposed part of Canada to an interruption of supply. But wait a minute? Couldn't the large coal deposit of Cape Breton be converted just as the Germans and the South Africans had so successfully done? Cape Breton had a mature coal mining industry. It also had some of the highest unemployment rates in the country. An opportunity beckoned.

Cape Breton had a refinery at Point Tupper which its owner Gulf Oil had mothballed. Point Tupper also had one of the best deep-water wharves and harbours on the East Coast of North America. It seemed to be an ideal situation. So I wasted no time in putting together a consortium of interests to examine the feasibility of a coal liquefaction plant. The consortium, called the Scotia Coal Synfuels Program, consisted of Gulf Canada Products Co. (the owner of the mothballed refinery and adjacent properties); two Crown corporations, the federal Petro-Canada and the provincial Nova Scotia Resources Ltd.; the Cape Breton Development Company (Devco), owner of the producing coal mines; Nova, an Alberta Corporation; and my own company, Alastair Gillespie & Associates Limited.

Each consortium member put up $150,000, which was matched by an equal amount from the federally-operated Oil Substitution Fund. My company participated as the manager of the feasibility study and as a junior investor. It was a time of political uncertainty. Pierre Trudeau and the Liberals had returned to power with a majority in 1980, replacing the Joe Clark government. Clark stepped aside as Conservative leader and began his fight with Brian Mulroney. The Conservatives were leaderless and turned to Erik Nielsen, their House Leader, a venomous character assassin, while they went about choosing a new chief in a bizarre contest now known to have been deeply influenced by mysterious German money. Little did I know that the German influence might profoundly affect my own business future. Several months after the consortium had been formed and publicly announced in the presence of Nova Scotia Premier John Buchanan and the federal Minister of Finance, Allan MacEachen, in March 1981, Nielsen took aim and accused me of breaking the conflict of interest guidelines. His histrionics were vicious and personal and hurtful – particularly as I was not in the House of Commons to defend myself and particularly, too, because I had always bent over backward to avoid any conflict of interest. Fortunately, a parliamentary motion disposed of the issue and I was able to get on with the consortium's work.

The consortium retained a reputable consulting engineering company to evaluate the available technologies for producing high-value refined hydrocarbons, such as gasoline, diesel oils and heating oils. The Sasol approach was considered but rejected in favour of a U.S. system developed by Hydrocarbon Research Inc. (HRI), of Princeton, New Jersey.

Coal, tar sands bitumen and heavy crude oils all contain a small proportion of hydrogen and a much larger portion of carbon. Gasoline and diesel oil, for example, have the reverse chemical structure, that is, a smaller proportion of carbon. They are created by changing the chemical balance, massively increasing the hydrogen and reducing the carbon proportions.

HRI had a patented hydrogen addition process as distinct from the tar sands' carbon rejection processes. The recommendation of the consultants was to adopt the HRI (H-Coal) and its companion (H-Oil) processes. I took this information to Bob Blair, who was president of Nova, a consortium member, and suggested he take a look at the report. It might, I thought, be of interest to him for his plans at the Husky Oil heavy oil upgrader, and it would be a useful confirmation if he chose it. It turned out that this approach proved to be a winner as Husky adopted the H-Oil process. Blair's action also gave me confidence in this approach, and I immediately decided that I would take the Cape Breton project forward.

The next steps involved retaining a Canadian consulting firm and testing our methodology. We selected Bantrell Engineering, an affiliate of Bechtel. A shipment of Cape Breton coal was sent to HRI's facilities to be tested for its convertibility. These tests proved to be highly successful. Cape Breton coal and the HRI technology would produce 5 barrels of oil per tonne of coal, almost 50 per cent greater than the South African coals yielded at the Sasol plant.

About this time, our technical consultant, Bob Shannon, became interested in doing a project in Ohio with Ohio coals. The U.S. Energy Department became a collaborator and a $45 million supporter, partly I believe under the U.S. "Clean Coal Program." Let it be said they were far more

accepting of innovative ways of using the coal resource to reduce dependence on imported oil than Canadian government agencies.

At this time there was also considerable interest in reducing – better
still, eliminating – acid rain. Sulphur dioxide emissions (SOX) and nitro-
gen oxides (NOX) were the precursors of acid rain. What was of particular
interest to us was that the HRI technology eliminated these air pollutants.
Elemental sulphur became a valuable by-product.

In the mid 1980s, I decided to carry on with the work of the consortium,
which had completed successfully its assessment of the potential for coal
liquefaction of Cape Breton coal, that from the Donkin mine in particular.
Some members, however, had new interests and fresh fish to fry. Nova was
concentrating on its Western opportunities, and Gulf sold its properties to
Ultramar. Nova Scotia Resources was preoccupied by the potential of the
offshore oil and gas fields – Sable Island in particular. Nevertheless, Petro-
Canada remained interested; so of course did Devco.

I therefore formed Scotia Synfuels Limited to buy out Ultramar's ownership of the unused marine oil terminal and adjacent lands. I also made
a deal with the Nova Scotia Power Corporation, a neighbour, with a coal-
fired plant that would allow a Synfuels plant to access its coal requirements using the coal offloading facilities. About this time, interest was
being shown by a number of U.S. oil firms, who were impressed with the
strategic location of the marine oil terminal and the storage possibilities
of the tank farm. They included Global Petroleum, based in Boston. It had
a far reaching trading and distribution business.

There is a certain mystique about oil. It is worshipped as an essential life
force, much like water, oxygen or food. Its owners derive great power and
influence through the control of its production and distribution. Modern economies are totally dependent on its availability. The preoccupation
of oil industry corporate leaders had been to ignore all other sources of
energy such as coal. To the oil barons, coal was regarded as an "old hat"
nineteenth-century source. It had been replaced by oil, hadn't it? But what
about coal oil? Was not the required fuel for lamps in the midst of the
nineteenth century made from coal? Interestingly enough, the first producer of oil for lamps was a Nova Scotian, Abraham Gezner. He pioneered

Two aerial views of Point Tupper, Nova Scotia, the finest ice-free, deep-water oil terminal on the east coast of North America.

a new technology that replaced whale oil as the chief source of fuel for illumination. He built a plant in the U.S., which thrived until the Rockefellers entered the market. It was John D. Rockefeller who created Standard Oil, the huge oil-based empire and putative father of today's giant producer, Esso. No one in an oil company had risen to the top because he knew anything about coal. The culture of the oil industry was an exclusive culture; new perspectives on the in-the-ground resource were slow to be accepted. The huge tar sands deposits, for example, were so different to the conventional oil-drilling culture that they were all but ignored except by a very few. But once recognized for what they were, one of the world's great sources of oil, they started to attract significant investor interest. Nevertheless, the Canadian and Alberta governments appreciated their importance before the oil giants did.

By the 1980s, two oil sands plants were in place, Suncor and Syncrude, and the Canadian industry was changing quickly. New institutions were born, such as the Canadian Energy Research Institute (CERI). This was a cooperative research organization sponsored by six parties: the federal government's Energy, Mines and Resources Canada, the Alberta Department of Energy, the Private Energy Research Association (composed of corporate and individual members from oil, gas, coal, electrical and nuclear energy and pipeline companies), the University of Calgary, the Ontario Ministry of Energy and the Saskatchewan Department of Energy and Mines. The objectives were "to develop an economic research capability and to conduct studies that will assist industry and government in dealing with energy problems." The research program was developed by a board of directors named by the sponsoring organizations. In 1988, CERI published under the authority of K. Morgan McRae "An Assessment of the Potential for Coal-Derived Syncrude in Canada." It was an important document that identified coal liquids technology as an important future source of energy. Indeed, it concluded that the co-processing of coal and heavy oil, the approach that SSL had been pioneering, was a more favourable prospect than new tar sands plants. Several extracts from the report make the point:

By all indications, coal/oil co-processing appears a near term application to the production of clean liquid fuels from coal. Current economics indicate that the cost of coal/oil co-processing is within reach of the
production costs of integrated, mined oil sands operations.... In Nova
Scotia, recent work has centred on the application of two-stage coal/oil
co-processing for the upgrading of Cape Breton coals, employing the
process technology to be used at the Ohio prototype commercial coal/
oil co-processing plant.

In its conclusions and recommendations, the report went on to say that

from a long-term supply option with questionable merit, coal liquefaction has reached the stage where it represents a potentially economic
and viable supply option for Canada in the mid to latter 1990s. Coal/oil
co-processing, simultaneous conversion of crude bitumen and coal, is
an upgrading technology of special, near-term merit....

On the basis of the analysis contained herein, it is strongly recommended that the Canadian government and the governments of the
major coal-producing regions of Canada combine to facilitate the
examination of all relevant issues prerequisite to the eventual construction of a coal/oil co-processing facility. Given the uncertainties a
co-sponsored government /industry initiative would seem to represent
the best possible combination of risk exposure and Canadian expertise
in such an undertaking.

The 200-plus page report also concluded that as a result of technical
improvements there had been a significant reduction in unit capital and
operating costs. "While direct liquefaction costs have fallen from US $60-
80/barrel to the range US $40-60 level, the costs of coal/oil co-processing
stand at some US $25/barrel."

The report listed a number of other advantages in the coal/oil co-
processing configuration that Scotia Synfuels had been developing. The
long and the short of it was that the coal/oil co-processing approach offered significant benefits to Canada and the report recommended that
"coal/oil co-processing, the simultaneous conversion of crude bitumen

and coal, is the technology of particular near-term merit. Unlike tar sands/ processing plants, bitumen upgrading and frontier resource development, coal/oil co-processing is economic on a relatively small scale, can be cited adjacent to existing infrastructure and, hence can be geographically distributed so as to minimize the economic boom/bust of dislocation effects associated with mega-project development."

A few years later, the Senate of Canada held hearings to assess the synthetic fuels option offered by Scotia Synfuels. Their report (see Appendix V), published in June 1992, endorsed the project under the title "Scotia Synfuels: A project for the 1990s." Our financial advisors reported that the project would create hundreds of new jobs where unemployment was high, and it would have been immensely profitable. In the mid-1990s, it would have reached profitability at a world price for crude of $22/barrel. The economic climate was favourable to our project, which seemed ready to go forward when the federal government of Brian Mulroney and later that of Jean Chrétien promised assistance under a variety of programs.

But breaking promises by governments is endemic. We learned the hard way that regional development policy was sometimes a fraud. My experience with governments as my partners and I tried to develop Synfuels was deeply disillusioning. Let me explain.

Commercial dealings between private sector parties are governed by rules that can be enforced in the courts. Dishonest practices can be the basis for fraud actions. The contract is fundamental in commercial relationships. It provides recourse in case of commitments made but not delivered. False or misleading advertising is a prohibited practice, and bait and switch practices of unscrupulous vendors are criminal acts. In the economic life of the country, business rests upon on reliability and trust. Promises and commitments must be kept and non-delivery is a cause for damages. And the damages and/or penalties can quite simply bankrupt a defaulter.

Governments endlessly proclaim these virtues and call constantly for trust. Yet they do not always practise what they preach. Why do they believe that their actions will not be judged against the value system of society for which they prescribe in legislation? Regrettably, my personal experience with federal government regional development initiatives convinces me that they are very little different from the "bait and switch" tactics of unscrupulous salesmen, hucksters of hope.

A good "bait and switch" artist starts his confidence game this way. He shows his target (his intended victim) a desirable product, service or proposition. He promises the client that it's all for real. Once the client is so persuaded the sale is made; but what is substituted at delivery is a far cry from what was promised. Fraud you say? Does it remind you of old-time fast-travelling "snake-oil" salesmen? Today, its modern practitioners would face serious charges for such misrepresentation, including false and misleading advertising.

Have the federal government's regional incentive programs for Nova Scotia been very different in character from these illegal practices? Let me describe some of these ploys.

In July 1985 the newly-elected Mulroney government announced a new package of economic incentives for the high-unemployment areas of Atlantic Canada and some additional particular incentives for Cape Breton. Most of the affected geography already qualified for investment tax credits under the Regional Development Incentives Act of the early 1980s. But more was considered needed: the government decided to increase the "bait."

New low-interest loans were to be made available for qualified projects throughout Atlantic Canada. In addition to recognizing the fragile economy of Cape Breton and its greater unemployment, a generous Cape Breton investment tax credit and financial assistance program was announced by minister Sinclair Stevens to spark new investment. Cape Breton had been hammered by the closure of the Gulf Oil refinery, the closing of the heavy water plants, and the cutbacks at other major employers such as the SYSCO and Devco coal mines.

Our synthetic fuels project fitted the government's plans perfectly – or so it seemed. We proposed to develop the area's natural advantages, notably the resources and location of Cape Breton. The deep water of the Strait of Canso and the proximity of that natural harbour to the world's great circle shipping lanes gave the area immense strategic advantages. All shipping across the Atlantic for the east coast of North America passed right by the door.

In the early 1980s, the U.S. east coast was the world's major importer of crude oil and petroleum products. What's more, these imports were growing annually. In no time at all imports would represent 50 per cent of U.S. oil requirements – the biggest cause of the growing U.S. trade deficit and a threat to American national security.

Against this background one could properly ask, "Could some of the large deposits of Cape Breton coal be converted into liquid hydrocarbons to supply part of the eastern North American market?" Our research and, of course, the German experience in World War II and the contemporary South African developments offered strong proof that such a solution to the American supply problem was at hand.

There were other indigenous advantages for a coal-based synthetic fuels plant at Cape Breton. There was an unused refinery at Point Tupper on the Strait of Canso, recently mothballed by its owners, Gulf Canada. It included a magnificent marine oil terminal and tank farm. Why not put it back to work? It was strategically located, and fully engineered. Many of the former employees remained in Cape Breton. There was a pool of trained and professional workers available. Recognizing the investment opportunity, I decided to buy it from Ultramar, who had acquired it from Gulf Canada. Ultramar had decided to break the marine oil terminal up and sell the steel; but they had a problem – the magnificent marine oil structure with 100 feet of water had originally been partly financed by the federal government. There was an obligation.

These new incentives announced by Sinclair Stevens sent the message that the federal government was serious about attracting fresh investment. We at Scotia Synfuels Limited (SSL) believed the message Stevens sent. We thought the investment tax credit approach, in particular, a very realistic approach. It placed the onus on the private investor to put his own money at risk first; the private investor would make the decision – not a bureaucrat committing taxpayers' money. Wasn't that inherently the right way to judge the soundness of a business proposition?

So SSL went ahead and raised some investor funds for the purpose of restoring the marine oil terminal to operability as an initial step to the building of a synthetics fuels plant. The project attracted U.S. partners. The first group was Global Petroleum Inc. of Boston, a leading distributor of refined products. A second major player was Statia Terminals, an international operator of ocean-based terminals. Statia brought the know-how and expertise for rebuilding and updating the massive oil terminal.

Investment tax credits are low-risk incentives for the government. The money to construct a plant must be raised from the private sector and spent on the plant construction before any benefit accrues to the investor or to the project.

But as the record shows, the federal government in the late eighties went off on a spending spree. Grants and low-interest loans were given to Hibernia and to Nova Scotia's Westray coal mine with no expectation of recovering these taxpayer funds anytime soon. And gradually after that, the investment tax credit programs were withdrawn or reallocated to other projects. Did Karlheinz Schreiber's Bear Head Industries located on land immediately contiguous to the Point Tupper refinery properties receive encouragement? Had the German money that brought Brian Mulroney to power come back to haunt me?

After SSL completed a successful test program of co-processing, that is, the simultaneous upgrading of Venezuelan heavy oil blended with Cape Breton coal, SSL's financial consultants concluded that a synfuels plant was economically viable. An application for the promised Cape Breton investment tax credit was made. The two raw materials, high-sulphur coal and high-sulphur, high-heavy-metals heavy oil were the cheapest and most abundant raw materials available.

For a year SSL was left dangling while it awaited confirmation of its status as a recipient of the Cape Breton investment tax credit. Then the program for the promised Cape Breton (45 per cent) investment tax credits was withdrawn completely. A promise broken! We were astonished, but other promises were also soon broken.

As consolation we were advised that the special 30 per cent investment tax credit under the Regional Development Incentives Act (RDIA) would continue to apply. That was the "switch." It was also the new "bait." Encouraged, we decided to continue. Again, we were led down the garden path.

SSL made very considerable investments on the strength of these federal government undertakings. For example, as I have mentioned, SSL purchased the former Gulf Oil refinery properties at Point Tupper. It took step one in the construction of a synfuels plant. It organized the restoration and reactivation of the storage and handling facilities, including the marine oil terminal, with U.S. partners. All told, new private investments of close to $100 million were made.

After an expenditure of close to $40 million for new processing systems SSL applied to the federal government's Department of Industry to obtain the promised 30 per cent investment tax benefits. These systems would be an important and an integral part of the Synfuels plant. What did the Federal government say? "Sorry, no dice." This decision was rendered days before a new Liberal government was sworn in on November 4, 1993.

"But don't worry," they told us, "the balance of the synthetic fuels plant investment will qualify for the special 30 per cent investment tax credit provided under RDIA." That was the "switch." It was also more bait for yet another switch.

As reassurance Jake Epp, the federal Minister of Energy, Mines and Resources, agreed to a cost-share partnership with Scotia Synfuels Limited and the premier of Nova Scotia for one third, one third, one third shares in the funding of the final pre-construction phase, a $15 million program of work. This program included further test work, engineering, environmental assessments, marketing and financing.

Once again the record shows how commitments made were soon dishonoured. We went forward with our plans. SSL negotiated an agreement with Corpoven, a component of the National Oil Company of Venezuela, as a partner in the project. Corpoven would supply the crude oil for the heavy oil component of the co-processing upgrader. At the same time, SSL reached a formal agreement with the province for its one-third share. All seemed to be proceeding smoothly.

But the federal government let us down once more. It continued to focus on Karlheinz Schreiber's dubious Bear Head Industries project. It withdrew from the funding commitment it had made for its one-third share. Another federal government broken promise! Despite this disappointment, the province of Nova Scotia and SSL decided to proceed with the first phase of the program.

But fear not, the federal government raised its voice once more. We were told by the newly-elected Chrétien Liberal government that the special 30 per cent investment tax credit would indeed apply to the balance of the synthetic fuels plant construction. By this time we were well into the co-processing test program at HRI using Cape Breton coal and Venezuelan heavy oil. Contracts had been made so we completed them.

The results were extremely favourable. We were optimistic that the policies and priorities of the Liberals' Red Book would govern the government's decisions. At the same time we learned that Hydrocarbon Research Inc. (HRI), the U.S. process developer and owner of the technology, was for sale by its owner, Canada's Husky Oil, which had acquired the company after adopting its technology for its newly-expanded heavy oil upgrader. We decided to purchase HRI and signed a letter of intent with Husky Oil for its subsidiary, which in our view was the leading developer of co-processing technology in the world.

But then came Minister of Finance Paul Martin's February 1994 budget. What did the author of the Red Book do? One of the provisions of that Liberal government budget abolished the RDIA special (30 per cent) investment tax credit! We requested specific grandfathering provisions to protect our investment and nearly fifteen years of research and development but this request was refused by the Minister of Finance. This single step was a final repudiation of incentive policies aimed at encouraging new investment. To add insult to injury, Anne McLellan, the Alberta-based Minister of Energy, took the ridiculous position that there was already a surplus of refinery capacity in Nova Scotia and that therefore a synthetic fuels plant would not be in the public interest.

So much for the rhetoric of growth, new jobs, new industries, environmentally friendly technologies, regional development, export encouragement. So much for the Liberals' Red Book! Not surprisingly, the Liberals lost their seats in Cape Breton; they had lost the trust of their constituents.

This sequence of "bait and switch" events was a monstrous betrayal of trust. Unfortunately, it doesn't end there.

When the Eastern Passage Refinery at Dartmouth, owned by the international oil company Ultramar, was offered for sale in 1994 (post–federal budget), SSL signed a letter of intent to negotiate the purchase of the refinery from Ultramar as an alternative site for its synthetic fuels plant. After all, it had been operational, not mothballed – there were some obvious advantages.

Ultramar, we were told, wished to close the plant down but first it had to offer it for sale. The Bureau of Competition Policy had imposed certain conditions on Ultramar back when Ultramar acquired the plant from Imperial Oil. These conditions were aimed at ensuring continued operation of the refinery to provide competition and alternative sourcing options for independent gasoline retailers. When Imperial Oil bought the Eastern Passage refinery in a basket of Texaco assets, it was not permitted to hold on to the refinery and Ultramar had assumed these competitive conditions.

SSL's proposed acquisition would have met not only competition policy requirements but also export trade policy objectives. In this connection, it's worth remembering that one of the few benefits obtained by Mulroney's Free Trade Agreement (Canada/U.S.) for Canada was "national treatment" for Canada's export of refined oil products. Such exports would enjoy a favourable duty-free access to U.S. markets. That U.S. East Coast market was one of the largest import markets in the world.

And of course the development of a synthetic fuels plant at that location would have served a number of other policy objectives. The labour union was solidly on side. But did these positive benefits interest the Department of Industry? Not at all. Ultramar was allowed to close the plant down. The federal government's Director of Competition Policy found that our offer to purchase was not adequate, despite all the evidence that our price was significantly higher than the price paid for operating refineries in the U.S. So what did Ultramar do? It did what it had set out to do. It closed it down, dismantled the refinery and shipped its main parts to a Middle Eastern refinery project. Canada lost a refinery, Cape Breton gained no jobs, and I and my colleagues were victims of a government which meddled in business carelessly and irresponsibly.

A reasonable person might say, "Well, you had the opportunity to criticize the advice tendered to the Director on what was a commercial price, why didn't you?" Of course, we asked for it. But it was denied. It was "Confidential," we were told. These bureaucracies and ministers within the federal government had apparently never heard about the government's agenda for growth in Nova Scotia. More likely, they simply didn't care.

Throughout this trying time, I was assisted by a staff of three: Bob Shannon, technical advisor; Eric Maki, project manager; fine secretaries Judy Colt and Susan Kerr; and a highly qualified group of businessmen on the board of directors, John Abell of Wood Gundy, Bill Wilder, Claude Allard, Fred Dickson, David Philpott, and Brian Bawden of Osler Hoskin. They had wasted too much of their valuable time and talents. If governments, those hucksters of hope, wonder why the public regards them with so much cynicism, scepticism and distrust, they should remember that "bait and switch" artists are considered society's enemy and their action criminal behaviour. I had had enough.

It was time to give up. The board of directors and I made the decision to sell the properties, the magnificent marine oil terminal at Point Tupper and the equally impressive tank farm, to Statia Terminals, the operator of the facilities. And here the story improves. The terminal has continued to grow and more than 100 people now have good permanent jobs. The facility can handle super-takers because of the depth of the Strait of Canso and the size of the terminal; it is the finest facility on the East Coast of North America. Today it handles more tonnage than any other port in Canada except Vancouver. The project brought disappointments, particularly with government, but its current success has brought me great satisfaction if not the monetary reward a businessperson values. Nevertheless, the sight of Karlheinz Schreiber in handcuffs as he went before the House of Commons committee investigating his bribery infuriates me. His shenanigans didn't help our project that offered hope to Canadians in general and Cape Breton in particular.

Although my experience with the Synfuels project was demanding, difficult, infuriating, but in the end rather satisfying because of the jobs and the great port that we created, I had many other business ventures, many highly successful. *Canadian Business* magazine in July 2005 even chose me as the poster boy for "Entrepreneur" in an article entitled "Prime time," about how some Canadians forgot the golf course and saw their "golden years as a golden career opportunity." What prompted the article was my partnership with my old friend Bill Wilder in buying the Creemore Springs Brewery, a highly regarded microbrewery, in 1995. It had been started by John Wiggins, its imaginative founder, and an associate of his, Donald Mingay, a retired businessman, whose nearby farm property provided the lovely clear spring water. We bought just under a 50 per cent share and arranged to purchase the remainder from John Wiggins at a later date. The product was acknowledged as one of the world's great premium lagers. It was merchandised as "100 years before the times," which reflected not only the classical method and purity of the ingredients but also the century-old heritage building where it was located. Wiggins, an accomplished artist and marketing man, had created an ambience of quality around the product. He launched it in 1987 and sold us his share in 2005. Year after year, Creemore gained in favour. Its property and equipment kept pace with the growing demand. Its managers and its methods were first class. Gordon Fuller was the brew master and the conscience of the firm. It didn't take long before the major beer companies started to take notice and to show an interest. It was no surprise to us when Molson's made a very attractive offer. I look back on this period and this firm with a healthy respect for the management and staff who collectively made it such a jewel.

When Molson's bought Creemore, Bill and I received assurance that the brewery would not move from its wonderful location in Creemore, Ontario. And there it has remained. I still drink only Creemore.

In fact, my first contact with the brewery sector came soon after I left politics. As I sorted through offers and possible connections, I received some bizarre proposals, notably from Nigeria. However, I received a substantial offer from Carling O'Keefe, one of Canada's largest breweries, that

I become its chair. David Nicholson, the British director and a member of the European Parliament, proposed my name, and I quickly accepted. Unfortunately, Erik Nielsen's assaults on me in the House of Commons politicized my position. Beer prices were controlled by the government of Ontario, which was a Conservative one. I resigned from what had been a welcome and rewarding association after I left political life. As I said, it's difficult to escape politics once you've been in it. I did enjoy another important chairmanship, the National Westminster Bank of Canada. My friend Arthur Scace, who had worked closely with me on the Rhodes Scholarship Trust, asked me on behalf of the bank whether I would agree to be the Canadian chair. I immediately accepted.

I had great respect for the National Westminster Bank, with whom I had banked since I was a student at Oxford. They had become one of the two leading banks of the world through a series of shrewd mergers. Robin Leigh Pemberton, their chairman, formally inducted me into my new role. Shortly after I became chair, Pemberton and senior bank officials came to Toronto for the World Bank meeting. They had rented a home in Forest Hill to entertain. I said to them, "Why don't you come out to the country and see a bit of Canadiana." And so Pemberton, his wife and other officials arrived in Claremont with six Rolls-Royces. I handed Pemberton a fishing rod and said to him and his wife, "Well now, try for a trout in the pond." Soon, they came back with a very handsome fish. They were an attractive couple, she a venturesome hang-glider and he a shrewd banker. His qualities attracted Margaret Thatcher, who appointed him chairman of the Bank of England. It was a personal loss for me because he had been a great supporter of my work as non-executive chairman of the Canadian bank.

As the chairman in Canada, I was determined to assure that there was more even-handedness in the way the government and the banking community dealt with foreign banks. The Canadian banks, in our view, were selfish, protective and fearful of competition. Unlike other Canadian sectors, where foreign companies could bully domestic companies, Canadian banks were strong and did not need excessive protection. They had bully power themselves. Where they had been timorous was in the support for Canadian manufacturers and resource developers. In this respect, National

Westminster could provide something Canadian banks would not do, and in this respect National Westminster contributed significantly to Canadian business.

I served as chairman of National Westminster in Canada from 1980 to 1995, but I had numerous other business responsibilities and activities in those times. My experience as energy minister brought me several consulting offers from energy companies, and I had a particular interest in the development of the oil sands, where I had played a large part in assuring Canadian government support when the project appeared ready to collapse in the mid-seventies. Syncrude remembered that I had been their strongest advocate within government when times became tough, and they maintained close ties with me. It was the success of the Syncrude development that prompted me to berate the Coal Association about the possibilities of coal liquefaction. The association focused upon the cost of transportation and paid no attention to the larger possibilities, and we still pay the price for their poor judgement. They are now paying the price themselves as they scramble to adjust to the criticisms of coal from envi-

My son, Ian. Still trying to turn dead wood into good board material.

At Matheson Lake in front of Gillespie Island with my brother Andrew
in October 2006.

ronmentalists and politicians. Missed opportunities sometimes have great
costs beyond the industry itself.

Globalization and competition challenged the manufacturing sector.
My work as Minister of Industry had attracted the attention of Claude
Allard, who was the president of Uniroyal Canada. Two good friends were
on his board, Gordon Osler and Bill Hartley, who had helped me in my
political campaigns. They told Claude, who was an American, that I could
help the firm navigate Canadian waters and that my background in business and politics was unique. I developed a great respect for Claude, who
headed Uniroyal's international chemical operations. When I formed the
Synfuels project, I therefore retained him as one of the directors to represent the chemical side of our interests. He had enormous integrity and
vision. The Canadian company itself was based in Kitchener, a city which
has the most complicated road system I've ever seen but I did manage

Governor General Roméo Leblanc presents me with the Order of Canada at Rideau Hall in January 1999.

In 2002, Diana and I with Jean Chrétien, whom I supported for prime minister.

to find the old plant on the oddly named Strange Street. I served on the board from 1982 until 1990 when Uniroyal was sold to B.F. Goodrich. The large old plant is now empty, a symbol of the fate of much of the traditional manufacturing sector in Canada.

Although I could move easily in more traditional circles, I always possessed an entrepreneurial spirit that sought out the unusual and the adventurous. I tried to take chances, as in the case of Petroferm, with which I worked in the 1980s. We created a Canadian sole-purpose company, Petroferm Canada, an offshoot of an American company based on Amelia Island, off the coast of Florida. It was a research company created by one of New York's leading patent lawyers, who saw a glob of oil on the beach during his morning walk on a European holiday. On his way back, he noticed the glob had changed and wondered why: "There must be something altering that glob, and it must be bacterial." He scooped up the glob and put it in a container. After he analyzed it, he had his suspicions confirmed: there were bacteria breaking down the oil glob. They became know as emulsans. He thought once the process was understood, it could be used to clean oil tanks and to emulsify oil and water, which, to that point, had not been done successfully. He persuaded one of the leading American companies to manufacture the particular bacterium, which was then used to emulsify oil in water in a number of different locations. The oil emulsions are widely used, particularly by New Brunswick Power Corporation, which emulsifies heavy oil in 30 per cent water and then burns it as a power source. It was a fascinating venture that brought monetary and intellectual reward.

Petroferm was one of the many projects of Alastair Gillespie and Associates Limited, the consulting firm through which I carried on most of my business interests. My consultancy gave me major insights into international business and the wonderful ideas, many unrealized, that entrepreneurs advance. I advised Iranian manufacturing companies trying to make Canadian contacts. One Vancouver client was trying to drill in new ways in the Arctic but found that neither government nor big business took him seriously. I used my contacts to open doors. I also found time to assist as a director of certain socio/medical associations, including Lyndhurst Lodge

Receiving an honorary doctorate at University of Guelph in the spring of 2007.

My grandson Ian's graduation at Queen's University, Kingston, in May 2009.

(Above) The first grand-daughter to be married, in May 2006, Dr. Katie Webb. From left, granddaughter Vanessa Webb, my son-in-law Ian Webb, Katie and her new husband, Dr. Nick Gambarotta, my daughter Cynthia and grandson David Webb.

(Left) With my grand-daughter Meredith on the occasion of her wedding, November 2008.

Hospital and the Gage Research Institute for Lung Diseases, and I served as president of the Canadian Opera Company when it began its successful attempt to build a ballet and opera house.

Membership in the C.D. Howe Institute and the British North American Association brought me to Europe and in touch with many active business leaders and sustained an ongoing interest and participation in public affairs. I have attended Liberal leadership conventions, including the 2006 convention. However, I remain a businessperson whose political life was informed by the way Canada changed during my lifetime. It's been a long journey but one that has brought sudden turns, some disappointments, but much joy. I remain overwhelmingly grateful for my family's presence at my side, my friends' support when needed, and my nation's strengths, which provided the wind at my back.

REFLECTIONS

Looking back, business and public service are the two strands that characterize my family's activities in Canada. It all started with the fur trade in the late seventeen hundreds. The Beaver Club medal best describes the ethos. On one side of the medal is a beaver felling a tree with the inscription "industry and perseverance." On the other side is a manned canoe of a fur trader and several voyageurs about to enter raging rapids with the inscription "fortitude in distress." These precepts have guided me, my family and countless others in both business and public service. Speaking of which, it was Cecil Rhodes, the great South African entrepreneur, who insisted that his scholars should "esteem public service as their highest aim." In that connection there were nine Rhodes scholars in the House of Common and the Senate and countless others in senior positions in the federal civil service during my term. Today public service through political office or the civil service lacks the appeal it had to earlier generations of Canadians and the country is poorer as a result.

I came into public service with a number of strong convictions about business and government. I believed then as I do now that businessmen have an important role to play in government, protecting Canadian interests and promoting Canadian advantages.

I believed then as I do now that competitive, world-class corporations are important commercial ambassadors as well as sources of economic strength. Canada has often been described as a country with a branch-plant mentality, inward-looking not outward-looking. I have never felt that inward-looking attitudes would maximize our potential as a nation. I believed then as I do now that Canada needs to capture more of the value added from the refining and upgrading and manufacture of Canadian resources in Canada. I am concerned that Canada has lost rather than gained major multinational corporations.

I used to get worried when some foreign policy pundit (inside or out-side government) ignored the "how" in favour of the "what." One couldn't ignore the argument that our foreign policy objectives were to protect and secure our interests and values. Fair enough. But I get worried when the "what" of foreign policy is not accompanied by the "how." That's where "influence" becomes a central consideration – and that's where large, Canadian-controlled multinational corporations have a role to play. We simply don't have enough of them today. What a tragedy that Nortel, the gem of Canadian technology and our largest company less than a dec-ade ago, has collapsed into bankruptcy. Despite an attempt by Research In Motion to stop the sale of prized parts of Nortel's technology to foreign companies, the Harper government failed to act, taking refuge in a dubi-ous and weak interpretation of Investment Canada's mandate on foreign takeovers. Nortel's technology was created largely by Canadian engineers

Reflecting – my colleague Barney Danson and I at a recent Remembrance Day service at the University of Toronto cenotaph.

and scientists, supported by generous tax policies and subsidies, and promoted by Canadian governments for decades. While Nortel's great competitors – Siemens of Germany, Ericsson of Sweden, General Electric of the United States and Philips of the Netherlands – have survived for over a century, Canada's standard bearer has stumbled badly and died. It should never have happened and it is an indictment of bad management, government ineptitude and a fundamental lack of entrepreneurial spirit.

I believe, moreover, that the take-overs of international, world-class, giant Canadian companies such as Inco, Falconbridge, Stelco, Dofasco, Alcan, Algoma Steel, Molson Breweries and Labatt's do nothing to strengthen the Canadian economy. These take-overs weaken Canadian influence in foreign affairs. The big retailers are gone, too – Eaton's, Simpson's, Hudson's Bay Company. These take-overs have occurred since FIRA was destroyed and the declaration of Mr. Mulroney that Canada was open for business. On the other hand, the financial institutions seem to have gained, no doubt in part because they have profited from the sale of Canadian companies. Head offices matter, and we've lost too many. Instead of building and encouraging sources of commercial countervailing force, our governments seem to react like the proverbial deer at night, paralyzed in the glare of the headlights.

Not surprisingly, I am very suspicious about the use of that ill-defined nostrum globalization. I'm sometimes reminded that a farmer who sells his topsoil gradually will lose the farm. And our farm is too heavily mortgaged today.

I believe it would be helpful if we were to replace the emphasis often accorded to our private enterprise system or free enterprise with an emphasis on what CBC manager Gladstone Murray called a responsible enterprise system. If "responsible enterprise" had been the hallmark of commercial activity in Canada and the U.S., I very much doubt that the prevailing culture would have become so corrupted by obscene salaries, bonuses and severance payments that it would have led us into the financial and economic mess from which we are now trying to extricate ourselves. Some boards of directors seem to be completely out of touch with what is appropriate remuneration for themselves and senior management. How often I used to hear the mantra from business people that the only responsibility of the management of a company was to make a profit. This is a view often put forward by members of the financial community. I used to weigh in with the argument that business had not just one responsibility, i.e. to its shareholders. It had five, listed not in any particular order of importance: the customer, the employees, the community, governments and of course the shareholders. Instead of accepting the prevailing mantra of free enterprise or private enterprise as the economic culture of our commercial system, Murray advanced the theory that we should adopt responsible enterprise as a much more appropriate banner for government and the business world. It was an approach that I liked to argue too. In this connection, I have been particularly impressed by recent statements of Barack Obama. He seems to have latched onto the need to elevate responsibility as a modus operandi in these trying times. The very notion of responsibility must include the presence of countervailing force.

Cultures, be they bacterial, sociological or economic, are all about protecting the perceived essence of that culture. Cultures grow and multiply in an effort to survive. Their defensive tactics can morph into a number of forms, such as a sense of entitlement when greed becomes part of the essence of certain cultures, sometimes associated with the plutocracy of the U.S. Then again, there's the aristocracy of the class system in the U.K.

Such is the predatory essence of certain cultures. When the separate elements are not controlled by a countervailing force, the culture will likely implode. Such was the case in the early '70s when oil prices created tensions between countries. Given the struggle with the realities of today's issues I am reminded that history can repeat itself. What then can we do?

The government of Canada, by that I mean the executive branch, operates through a civil service, a bureaucracy. Few if any of the bureaucrats have had business experience. Many have chosen to become part of the bureaucracy because they sought security and not rewards for risk-taking. Legislatures make the law; they are the vehicle for making choices and holding the executive accountable. They are mostly peopled by lawyers, with few businessmen or businesswomen. Yet much government policy and the incidence of government programs involve business.

Such is the anomaly: the experience of businessmen and businesswomen is seldom tapped in the House of Commons or by the civil service even though so much of the business of government deeply affects the business world. I hope more businessmen and businesswomen will opt for membership in the House of Commons; although the pay may fall short of even moderate salaries now paid to executives, it's a lot better than it used to be. Moreover, they will learn, as I did, that politics has many rewards, and their lives will be richer for the experience of public life.

As election turnouts fall and so many shun politics, I recognize that differences among Canadians seem greater. As a born Westerner, I was always somewhat apprehensive about the power and controlling interests of Eastern Canada. This apprehension of course is shared by many in Western Canada today. I remember a meeting with the editorial board of the *Vancouver Sun* after becoming a minister. We had covered a number of issues and one about which I was particularly emphatic was voting day. I argued that, historically, voters in B.C. knew the result of the general election before they had even voted. How could they feel that they were part of the decision? I proposed that this could be alleviated by different voting times in different parts of the country so that the results would all be recorded if not simultaneously, at least within a similar time frame. After politics, I was active in an all-party group based in Toronto called the Institute for Political Involvement (IPI). One of our first submissions to an official reform of Parliament commission was just that. It took close to twenty years for the government to adopt the recommendation.

I also believe that the Senate badly needs reform. My views derive from my experiences In Ottawa. Too many senators were inactive, serving out their years in comfortable semi-retirement, members of probably the best club in Canada. I argued that the beginning of Senate reform should start with rules that would limit Senate membership to seven years. Recently – the Harper government has been talking about eight years. In this case, Harper's ideas have considerable merit and it will be a test of our political system whether an antiquated and ineffective body can be successfully reformed.

Ademocracy is only as strong as its citizens' commitment to participation in its life. From the arrival of my ancestors on Canada's shores two centuries ago, public service has been an important part of my family's focus. I was fortunate to have the opportunity to do my part as my forefathers did in the fur trade, the wars and the public service. And I'm proud that the tradition has continued with my children. My daughter, Cynthia, has made a very focused and effective career in health care My son, Ian, devoted most of his working life (twenty-five years) to government service. He worked his way up to leadership as CEO of Canada's export development and financing agency. My beautiful and lively wife, Diana, was always a much remembered Canadian ambassador wherever she went. She was a strong nationalist and advocate for her country. Yes, public service may not pay big salaries but it contains its own rich rewards.

A successful journey doesn't require a good road map. And so it is with a career. Good luck helps but so does a sense of direction. I've often preferred the less-travelled road – the naval air service, small business, publishing, politics, coal liquefaction, breweries. It's brought surprises but also wonderful experiences and, I hope, a real contribution to my country.

The citation on my appointment as an Officer of the Order of Canada described me as a maverick entrepreneur. It's not a bad description of a life where business, science, politics and war mingled together. Made in Canada, a country of great challenges and possibility, I proudly and truly am.

MAIDEN SPEECH TO
THE HOUSE OF COMMONS

HOUSE OF COMMONS DEBATES, 1ST SESSION,

28TH PARLIAMENT, TUESDAY, NOVEMBER 5, 1968

Mr. Alastair Gillespie (Etobicoke): Mr. Speaker, in this my first speech to the house I should like to draw your attention to the fact that Etobicoke is a new riding. It forms a large part of the old riding of York West which was represented with such distinction in this house by Mr. Robert Winters.

The lands, rivers and people of this area played an important role in the early development of our nation. Over three centuries ago it was the place for commerce, exploration and discovery. Its people looked to the future rather than to the past. They looked for and sought a future better than they had. They sought the good life for themselves and for others.

And so it is today, Mr. Speaker. Our concern for the future must be based on the same principles; and it is in this context that I should like to talk about some of the conditions that we have to create in Canada for our future development. In particular I want to refer to creating conditions for investment, for fostering a strong Canadian point of view, and for sustaining confidence in our institutions, starting with the need to reform this house and its procedures.

The case against inflation has been made so many times and so cogently, Mr. Speaker, that I do not propose to repeat the arguments here except to draw your attention to the problems of government financing and of financing our future economic growth in the private sector.

There are some who say that full employment and inflation go hand in hand, that one cannot enjoy the benefits of the one without paying the price of the other. They would promote the idea that a little inflation is a good thing, that it is good for business, that it promotes prosperity and keeps things going. In my view, Mr. Speaker, nothing could be more dangerous. This is the most corrupting philosophy of them all – short term euphoria, like the pathetic rationalization of the addict in the early period of his addiction protesting the wisdom of his own foolishness. Over a period of 15 years a one per cent deterioration per year in the value of our money amounts to a discount of 15 per cent. What man is going to lend $100 now, Mr. Speaker, if he can expect in return only $85?

The funds that are used to finance government deficits and extra budgetary needs, to purchase government bonds, federal, provincial or municipal, are mostly the collective savings of millions of Canadians. They are the premiums that are paid on life insurance policies and the deductions made from the weekly pay cheque for future pension benefits. Yet there has been a tendency in many quarters to identify those who purchase bonds with the "haves", as if the beneficiaries of the borrowings were the "have nots". Surely it is time to recognize that they are one and the same person.

The point to be made is this. Federal government extra budgetary needs plus provincial and municipal government spending are going to require enormous sums each and every year. Little of this development can take place unless we show the lenders that we can control inflation. And for the same reasons, Mr. Speaker, corporate expansion will be curtailed unless we prove to those who would finance corporate borrowings that we are serious about controlling inflation. Obviously the uninterrupted series of budgetary deficits over the past ten years does not build confidence. That is why the minister's program for a budgetary balance by the end of the next fiscal year is so important.

Federal government policy must be designed to bring about and preserve an orderly capital market. This requires not only the management of its own debts and its own budgetary requirements; it requires on the part of the federal government a full appreciation of the capital needs of the provinces and municipalities and also the needs of the private sector. Just as in the tax fields arrangements must be worked out with the provinces so, too, is it important that there be collaboration on capital needs. There is, after all, a limited supply of money.

Nor can Canada rely solely on domestic sources of capital. Indeed, in recent years Canadian borrowings abroad have averaged close to $1 billion a year. Our ability to go to the United States market or to European markets will depend on the confidence we earn abroad, on confidence in our competitive position which must not be eroded by inflation at home, on their confidence that the risks of devaluation are negligible and that we are not always just about to change the rules. Canada cannot insulate itself from world economic conditions and there is no use pretending that we can. This is all the more reason, therefore, to examine our vulnerability in areas which we ourselves do not control.

Within the last year there were three major international developments which seriously damaged confidence in the world's monetary system and in the Canadian dollar. I refer to the devaluation of sterling, to the United States guide lines and to French efforts to force devaluation of the United States dollar in terms of gold. Fortunately, after a rather uncertain period the value of the Canadian dollar has strengthened. This is not a time for complacency. There are many uncertainties facing the world monetary system today. Let us not forget that Canada is more vulnerable than most countries because of the large part, the enormous part, proportionately four times that of the United States, that foreign trade plays in our gross national product. Let us recognize that we rely at the present time on foreign capital flows to finance our balance of payments. For these reasons we are vulnerable. For these reasons, too, I hope it will be possible to negotiate with United States authorities the removal of the upper limit of $2.6 billion on our foreign exchange reserves. We need this flexibility.

These truths, the need to establish confidence in our capital markets, the need to recognize the dangers of inflation, are central to the whole question of the future development of Canada. Yet in this area the two main opposition parties seem to me to be peculiarly inconsistent, though consistently ambiguous. They appear to have turned their backs on both monetary and fiscal measures. They seem to have discarded completely the idea that interest rates are an effective tool of monetary policy. Equally, they appear to ignore fiscal measures. They have been curiously silent on the desirability of a balanced budget. They deplore the effects of inflation but ignore even more doing anything about it. They profess, but they do not inform. Is this Progressive Conservatism at its modern best?

The NDP, on the other hand, seem to regard deficit spending as a way of life. They remind me of a man who would write a cheque for his favourite charity on a bank account that did not exist. Yet they talk of the eroding effects of inflation like the convivial roustabout who, anticipating his own overindulgence, lectures others on the predictable after-effects. When, for instance, has a spokesman for the New Democratic party publicly taken a position against wage increases which exceed productivity increases? When has a spokesman of the New Democratic party stated publicly that wage increases which exceed productivity increases are inflationary and therefore have to be paid for by every other wage earner in Canada – indeed by all Canadians? The NDP behave as if cost-push inflation never existed.

I should like, Mr. Speaker, to turn now to the question of entrepreneurial spirit, initiative and enterprise from the Canadian point of view. As Canadians we need to concentrate on doing what we are best equipped to do. We can stimulate entrepreneurship through leadership by government, by insisting on a more efficient use of our research and development efforts and by insisting on a more selective effort. We have too often tried to cover too broad a spectrum and we have not concentrated on certain unique opportunities. Somehow or other we seem to have got caught up in a share the wealth approach to investment in research, a something for everyone philosophy. I think the time has come to apply a very much more selective approach to research expenditures, and I think this approach should be tied directly to the idea of originality, to sponsoring Canadian originality.

It seems to me that we need to give our investment a Canadian slant. The character of a nation, the distinguishing quality of its people, is to be found in how it comes to terms with its environment, how it responds to the land, to the weather, to climate, to nature, to its natural resources, what it builds its houses out of, what it eats, how it works to sustain life above the subsistence level, how it plays, what it writes, sings and paints – in a word, in its capacity for originality.

We should realize that our originality has been subverted by our ability to obtain the benefits of foreign innovation. The Watkins report focuses on one aspect of this, the prevalence of the manufacturing licence, of the royalty agreement and of the engineering agreement. In return for a royalty on sales and, usually, an undertaking not to export, a Canadian company obtains the benefits of foreign research and development for its exclusive use in the Canadian market. This is the easy way; it takes the risk out of research because it requires none. In my view this particular device for obtaining foreign knowhow has had a more serious effect on Canadian entrepreneurial attitudes than any other single factor. The effect has been far greater, for example, than that of foreign ownership.

At the same time we must continue to concern ourselves with the development of our resources with Canadian ownership. That is not to say that we will be able to do the job alone. We must provide an hospitable climate for foreign investors, but we must also insist that future Canadian resource development will be undertaken in partnership with Canadians.

In this connection I think it most significant that the recent study completed by York University for the Toronto Stock Exchange indicated that there would be a serious lack of Canadian equities within five years. More particularly, the demand on the part of Canadians for equities will outrun supply in a ratio of approximately two to one. This has serious and far reaching economic implications in terms of foreign ownership and balance of payments difficulties.

One does not have to argue the case for efficiency in industry, nor does one have to argue the case for efficiency with the Canadian public. How curious, Mr. Speaker, that one should have to argue the case for efficiency in this house with hon. members opposite.

At a time when man can contemplate the surface of the moon from a transmitter he has planted there, when he can watch in the comfort of his livingroom the carnage of war as it happens on the other side of the earth, when jumbo jets and supersonics will shortly revolutionize his mobility in the air and shatter his tranquility on the ground –

Mr. Winch: But you cannot even balance the budget.

Mr. Gillespie: – when man can destroy himself with the bomb and depopulate with the pill, when the sexual revolution can rock the very foundations of great religions, when the gap between the rich nations and the poor nations grows wider and when against this background, even the most tentative steps in the direction of parliamentary reform are resisted in the name of freedom, is it any wonder that people ask how contemporary is the parliament of Canada today and, worse still, how relevant is it?

This sovereign body, it has been emphasized, protects our freedoms and the personal liberty of all Canadians as no other agency or institution does. Its ritual, its procedure, its symbols all emphasize that it won its freedom from executive power. Yes, Mr. Speaker, but the pace of events has quickened. What is needed now is a realization that the freedom to change is the most important freedom of all. What is needed now is the power to engineer change. I say to the opposition, do you not recognize change when you see it?

We operate as if television had never been invented, with no apparent awareness that a two-minute interview on the national network is more effective than an hour's debate. Let us recognize the importance of the electronic media. And let us be thankful that it can inform the people in a way that we cannot.

There is an enormous credibility gap in connection with the question of government efficiency, and it will remain a yawning chasm until such time as we place first priority on the efficiency of our own operations in this house. How can we criticize waste and poor productivity in the government service if we do not first of all raise the level of our own productivity? If we fail to convert this house into an effective instrument of change we shall have failed ourselves, we shall have failed to extend democracy, we shall have failed to extend the maturity of our country, we shall have failed the people of Canada.

We must be acquainted, Mr. Speaker, with the available opportunities to build a stronger country with a greater culture by having a truly bilingual government. Thus, here and abroad, Canada will be recognized as a progressive country.

Let us, as Canadians, welcome change for the opportunities it provides. Let us build our country in a distinctively Canadian entrepreneurial spirit.

NEW PRINCIPLES OF INTERNATIONAL BUSINESS CONDUCT, JULY 18, 1975: "THE GILLESPIE GUIDELINES"

Foreign-controlled businesses in Canada are expected to operate in ways that will bring significant benefit to Canada. To this end they should pursue policies that will foster their independence in decision-making, their innovative and other entrepreneurial capabilities, their efficiency, and their identification with Canada and the aspirations of the Canadian people.

Within these general objectives, the following principles of good corporate behaviour are recommended by the Canadian government. Foreign-controlled firms in Canada should:

1. Pursue a high degree of autonomy in the exercise of decision-making and risk-taking functions, including innovative activity and the marketing of any resulting new products.

2. Develop as an integral part of the Canadian operation an autonomous capability for technological innovation, including research, development, engineering, industrial design and preproduction activities; and for production, marketing, purchasing and accounting.

3. Retain in Canada a sufficient share of earnings to give strong financial support to the growth and entrepreneurial potential of the Canadian operation, having in mind a fair return to shareholders on capital invested.

4. Strive for a full international mandate for innovation and market development, when it will enable the Canadian company to improve its efficiency by specialization of productive operations.

5. Aggressively pursue and develop market opportunities throughout international markets as well as in Canada.

6. Extend the processing in Canada of natural resource products to the maximum extent feasible on an economic basis.

7. Search out and develop economic sources of supply in Canada for domestically produced goods and for professional and other services.

8. Foster a Canadian outlook within management, as well as enlarged career opportunities within Canada, by promoting Canadians to senior and middle

management positions, by assisting this process with an effective management training program, and by including a majority of Canadians on boards of directors of all Canadian companies, in accordance with the spirit of federal legislative initiatives.

9. Create a financial structure that provides opportunity for substantial equity participation in the Canadian enterprise by the Canadian public.

10. Pursue a pricing policy designed to assure a fair and reasonable return to the company and to Canada for all goods and services sold abroad, including sales to parent companies and other affiliates. In respect of purchases from parent companies and affiliates abroad, pursue a pricing policy designed to assure that the terms are at least as favourable as those offered by other suppliers.

11. Regularly publish information on the operations and financial position of the firm.

12. Give appropriate support to recognized national objectives and established government programs, while resisting any direct or indirect pressure from foreign governments or associated companies to act in a contrary manner.

13. Participate in Canadian social and cultural life and support those institutions that are concerned with the intellectual, social and cultural advancement of the Canadian community.

14. Endeavour to ensure that access to foreign resources, including technology and know-how, is not associated with terms and conditions that restrain the firm from observing these principles.

CITATION OF THE ORDER OF CANADA

The Honourable Alastair W. Gillespie, P.C., O.C.
Toronto, Ontario

Officer of the Order of Canada

He has excelled in all of the many initiatives he has undertaken in the private and public sectors. As a Minister of the Crown, he served with distinction in a variety of portfolios. After leaving politics, he returned to business where he carved out a unique niche in the fossil fuels industry. His record of community service spans four decades and includes a leadership role as Director of the Spinal Cord Centre at Toronto's Lyndhurst Hospital, Director of the National Ballet School and President of the Canadian Opera Company. His tenacity, coupled with a maverick entrepreneurial spirit, has earned him the respect and admiration of Canadians from coast to coast.

CITATION OF THE D.LITT., UNIVERSITY OF GUELPH

Madame Chancellor: In accordance with a recommendation from the Senate of the University of Guelph, it is my great honour to present to you the candidate

Alastair Gillespie

for the degree of Doctor of Letters, *honoris causa.*

Alastair Gillespie is recognized and admired across Canada for his outstanding contributions to the public and private sectors and is greatly respected for his entrepreneurial spirit and dedication to community service.

Mr. Gillespie was educated at Brentwood College School and the University of British Columbia before enlisting in World War Two. He served as a pilot from 1941 to 1945, reaching the rank of Lieutenant with the Royal Canadian Navy. He earned a Bachelor of Commerce degree from McGill University in 1947 and attended Oxford University as a Rhodes Scholar. He later graduated from the University of Toronto with a business degree.

Mr. Gillespie's drive and initiative have earned him a great deal of success in the private sector. He has been a director for a great variety of companies and was chairman and director of Creemore Springs Brewery Limited and Scotia Synfuels Project. He was a vice-president and director at Canadian Corporate Management Company Limited and at W.J. Gage Limited.

Mr. Gillespie was elected as a Liberal Member of Parliament for Toronto's Etobicoke riding in 1968. He was re-elected twice and served as the Minister of State for Science and Technology; the Minister of Industry, Trade and Commerce; and the Minister of Energy, Mines and Resources. After leaving politics he returned to continued success in the private sector.

Mr. Gillespie has a history of passionate involvement in community service. He has served as a director for a variety of non-profit organizations including the National Ballet School, the Ballet Opera House Corporation, the Canadian Opera Foundation and the Gage Research Institute. He is a former president of the Canadian Opera Company and served on the Board of Governors for the Lyndhurst Hospital, where he also served as a director of the Spinal Cord Centre. He is an Honorary Vice-President of The Champlain Society and Patron of the environmental think tank Green Door Alliance. Mr. Gillespie was awarded the Centennial Medal in 1967 and was named an Officer of the Order of Canada in 1998.

Here at Guelph, we are particularly grateful for his role as a lead fundraiser for the Chair in Scottish Studies. He served as a director for the Scottish Studies Foundation and won the Scottish Studies Society's 'Scot of the Year Award' in 2003.

For his many distinguished contributions to the public and private sectors and for his enduring commitment to community service, I ask you, Madame Chancellor, to confer upon Alastair Gillespie the degree of Doctor of Letters, *honoris causa*.

INDEX